America! What Were You Thinking?

Emancipating 3,953,761 enslaved Africans and African Americans and then leaving them to live in the same general population alongside their former enslavers, overseers, drivers, and various other proponents of slavery in the hopes that everyone could all just let bygones be bygones.

How has that worked out for you?

America! What Were You Thinking?

Emancipating 3,953,761 enslaved Africans and African Americans
and then leaving them to live in the same general population alongside
their former enslavers, overseers, drivers, and various other proponents of
slavery in the hopes that everyone could all just let bygones be bygones.

How has that worked out for you?

TERRY DEADRICK-LEONARD

Cartelyou & DeSoto

Cartelyou & DeSoto
cartelyoudesoto.com

Copyright © 2020 Terry Deadrick-Leonard
Request a Lecture: deadrick-leonard@torontomail.com

ISBN: 978-0-578-79535-5 (hardcover)
ISBN: 978-0-578-79594-2 (paperback)

Cover image © Ocusfocus

Limit of Liability/Disclaimer of Warranty

The advice and strategies contained herein may not be suitable for your situation. Neither the publisher nor author shall be liable for any loss of profit or any other commercial damages, including but not limited to special, incidental, consequential, or other damages.

Disclaimer

This publication is designed to provide accurate and personal experience information in regard to the subject matter covered. It is sold with the understanding that the author, contributors, publisher are not engaged in rendering counseling or other professional services. If counseling advice or other expert assistance is required, the services of a competent professional person should be sought out.

DEDICATION

FLIGHT

To those Americans who choose to leave the experiment:

Here's to your health and your family's,

and may they live long and prosper.[1]

FIGHT

To those Americans who choose to remain a part of the experiment:

If you want to know the end, look at the beginning.[2]

CONTENTS

INTRODUCTION

The strangest disease I have seen in this country seems really to be broken heartedness . . .[1]

—Missionary Herald 1880

The research question or problem, "America! What were you thinking? Emancipating 3,953,761[2] enslaved Africans and African Americans and then leaving them to live in the same general population alongside their former enslavers, overseers, drivers, and various other proponents of slavery in the hopes that everyone could all just let bygones be bygones" is a story that just happens to contain its share of the gloom, despair, and agony[3] of a great American blues song. But, it is perhaps, more importantly, a story about regrets. No, not like the regrets that seem to be induced by a seemingly unending physical and emotional hangover after attending a bachelor or bachelorette party in America's Las Vegas, Nevada, or China's Macau, both with their endless options for unadulterated revelry. Nor is it like regretting investing too much time focused on career and not investing enough quality time with family and close friends. Yes, these ideas are all the kinds of thoughts and feelings that lead individuals to ask themselves, ultimately, What was I thinking? or better yet, How did my thinking become so skewed as to think that this was going to end well? However, this problem is not about an individual, a person, a singularity, or Sherlock Holmes's insoluble puzzle.[4] Nor is it William Winwood Reade's enigma.[5] It is instead a problem of Holmes's aggregate and of Reade's species. It is a nationhood problem and one only need to do the math in order to understand the perplexity of the emancipation of 3,953,761 enslaved Africans and African Americans and then leaving them to live in the same general population alongside their former enslavers, overseers, drivers, and various other proponents of slavery in the hopes that everyone could just let bygones be bygones.

This is also about recollecting almost every cliché that has to do with the idea of being dissatisfied with something, such as the last straw, the tipping point, the point of no return, and the list goes on and on. So, in some regard, this book is dedicated to any and all Americans who say that they have had more than their fill of being treated like guinea pigs in the great American melting pot experiment. Which is not unlike the main character in Israel Zangwill's play, *The Melting Pot*,[6] who eventually triumphs over the tragedy of ethnic cleansing. This book's dedication also extends to those who feel as though this is the ending of what was a very long and committed relationship between citizen and country. Those who get the sense that this is like the chaotic estrangement that precedes an even messier divorce. Those whose emotions are being or have been severed from their partner and at this point it is just about the division of community property and of course, the custody of the children.

However, this is not a relationship between two individuals, but between a nation and a large segment of its population and like most relationships, this is about feelings and attitudes. Like the feelings and attitudes Chicago syndicated columnist Sydney J. Harris in 1953 was trying to explain regarding the distinction between patriotism and nationalism. Many believe that Harris was spot-on when he described the importance of the two words attitude and feeling in his contrast, expositing that, "[T]he patriot is proud of his country for what it does," but "[T]he nationalist is proud of his country no matter what it does" with one attitude leading to a feeling of responsibility and the other blind arrogance.[7] Harris seemed to express a belief that, "[Patriotism] creates a feeling of responsibility . . . and [Nationalism] a feeling of blind arrogance . . . "[8] Thus it is not the Great American Novel, where all's well that ends well,[9,10] but is instead America the great, a novel, where all *ends*, not unlike most empires. Which is a double entendre, to say the least with regard to the drama of emancipating of 3,953,761 enslaved Africans and African Americans then leaving them to live in the same general population alongside their former enslavers, overseers, drivers, and various other proponents of slavery in the hopes that everyone could all just let bygones be bygones.

Just as art often imitates life there are scores of theatrical analogies and metaphors that can be used to sum up the overall sentiment of this break-up between America; or "Amerige, i.e., the land of Amerigo"[11] in reference to Amerigo Vespucci the Italian Explorer who named America; and many of its citizens. Namely its citizens who fear social and political "atavism" and those who sympathize with both their plight and their fear. It is kind of like the breathtakingly emotional scene from the cult classic American film *The Jacksons: An American Dream* where the family matriarch finds out that the family patriarch is having an extramarital affair. She confronts him and says, "You're a liar, and a cheat and I don't want you no more."[12] So, when a person or in this case, a people have been emotionally or physically wounded by someone, in this case, a nation they believed had their best interests at heart, the uncovering of the deception can be devastating and the wounds, even though healed, leave gruesome scars. And not to gloss over the fact that yes, of course, humanity resides within an apparently fallen world in which human beings are capable of committing the vilest of acts against other human beings. However, if the emancipation of 3,953,761 enslaved Africans and African Americans and then leaving them to live in the same general population alongside their former enslavers, overseers, drivers, and various other proponents of slavery in the hopes that everyone could all just let bygones be bygones were not cruel, not vile enough, the rub is that the victims were specifically and purposefully targeted as part of a so-called race or ethnicity-based selection system.

It has been said that life is all about perspective. Take, for example, the saying that, one person's pain is another person's pleasure[13] or that one person's comedy is another person's tragicomedy such as in the American film *Trading Places*. In the film one of its two main antagonists, Mortimer, is overheard saying that he does not want the film's protagonist, Winthorpe, who was purposefully framed to look like a thief and an illicit drug dealer, to be restored to his former successful life after the conclusion of an absurd social experiment and the wager of one dollar. However, before dysfunctional could become functional again and before the abnormal could become the new normal and Winthorpe could be restored to his former life of wealth and prestige, Mortimer says, "I don't want Winthorpe back after what he's done."[14] This, in spite of the fact that Mortimer was the catalyst behind Winthorpe's challenges in the first place. And so, it is this absurd fictitious rejection of normalcy which is perhaps not completely unlike the idea of transference psychology that has been associated with the pathology of the enslavement of human beings. A pathology that creates within the enslaver a fear of future retribution through either reaping or karma for the dastardly deeds done to the enslaved. It also uncovers the often-complex set of emotions involved when an antagonist blames the person they are antagonizing, the protagonist, for the predicament that the protagonist finds her or himself in.

So, even though the previously mentioned film is amusingly levitous, Mortimer represents an archetype of not just irresponsible wealth and narcissism, but of skullduggery and a frivolous view of the lives of other human beings. One moral to the story is that the lives of some people have, as fictitious as it may sound, essentially been introduced to a life of challenges, not because they lack personal responsibility, but because they were born into a particular system. Another moral to the story is the suggestion that people often do not initially have a clue that hidden forces are constantly acting against their best interests. And perhaps the real irony whether in fiction or reality is that sometimes there is no turning back after so much upheaval has been heaped upon the soul of a person or in this case, the soul of a nation of people. So, is it really possible that a large segment of America's population does not *want* America back? Does not want back the America that they thought they loved, not now, not after all that it has done. And can restoration really be as simple as a political course correction, heartfelt repentance, and even groveling on hands and knees in order to repair the damage that has been done to the psyche of a people?

Using a fair share of allusion, thoughts and ideas from antiquity that are harbingers and progenitors of America's challenges, chocked full of Antebellum narrative, flash-forwards into a more contemporary America for contrast and comparison, all with the goal of simply being a survey course of sorts, this book repeatedly asks the question, "America! What were you thinking? Emancipating 3,953,761 enslaved Africans and African Americans then leaving them to live in the same general population alongside their former enslavers, overseers, drivers, and various other proponents of slavery in the hopes that everyone could all just let bygones be bygones." But it also begs follow up questions such as, What if the "woe due"[15] which the American president who emancipated the enslaved, Abraham Lincoln, spoke of regarding the horrors of America's 1861-1865 Civil War was somehow not a true reckoning? and What if the idea that 'imperfect action being better than no action'[16] was in this case, simply inadequate? Perhaps it was the notion that it was political negotiation and not a true repentance and change of heart[17] that seems to have doomed America to be trapped in perpetuity between two warring factions. One faction interested in the sincerity of heart that leads to Lincoln's "new birth"[18] or "The abolition of slavery by the spirit of repentance"[19] which abolitionist William Lloyd Garrison so forcefully declared nearly three decades before the Civil War began. And the other faction interested in the political and economic expediency that might entrench and preserve patriarchy and privilege.

CHAPTER 1

SOCIAL CHANGE

[E]ternity is simply too long to wait for the horrors of history to settle into a meaningful pattern.[1,2]

—E. Elaine Murdaugh 1979

What was America thinking when it emancipated 3,953,761 enslaved Africans and African Americans and then left them to live in the same general population with their former enslavers, overseers, drivers, and various other proponents of slavery? Yes, what was America thinking when it was creating the living, breathing, Utopian nation in which as its Declaration of Independence declares, "[A]ll men are created equal" (US 1776) on parchment paper, while simultaneously building America's social constructs of race and color? During the incipient stage of nation-building, did America not already have an inkling that the purported notion of the inferiority of Africans and African Americans would be the perfect ruse in light of the phrase, "[A]ll men are created equal" in order to justify the enslavement or human trafficking of Africans and African Americans?[3] If one were really and truly trying to personify America through anthropomorphism as a living, breathing organism, and if one were trying to (with plenty of stress on the word *trying*) take the pulse of America, it would be beneficial to know that science has now confirmed that a heart starts to beat even before it is fully formed. This means that individual cells, even though immature, can pulse or beat and contract and relax independently before they eventually interconnect to beat in unison and form a mature heart.[4,5,6] So, even before America was fully birthed as a new nation, it had a heartbeat.

Before trying to take the pulse of America, it might also be advantageous to understand that the pulse is considered to have its own character. And just like an individual's character, America can be described as having complex mental and ethical traits that distinguish it from other nations.[7] It appears to vacillate between the strong pulse and the weak, the paradoxical, the genetic restricting, the forcefulness, the collapses, the slow rising, the flatness or the backflow pulses.[8] So, what kind of living, breathing being, or entity is America? America is perhaps best described as a conglomerate. Not quite like Shelly's Frankenstein,[9] but arguably not too far off from Stevenson's Jekyll and Hyde[10] because it is not one–distinct–individual nation or the infamous, mythical melting pot,[11] instead it contains nations within a nation based upon the notions of race, ethnicity, religion, gender, sexual orientation, and socioeconomic status. And after understanding what America is, one might simply ask the questions, Is America as a nation progressing? Is America somewhat stagnate? Is America regressing?

In other words, what is the pulse, the proverbial heartbeat of America after the Civil War? After the so-called Reconstruction of the divided nation era? After the implementation of the Black Codes and later the Jim Crow laws, which were codes and laws implemented by states as a way to nullify the freedoms gained by newly emancipated Africans and African Americans? After the 1950s-1960s Civil Rights Movement to gain equal rights for African Americans? How does the melting pot[12] experiment look after more than one hundred and fifty years of reflective observation? For example, it has often been implied that it is not that African Americans or people of color think that they are somehow above the law or that criminal offenses should not have consequences simply because African Americans or people of color have historically endured oppression. No, the real complaint of African Americans or people of color is that the consequences and punishments meted out to them as a group tend to be much harsher than the punishments given to those who self-identify as White and have or lack similar criminal records for committing the same offenses.

So, have things gotten better, worse, or remained the same since the Louisiana parish of St. Landry implemented its post-Civil War Black Code in 1865 stating that "[N]o negro shall be allowed to pass within the limits of said parish without special permit in writing from his employer. Whoever shall violate this provision shall pay a fine of two dollars and fifty cents, or in default thereof shall be forced to work four days on the public road, or suffer corporeal punishment as provided hereinafter . . . "[13] The simple answer to this question is that, of course, the letter of that law as well as many like it; the bare legal instruments; have long since been done away with. However, the more complex answer should include the question of whether or not the spirit of those laws still remains.[14-17] So, in some regard, things have gotten better, but just like beauty is in the "[E]ye of the beholder,"[18] social change is relative to either the lack or the abundance of freedom and liberty which an individual or group possesses.

Who is to say whether the lawmaker's motives were pure or nefarious and whether the enacted laws intent was inspired from an honest desire to maintain civil order or if there was an underlying theme of subjugation and humiliation present? It has been said that if you are careful not to "strip a man of his dignity in the first place, you won't have to worry about trying to restore it to him in the future."[19] One could ask whether or not legal subjugation, followed by social humiliation, followed by an attempt to restore dignity, was or is a recurring theme in America. Take, for example, the more contemporary practice of jails and prisons forcing new inmates to strip naked, submit to a body cavity search, and then have their bodies sprayed with insecticides[20] to kill any lice that the individual might be carrying. This, in spite of the fact that only a small percentage of the population does, in fact, have lice, or that head lice are not known to spread disease.[21] Also, worth mentioning is the fact that the spread of lice through contact with inanimate objects and personal belongings is rare.[22]

Again, this repetitive motion of legal subjugation, followed by social humiliation, followed by an attempt to restore dignity begs the question, How is dignity restored once the chains are loosed? It also asks whether or not the spirit of the slave laws, the Black Codes, and Jim Crow laws is so deeply entrenched and embedded in American society that it will never be able to recognize the common humanity and common destiny[23] of all Americans. Whether referred to as recurring themes, repetitive motions, or paradise lost, found, and then lost again,[24] a lot is often said about the pitfalls of history repeating itself simply because previous lessons that had poor outcomes were not learned from. Science now says that the age-old problem of repeating the same mistakes lies within the realm of cognitive neuroscience and neural pathways. New research suggests that the best way not to repeat the same mistakes over and over is actually not to try to necessarily learn from them, but instead to focus on the positive future outcome that is wanted.[25,26,27] Yes, but how? Even with science, technology, and a library full of research at its disposal, how can America focus on a "better and richer and fuller"[28] American

Dream? One that is filled with life, liberty, the pursuit of happiness, and of course prosperity for all when a large majority of those who self-identify as White want the Dream for themselves and those that belong to their tribe, but either in their conscious or subconscious minds they do not want the same Dream for people of color?

Suppose the underlying motives of the slave laws, the Black Codes, and Jim Crow laws were at their core attitudes of subjugation and humiliation. Then should not America have known that just because you *break* a human being or push them to the point of being emotionally exasperated does not mean they naturally become docile or passive? Because as a matter of fact, they often become passive-aggressive. The kind of people who might even become the leaders of a resistance because they have learned to withhold their desire to act out when prodded or provoked. Likewise, just because a humiliated person seems even angrier than ever before after humiliation does not necessarily mean that the person now lives each waking moment thinking of or plotting ways to extol revenge. Suffice it to say that human beings are individuals, singularities, or Sherlock Holmes's insoluble puzzle,[29] and William Winwood Reade's enigma.[30]

Destruction and chaos completely break some individuals, but it makes others harder and more fervent. An instance of this theory played out in an episode of the American television spy-drama *Burn Notice*. In this particular episode the main character's mother asks the man who trained and mentored her son to be a world-class spy, how is it that her younger son, who grew up in the same home, could have turned out "so different" from his older brother? The explanation she was given was a word picture imagining what it looks like to hold two glass bottles up in the air and then letting them both drop to a hard floor. What happens to the glass bottles? Of course, they break. However, they do not break in the same way. While one crumbles into nothing more than a pile of glass, the one other one breaks in such a way as to have the potential to be used as a jagged-edged weapon. The same environment that turned one son into a warrior-hero is the same environment that crushed his younger brother. People do not break the same.[31] So, as this book's title so aptly asks, What was America thinking? Whether its laws were written on stone tablets, papyrus, or parchment paper, was there absolutely no forethought that went into the future ramifications of the slave laws, the Black Codes, and Jim Crow laws? Who could not predict that abolishing, repealing, and replacing laws written down on paper might never undo those laws already written on the hearts of men and women.[32] There have always been pivotal points in American history where those on the outside looking in at America would have thought Africans and African Americans were surely going to promulgate an exodus after the conclusion one of its many different cataclysmic color-prejudice induced events. Not simply a migration to another part of the nation, such as from south to north or east to west. Nor a retreat or separation such as Madison Park in Alabama in 1880[33] formed by former slaves. Nor freedmen's towns and communities such as Tulsa, Oklahoma's Greenwood, better known as America's Black Wall Street until 1921 when it was razed by mobs of White residents who killed as many as 300 African Americans.[34] Nor the formation of towns like Rosewood in Florida struck down by White vigilante terror in 1923, killing dozens of African Americans and essentially breaking the will of the thriving all African American community.[35] No, this was not the ethnic or "racial cleansing"[36] by White vigilante groups, which was not uncommon in nineteenth and twentieth-century America. No, this would have been an actual exodus, en masse, from America, a divorcement. One obvious red-flag to those on the outside looking in at America, as a tell-tale sign of whether or not there would be an exodus might have been the idea that for the melting pot[37] experiment to continue, people of color would have to be willing to make their contributions to society while being handicapped by a lack of autonomy dealt them by hindrances such as the post-Civil War Black Code work travel permits.

The interjection of the necessity of a permission slip from an employer seemed to make it plain and clear that African Americans were only going to be tolerated out and about in the vicinity of the general White public if said African Americans were in the course of fulfilling their employment duties. Thus, a permission slip was needed by African Americas to be out in public, whether in the middle of fulfilling their employment obligations or on their way to or from that employment. This requirement implied that any unemployed African American was subject to incarceration and not just incarceration but forced time as laborers for the municipality or to be hired out to local private business enterprises through a system known as convict leasing. As a matter of fact, "Florida's incarcerated population increased from 125 in 1881 to approximately 1,071 in 1904."[38] It was as if the powers that be, in this case, the criminal justice system said that if Africans and African Americans could no longer be bought and sold, they could at least be leased or rented. Louisiana, mentioned previously, and Florida are just a couple of examples. Still, all of the former enslaving states have been accused of using the Black Codes and Jim Crow laws to not only oppress free Africans and African Americans, but to make a profit through convict leasing while doing it.

It does not take a lot of imagination to conjure up images of the plethora of melee's that must have been common during that time. Perhaps not unlike the more modern law enforcement policies of some of America's larger urban centers, commonly known as "stop-and-frisk."[39,40] But in the case of the Black Codes and Jim Crow laws, the goal was not crime prevention in any way, shape, sense, or meaning of the term. It was about the powers that be, in this case, the criminal justice system, regaining some of the authority it lost with the Emancipation Proclamation and the ratification of the Thirteenth Amendment. It also symbolized for many Southerners, who self-identified as White, the reiteration of the fact that the primary purpose for Africans and African Americans, whether enslaved or free, was to provide labor. Later it would be psychiatrists like Norman Humphrey in the 1940s who began suggesting that the whole social construct of race, at least as it related to racialized culture in America, was simply the equivalent of a caste system[41] in which people of color could be arrogated for service as free or cheap laborers. It begs speculating whether or not in contemporary society, the harassment, brutalization, and incarceration of the African American population on such a large scale would be enough motive to see an exodus of citizens who essentially want to be left alone while they go about living their lives.

One need not have a formal degree in sociology, anthropology, social studies or have an advanced understanding of social constructs or the pseudoscience which helped carry the myth of race into the twenty-first century to be able to locate one of the five arterials or flow systems where America's pulse can be found. Social Change is best described as the radial artery–located at the wrist, it is the most common location for taking the pulse and the easiest to read and understand. The other pulse points are: Politics, Economics, Religion, and Sports as entertainment will also be explored in this book, respectively. So, just like the pulse at any artery is an indication of the condition of the heart of a being no matter where it is taken, the pulse of America can be felt everywhere.

For example, some Americans think America's National Football League (NFL), the league for American styled gridiron football as opposed to Association football or soccer, is simply a sports issue, and it is not. Quarterback Colin Kaepernick and the whole national anthem of the United States protest issue is about much more than just sports. It also relates to social change, politics, economics, religion, and entertainment. Kaepernick declared that his non-violent protesting was in opposition to the systemic oppression of people of color in America and not opposition to the United States flag or its military.[42] But judging from some of the backlash he received, including death threats, a particular segment of the American populace either do not trust his sincerity or do not care about his First Amendment rights. Kneeling as Kaepernick did as opposed to standing during the playing of the Star-Spangled Banner, the national anthem of the United States, is seen not exclusively, but primarily, by those who self-identify as White as not only disrespect but as a sign of ungratefulness as it were on the part of African Americans; who are the descendants of enslaved Africans; and people of color in general. The conversation is much bigger than sports as this book will attempt to demonstrate in a chapter dedicated to sports. Kaepernick's protesting became such a polarizing topic that even the forty-fifth president of the United States time and time again suggested that players who kneel during the anthem should somehow be punished by the owners of their respective teams. This inference that the forty-fifth president of the United States and many, if not most of his followers and loyalists made was that people of color should all just be grateful to live in the United States, in so-called relative freedom. That people of color should stop complaining is what many were suggesting, and some of the bold individuals like the forty-fifth president of the United States himself even demanded it.

Yes, America is a great place to live. Yes, given the option to live anywhere else in the world, it could be argued that the vast majority of African Americans (who are the descendants of enslaved Africans, people of color, and those who have been oppressed and marginalized for decades if not centuries) would choose to remain in America even if given the means, motive, and opportunity to leave.

So, it is quite unsettling when many who self-identify as White bring up the idea that if the complaints about America are so unbearable, then perhaps those people should simply leave America. Well, first of all, enslaved Africans were brought to America. A better way to explain it is that they were literally forced to make the arduous journey from the continent of Africa to the New World. It was a practice and a journey that was at times legal and at other times illegal, but it was always against their wills. They were not given any choice. So, to insinuate that African Americans; who are the descendants of enslaved Africans; could or should go back to, as in back to another country, is ludicrous. When speaking of generations and generations of people of color who were all born in America, whose mothers and fathers were born in America, as were their parent's parents, and their parent's parent's parents, and so on and so forth, are by definition indigenous in every sense of the word. They can never be viewed as foreign just because their ancestors, many of whom were kidnapped, by the way, were forced to come to the Caribbean, to Central and South America, and ultimately to the United States.[43] They are no more foreign than those who self-identify as White are foreign simply because their ancestors arrived in America as part of the original Thirteen British Colonies, also known as the Thirteen American Colonies, or arrived much later on New York Harbor's Ellis Island from various parts of Europe.

With often venomous displays of division and partisanship one might expect America's pulse to constantly race with uncontrolled passions and spiritual turmoil. However, it has been postulated that it is not uncommon to run across a man or woman who self-identifies as White, who appears, at least on the surface, to be a staunch supporter of the African American or Afro-American movement. Usually, they are not just necessarily lovers of the *brethren* or truly believe in equality between the so-called races. In fact, these often-staunch supporters of the African American or Afro-American movement are quite often just very legal minded individuals. They are often simply people of principal when it comes to rules, regulations, and the letter of the law. It is kind of like the overarching premise in the American film *A Time to Kill* where one of the film's main protagonists kills two White men who viciously beat and raped his daughter. And then a White lawyer, Jake, in spite of the backlash he endures from a violent White Supremacist ideology group, defends this act of revenge by an African American man against two White men in racially charged Mississippi in the 1980s.[44] So, there are men and women who self-identify as White who are just people of principal. Whether lawyers, lawmakers, or the least educated among them, they understand the core concepts of America's laws and believe they should be applied evenly, regardless of the notion of race. And while they may not really and truly see African Americans and people of color as brethren, many of them can, in most instances, respect them. Arguably in the minority, these are quite often simply fair-minded individuals who are willing to buck the system of racism and pervasive societal prejudice that view fellow citizens based on tribalism.

However, if America is going to or cares to survive the new world order in which people of color unseat those who self-identify as White as the largest population in America, does it not need to change the way it views the idea of color as a social construct? Often, America's problems with skin color are not even really about the inability to be politically correct or about a lack of tolerance per se. It is instead about not being self-aware. Historians and scholars suggest that instead of a *reconstruction* by means of the 1867-1868 Reconstruction Acts after America's Civil War, there should have been a *deconstruction*. There should have been a tearing apart of the ethnocentric view toward people who are either mildly or radically endowed with melanin. In building or rebuilding a more perfect union, all so-called race and ethnic related pejoratives should have been done away with, especially when referring to fellow citizens. After all, labels are made to be embraced, hated, then discarded only to be replaced by different labels that are embraced, then despised, and ultimately done away with. So, why does it make sense to refer to White people as "those who self-identify as White" instead of referring to them as Caucasian–Anglo–of European descent? Well it is mostly about the fact that color is not only a social construct, but the term White in particular within that social construct denotes a certain amount of power attributed to the so-called color White.

So, at least in the minds of many, this is a way of removing, lessening, or mitigating some of that word's power, whether that power is real or perceived. Also, to be quite frank, the term White is quite ambiguous. Does it refer to Anglo-Saxon? European? Does it refer to a person who is simply not Black–not brown skinned–not Latino or Hispanic in the United States? Is it simply someone whose ancestors arrived on Ellis Island from some other part of the world? So, with that being said, some Americans self-identify as White by default because their ancestry is heavily steeped in Europe and others because it was simply ingrained in them by default.[45,46] Historians and scholars corroborate American activist and writer Theodore W. Allen's assessment that, "The plantation [middle-class] deliberately extended a privileged status to the White poor of all categories as a means of turning to African slavery as the basis of its system of production.[47] So it was America's shift from socioeconomic status or class to a melanin based "pigmentocracy,"[48] which assisted in the creation of a distinct division between the so-called African-Negro-Black American and the so-called White American.

It makes sense not to say a person is White. Because the truth of the matter being that it is presumptuous to assume a person's true ancestry simply based upon superficial physical characteristics. However, it appears as though it is quite often the persons themselves, who are calling or referring to themselves as White. It may be that step one in knocking so-called "White privilege;"[49] invisible racialized advantages; down a notch or two is by referring to people as *self-identifying* as White and not *being* White. Because it is this term White that often denotes an invisible sense of belonging to a dominant status group with regard to titular racial hierarchy.[50] This just goes to help underscore the power of words. Take, for example, a scene from the American film *The Matrix Revolutions* where the film's main protagonist insists that "Love is a human emotion,"[51] implying that a computer program cannot feel love. To which the film's holographic computer program character replies, "Love is a word,"[52] but what matters most is simply, "The connection that the word love implies."[53] The computer program goes on to say that he can see that the protagonist is in love and asks, "What would you give to hold on to that connection?"[54] To which the protagonist replies, "Anything."[55] So, the term White, at least in America, is much-much more than just a word. It is more than just a way to help distinguish or differentiate people visually. It is more than just something used purely for the sake of positive visual identification.

Like in *The Matrix* film, it is about the connection that the word White implies. It implies that if a person self-identifies as White then they are one of *them*, part of *them*, they belong to *them*, and perhaps even if forced to choose a side, are with–*them*. Who is them? Them is the proverbial powers that be, whether it is referring to the courts, government bureaucracies, or the controlling bodies of essentially any public or private organization or corporation. It can be overt acts of racial bias, mortgage algorithms that charge higher interest rates for African Americans and people of color,[56] or those individuals and bodies in America who are still trying to understand the meaning of diversity while other Western nations are already well into understanding "inclusion."[57] However, even if someone who self-identifies as White denounces those powers, even if they were to figuratively run away from home, change their name, they will always be part of that *family* as it were.

From Jack Johnson becoming the first African American world heavyweight boxing champion in 1908 to Jackie Robinson breaking the invisible baseball *color line*; a phrase which will be described further in subsequent chapters of this book; when he started for the Brooklyn Dodgers in 1947, the moral to the story is rather obvious. The outlawing of the dirty business of human trafficking, (which was the import of Africans via the Atlantic Ocean to be used as chattel slaves), the Emancipation Proclamation of 1863; which in itself did not free the enslaved, it took the Thirteenth Amendment in 1865, the 1954 United States Supreme Court decision of Brown v. the Board of Education which ruled public school segregation unconstitutional, the Civil Rights Act of 1964, the Voting Rights Act of 1965, and the Hate Crimes Prevention Act of 2009 were all great achievements. They were very necessary for freedom and for democracy and those men and women who self-identify as White who were on the right side of these monumental accomplishments should be applauded.

However, it is also especially important to make sure that women get their just due, not just in order to be politically correct or to necessarily support the feminist movement. But because on the other side of the battle for America's soul, while White men, instead of reconstructing to be a more perfect union after the Civil War, were instead constructing the Black Codes of Jim Crow laws, their significant others, women, were not sitting at home twiddling their thumbs. They, too, were advancing the White Supremacist ideology. It has been argued that the idea or the narrative that so-called White Supremacy is patriarchal is false. The vast majority of White women adhere to the same or similar ideologies as their White male counterparts, including the idea that the former enslaving South did not in fact lose the Civil War.

The Daughters of the Confederacy is a group of somewhere north of twenty thousand[58] White women who claim to be able to trace their familial lineage back to White men who actually fought in the American Civil War on the side of the Confederacy. The Confederacy was the southern states that seceded from the United States, more commonly referred to as the Union. The Daughters of the Confederacy is still alive and going strong in their attempts to defend their belief in the Lost Cause ideology. An ideology which falsely paints a revisionist history of the Confederacy's role in the Civil War as one of virtuosic and of heroic proportions while denying the role that the enslavement of Africans and African Americans played as a major reason for the war.[59] Most of their contemporary efforts involve funding the erection of statues and other memorials that commemorate Confederate soldiers. However, perhaps their greatest influence in American culture is felt through influencing and rewriting or slanting the Civil War through the glossing over of the Confederacy's true role in the Civil War. They attempt to marginalize America's violently racist past as presented in public school textbooks by not painting the Confederacy and its acts of war as rebellious and treasonous, due in large part to its pro-enslavement stance. But critics argue that the Lost Cause ideology was simply an attempt by White Southerners after losing the Civil War to save face and keep up the appearances of dignity by doubling down on an unfounded notion of honor that they gleaned from the outcome of the war.

There are historians and scholars who argue that the indoctrination of millions of Southern children through the so-called Lost Cause is perhaps why even after over one hundred and fifty years have passed, the attitudes of those who self-identify as White in the South has not changed much. Those children who were either indoctrinated with the Lost Cause ideology directly or indirectly grew up to be mayors, governors, congressmen, and women, and even presidents of the United States. This might help explain why the United States Congress has soberingly been referred to as "a little bit of an ugly institution" because it is "designed to be a mirror" of American voters as a people.[60] Perhaps this helps further explain why abolitionist Angelina Grimké and other loyalists of African and African American freedom like her were so opposed to the enslavement of Africans and African Americans in the first place. Grimké believed that being enslavers corrupted the souls of White people[61]—in a sense desensitizing them.

One of the steps in ego identity indoctrination[62,63] is either through blatantly rewriting history, primarily through key redactions, or through various other storytelling methods capable of at a minimum blurring truthful narrative through linguistics. America's fortieth President, Ronald Reagan, was himself considered very adept at parsing words and phrases, often called coded language, to infer the notion of race or ethnicity. His infamous syntax of the "Welfare Queen"[64] trope in both his 1976 and 1980 campaigns was considered genius by his followers and loyalists. Political scientists point out that Reagan managed to turn a lack of oversight of the public, state, and federal systems designed to financially assist low-income individuals, families, senior citizens, and military veterans into a bogeyman. Thereby villainizing the average recipient of public assistance because of the shenanigans of a reputed criminal who was guilty of many other and arguably much worse crimes than welfare fraud.

Even before he formally entered politics, Reagan had already become acquainted with the ideology of the Southern Strategy of the 1960s. As a matter of fact, he may have even been familiar with the predecessor to the Southern Strategy, which was the Declaration of Constitutional Principles, also known as the Southern Manifesto of 1956. Signed by approximately twenty percent of the members of the Eighty-Forth United States Congress, all from the former enslaving states;[65,66] the Southern Manifesto urged all Southern Congressmen to "exhaust all 'lawful means'"[67] in resistance to the 1954 court decision of Brown v. the Board of Education mentioned previously. But the Southern Strategy or the White Southern votes strategy was an ideology that embraced a particular segment of the population, comprised primarily of the electorate and the elected who self-identified as White. Those who realized that their political messaging could no longer get away with publicly espousing their racially motivated biases, bigotry, and overt racism, not just socially but also in terms of public policy.

So, over the course of years and decades part of the common vernacular of this political ideology was changed. Strategically implemented through the clever coding or disguising of both racially motivated social language and racially motivated political language. Using semantics, political dog whistles; words and phrases that on the surface appear benign, but to both the base of a political party and to its opposition, it is understood to be nefarious.[68] Through tropes and the parsing of words, synonyms made their agenda more palatable to the untrained observer, but their underlying racially tinged motives remained the same. It may have well been called hiding in plain sight. Some historians and scholars believe that when it came to the Strategy, it was not just what came out of the mouths of the electorate and the elected that associated them with this ideology; it was also how they voted.

So, there was no hiding Reagan's association with the Southern Strategy starting with his public support of California's 1964 Proposition 14. Proposition 14 was a state ballot proposition that amended California's constitution and nullified the state's Fair Housing Act. The amendment was defined by its supporters as merely "a matter of homeowner's freedom,"[69] while those who opposed it like civil rights leader Dr. Martin Luther King, Jr. saw it as simply a strategy devised to discriminate against people of color by allowing White property owners and landlords the right to deny people of color opportunities to rent real estate in the state of California. For decades, amendments like this were part of the Strategy to win White Southern votes and have been impugned as racially divisive by historians and scholars.

The Strategy's deniers say that it never happened, even though Kevin Phillips, the former political strategist for America's thirty-seventh President, Richard Nixon, admitted in 1973 that the Strategy was real. And that part of the Strategy was in fact for Republicans to encourage large numbers of African Americans, who Phillips referred to as Negroes, to register as Democrats. This, in theory, would drive White voters, who Phillips referred to as Negrophobes, away from the Democratic Party and into the Republican Party.[70] Meanwhile there are electorate, elected and their progeny who do not deny that the Strategy existed, but they attempt to defend or deemphasize any perceived malevolence in the Strategy, describing the Strategy as merely a nuanced facet of conservative ideology hated by opponents whom they label as progressives, and whom they also accuse of race-baiting.[71] The Emancipation Proclamation of 1863, the 1954 court decision of Brown v. the Board of Education, the Civil Rights Act of 1964, the Voting Rights Act of 1965, and the Hate Crimes Prevention Act of 2009 were all great achievements. However, these were only *legal* statutes and precedents. These things were simply designed to force bigots, racists, and those who hold biases against people of color to think twice before openly discriminating against people of color. It created a certain amount of tolerance, but part of the problem is that many people of color over time began to mistake this simple tolerance for bonafide goodwill, for true equality, and even for brotherhood–as bonafide fellow citizens of the United States. Unfortunately, the idea that "all men are created equal" is not without its own sense of irony because the word "equal" appears to have morphed into the concepts of a socioeconomic equality and inequality approach instead of an equity and inequity approach. And perhaps it was the inherent challenges of socioeconomic equality and inequality which motivated the Greek philosopher Aristotle to clearly demonstrate that equality births conflict, especially when supposed equals possess unequal shares or when supposed unequal's possess equal shares.[72] For that matter, even the concept of equity in terms of "equal pay for equal work" and "equal reward for equal preparation"[73] does not fully demonstrate the idea of fairness; a synonym for equity.[74] Because it does not delve deep enough into the underpinnings of socioeconomic fairness with an understanding that "equality is the goal, not the method."[75] And if an egalitarian society is truly the goal, then every citizen has to have equal access to "wealth, power, or prestige."[76,77] Which would render the equity approach in its purest form as simply the fact that all individuals have what they need in order to be successful.

Perhaps the election of the forty-fifth president of the United States was simply a harsh reminder of the case made by historians and scholars laying out facts that suggest that America is not really the nation of goodwill or brotherhood toward each other, a mask it often dons in the presence of both its enemies and its allies. This all suggests that if America's affinity for embracing language that touts unity as in pledging, "[O]ne Nation under God"[78] or the beauty in "[C]rown thy good with brotherhood,"[79] were cast aside, then perhaps America is really just a nation of limited tolerance for each other. And as painful as it is for Americans to talk or think about, it begs the question, If America can do better as a nation, then why is it not in reality, doing better?

People not only stereotype other racial or ethnic groups, but they also have preconceived notions or stereotypes about their own group, forming often erroneous and harmful ethnocentric views of the world in which they live. Take, for example, the fact that the unemployment rate among people of color is typically considerably higher than it is for those who self-identify as White. From this fact, mixed with the self-stereotype that White people are more industrious, many Whites conclude that the high unemployment rate for people of color equates to people of color not being as industrious as those who self-identify as White.[80] And because particular stereotypes have stood for so long, they often become so entrenched in the thinking of those who self-identify as White that even when African Americans excel, they are simply seen as "[E]xceptions that prove the rule."[81]

Studies have suggested that one plausible reason certain minority groups seem to fare better than others depends upon whether they belong to a group that immigrated to America voluntarily, meaning those who voluntarily immigrated to America in hopes of securing a better life. Which is then contrasted with those who would be classified as involuntary minorities, namely Africans and African Americans who came to America by force.[82] It has been postulated that African Americans may have developed such a disdain for soi-disant White culture in general because of enslavement, the Black Codes, and later Jim Crow laws, that some of them in a desire to not want to take on the attributes of their oppressors, were not as motivated as they could have been. This, in spite of the fact that one study shows that the desire for higher learning amongst African Americans was so great that from 1910 to 1930, there were statistically more African Americans in school than there were Whites.[83]

The moral to the story is also that it is not just the skin color—the different shades of brown or the African ancestry that makes people of color part of the diaspora. Instead, it is the idea that no matter how much people of color integrate with society at large, America is made up of and continues to hold onto the idea that it is made up of nations within a nation and cultures within a culture rather than that mythical melting pot.[84] Even the proverbial bright-eyed and bushy-tailed optimist who does not take bad news or negative news very well has to reckon that it appears as though unless America submits to some type of soul searching, spiritual revival, some form of a new awakening; skin color will for the foreseeable future prevent not the diversification of America; that has already taken place, but the total cultural inclusion of people of color into the greater American collective. This suggests that Emma Lazarus' Statue of Liberty sonnet, New Colossus, that says, "Give me your tired, your poor, your huddled masses yearning to breathe free,"[85] should be revalued or viewed in proper context. While both inspiring and endearing, those words were most likely not representative of a general yearning or a broad desire to extend a heartfelt invitation to just anyone who happened to grace America's shores. No, that open arms welcome was specifically meant for Europeans, not for the descendants of enslaved Africans and African Americans. On the contrary, the invitation for Africans was arguably loftier and more purposeful and would have sounded more like English Bishop and hymn-writer Reginald Heber's hymn "Brightest and Best:"[86]

> Brightest and best of the sons of the morning,
> dawn on our darkness and lend us thine aid . . .

Yes, America had truly enslaved some of the African continent's brightest and best, those whose progeny would lead to a long list of African America firsts like the Jack Johnson's, the Jackie Robinson's and thousands of others like them. Enslavers were not interested in Africa's "huddled masses yearning to breathe free," and perhaps it is notions such as this one that may help present the ongoing case for why there is a Black History Month in America. And why it is that accomplished African American men and women; the descendants of enslaved Africans and African Americas; tout their often innate as well as quantifiably rich family histories. It is almost as if even one hundred and fifty years after the Emancipation Proclamation, there is still an inherent desire to prove their worth, to prove that their accomplishments further justify their being in America. As if they are saying they belong in America because they are substantial contributors to society, and while this is to be applauded, those who self-identify as White do not have to do that. It is as if those who self-identify as White feel they belong even if they are average. Even when many who self-identify as White are literally or figuratively indigent, they still feel worthy. They still feel superior to people of color even when people of color are more educated and financially well off than themselves simply because of the remaining vestiges of the enslavement of Africans and African Americans.

Perhaps this is why it makes more sense to think that 3,953,761 newly emancipated Africans and African Americans; people who were quite often simply snatched or kidnapped from the African continent; should have been given their own state or a couple of states in America to pull themselves together as it were. This, as opposed to thinking that they should straightway be inserted into the general population. It makes perfect sense that after centuries of subjugation and brutality, they needed both the time and the space to learn or relearn how to once again live like most of their African ancestors lived–free. Reasonable arrangements should have been arranged for at least a few generations before they were expected to fully integrate into the general populace with those who self-identify as White after centuries of enslavement. It stands to reason that regardless of color or ethnicity, what group of people anywhere around the globe, in similar circumstances, could be expected to thrive when left at the mercy of a numerical, economic, and political majority? In a land where very few of that majority felt bound by duty to protect them from being preyed upon by "swindlers and rascals."[87] Yes, What was America thinking? Did it not have the slightest clue that these newly freed men and women would need time for "slow and careful internal development,"[88] versus being heaved immediately into economic and political competition with their former enslavers, overseers, drivers, and various other proponents of slavery, the majority of whom could not fathom living amongst free Africans and African Americans? So, as this book's title so aptly asks, What was America thinking, and was there a genuine hope that everyone could all just let bygones be bygones?

So, have things gotten better, worse, or remained the same in America since the Louisiana parish of St. Landry implemented its post-Civil War, 1865, Black Code? Well, that depends upon whether speaking in terms of perception, as in how do things feel to the senses? Or speaking in terms of reality as in questions of, What does the analytical data say? Was the study purely academic or funded by government grants or private enterprises? What exact time frame is being studied and evaluated? Does it possess a macro or a micro view? Should the numerical data conclusions be rounded up to make things appear worse or rounded down to make things look a little better? Should the study be Faith-based, secular, or both? Take, for instance, the study of the criminality of the use of illicit and prescription drugs and how the social construct of race or ethnicity of the user influences general public opinion and media coverage. African Americans and people of color are often portrayed not just in the general public, but also in the media, within the halls of congress, and even within the White House as criminals rather than as victims of drug addiction, unlike those who self-identify as White who are addicted to drugs such as opioids.[89]

The eradication of tribalism or changing the condition of the human spirit of Americans will not be done using statistics and comprehensive research reports. Nevertheless, peer reviewed and credibly sourced data is an indispensable tool for illuminating historical truths. Take, for example, the research which suggests that nearly eighty percent of opioid-related overdoses in America were White people, while only about twelve percent were African American.[90] Yet when large percentages of White people have drug addictions, such as either the methamphetamine use crisis or the more contemporary opioid abuse crisis, it is considered to be a national health crisis, worthy of special funding for special dependency recovery programs. But when people of color have drug addictions, such as the crack cocaine epidemic, they were castigated as simply individual criminal acts worthy of the full penalty of criminal law.[91] So, those who self-identify as White should not be even a little surprised that just over one hundred and fifty years after the Emancipation Proclamation and a little over fifty years since the Civil Rights Act of 1964, that even America's drug addicts are caught in the crossfires of racial disparity.

The social construct surrounding skin color; the quantity of melanin possessed by all human beings, who are scientifically speaking ninety-nine point nine percent genetically similar;[92,93] is going to continue to perpetuate dueling or multiple perceptions and multiple realities. Realities that influence the way America views everything from the way it judges its lawbreakers to the way it examines its sick. Ideas which lead to the argument suggesting that the Declaration of Independence's "self-evident" (US 1776) concrete truths of equality and inalienable rights are in fact not concrete, but arbitrary. That perhaps the words should be blasphemously replaced with words that are a more reflective of the Declaration's often racially biased interpretation. The same can be said for the terms America or American, which, much like the terms freedom and liberty, are subjective, dependent almost exclusively upon the individual "[E]ye of the beholder."[94] Based not upon a singular worldview, but upon the plethora of social, economic, political, and religious views that make up the many different cultures or sub-cultures within the so-called melting pot[95] experiment.

Historians and scholars have frequently noted how America's Founding Fathers, or simply the Founders, a term typically reserved by historians to designate the most noteworthy protagonists in the formation of the nation, used the word *experiment* with regard to America. In his farewell address printed in the American Daily Advertiser, George Washington noted that "It is well worth a fair and full experiment."[96] President John Adams exclaimed somewhat prematurely that "The experiment is made and has completely succeeded; it can no longer be called in question."[97] During his second inaugural address, President Thomas Jefferson told his audience that, "[t]he experiment has been tried; you have witnessed the scene..."[98] And about a century later, William Jennings Bryan, before he was appointed Secretary of State under President Woodrow Wilson, would denounce the experiment when referring to his opposition to the annexation of the Philippines stating that, "Our experiment in colonialism has been unfortunate. Instead of profit, it has brought loss."[99] In fact, the idea of America being a "[T]wo hundred-year experiment in self-governance"[100] is still being discussed today.

CHAPTER 2

ECONOMICS

*The debate over the profitableness of slavery has been going
on... for almost one hundred and fifty years.*[1]
    –Thomas P. Govan 1942

hat was America thinking when it emancipated 3,953,761
enslaved Africans and African Americans and then left
them to live in the same general population with their
former enslavers, overseers, drivers, and various other proponents of
slavery? What was it thinking when it promised enslaved Africans and
African Americans Forty Acres and a Mule[2] after the Civil War ended
but did not deliver? Yet it still expected 3,953,761 former enslaved
Africans and African Americans to prosper economically living in the
same communities with their former enslavers, overseers, drivers, and
various other proponents of slavery. Those who wished them no
good–those who wanted to see them fail? Not only were they starting
from scratch without land or capital in a land that was in some regard
foreign to them, not foreign because they were not born on American
soil, but because they were treated as the "necessary evil"[3-9] spoken of
by enslaver and Associate Justice of the United States Supreme Court
William Johnson. Johnson was of course not alone in his "necessary
evil"[10] opinion. Because with the exception of only the most strident
of abolitionists and anti-slavery proponents, the "necessary evil"[11] was
arguably the majority sentiment or something close for the Southern

states where the enslavement of Africans and African Americans was most widely practiced as well as Northern states. All of whom realized that America needed Africans and African Americans to provide the necessary labor to help build a nation, in particular, to help build its "Sugar Empire"[12] and later its "Cotton Kingdom."[13] But America was also familiar to the newly emancipated Africans and African Americans, not only because they may have been first, second or even twelfth generation born on American soil and survived generations of subjugation and brutality, but also because they multiplied in numbers in spite of their living conditions and they did indeed literally and physically speaking help build a nation.

Even after the Emancipation Proclamation, the Black Codes in states like South Carolina, nullified the state's so-called slave statutes, statutes which in terms of economics were regulations that deprived enslaved Africans and African Americans of their rights to buy and sell property and to enter into contracts. However, as mentioned in the previous chapter on Social Change, there is quite often a difference between the letter of a law or, in this case, a code and the spirit of that particular law or code. So, slave statutes were strategically replaced by synonymous and nuanced Black Codes. It is quite often perception versus reality and at other times it is attribution theory. Take, for instance, the fact that South Carolina, in nullifying the slave statutes and implementing their Black Codes, stated that "persons of color" have the right to buy and sell land, to enter into contracts, to enjoy the "fruits of their labor" and to receive "protection" under the law regarding both their property and their lives. This code at face value suggests an improvement for newly emancipated Africans and African Americans as opposed to their previous condition. However, in the very same document, it was declared that "persons of color" were "Not entitled to social or political equity with White persons."[14] So, newly emancipated Africans and African Americans would no longer be subject to the slave statutes and regulations as far as South Carolina was concerned, but neither would they be afforded full equity with Whites. To borrow a term from the previous chapter on Social Change, this was another red-flag, a warning sign. It meant that if the melting pot[15] experiment were to continue past this point, people of color would be investing their hard-earned dollars in an economy that offers them mere pennies on the dollar for their investments compared to those who self-identify as White. This was in addition to the fact that their right to vote for meaningful change would never be fully protected.

Fast-forwarding into a more contemporary economic time frame by using the refrain from the American football film *Jerry Maguire*, "Show me the money,"[16] is facetiously eloquent. However, witticism notwithstanding, the forensic accounting phrase of, "follow the money," is a more appropriate description of this chapter's attempt to demonstrate that the economic playing field in America has never truly been level for all of its players. And just like this book has alluded to in the previous chapter on Social Change; the fact that America needs to change the way it sees color as a social construct and how America's issues with skin color is often not as much about the inability to be politically correct or about a lack of tolerance per se; there is a lack of self-awareness with regard to America's unlevel economic playing field. However, what happens when the forty-fifth president of the United States—the "Leader of the Free World"[17,18] —is not self-aware? What if a president believes that the way America can appease African Americans; who are the descendants of enslaved Africans; for racism issues in America is simply by creating jobs? Although job creation at face value suggests a welcome improvement for African Americans who are either unemployed or underemployed.

However, again, as previously mentioned, the philosophical question often relates to the idea of there being the letter of the law, or in this case, economic stimulus, and the law's spirit, or the motivation or impetus. In this case, at least on the surface, a president's job creation impetus might suggest that the only problem African Americans and people of color have in America is a lack of jobs. Yes, a lack of jobs for African Americans and people of color is an issue.

However, to be quite clear, an uptick in new job creation by itself does not quell America's racism issue. This was the point of those who suggest that presidents should tamp down on rhetoric that paints the lack of employment opportunities for African Americans as having miraculously been solved when there is even the most minute increase in new job creation. It seems obvious that employment is not the magical elixir that will make the oppression or people of color disappear. Simply enjoying a regular salary will not end systemic racism. Furthermore, it has even been suggested that America, while employing top economists to try to encourage economic growth through various Executive Branch led policies, should also employ industrial and organizational psychologists. With the goal being to get to the actual root cause of racialized economic disparity. Because a fundamental question that almost every African American or person of color, even those who are highly educated top earning professionals, have probably had to ask themselves is: What happens when I get the job I have either dreamt about or perhaps desperately needed, but soon realize that I still have to deal with averse or explicit microaggression[19,20] from associates who self-identify as White? So, this topic is really about more than just the macro view of the economy and the braggadocios ranting of "Jobs, Jobs, Jobs!"[21] hyperbole of the forty-fifth president of the United States. Because even though the unemployment rate may decline, in ten of America's cities in which African Americans represent a majority of the population, the unemployment rate is still typically higher for African Americans for Whites by approximately four to nearly eleven percent.[22,23]

This is, of course, not suggesting that economic inequities, which may be the residual effect of the Black Codes and Jim Crow laws, are alone solely responsible for what prevents many people of color from being able to narrow the wealth creation–prosperity gap[24,25] that exists between themselves and those who self-identify as White. For there is an abundance of scholarly research as well as an abundance of books[26-29] written by people of color about the subject of personal responsibility or self-help as a community. A community which exists as the nation within a nation previously expounded upon in this book in the chapter on Social Change. From the economic topics of so-called "entitlement programs"[30,31,32] or federal safety net programs to education and small business development, it is a universally recognized given that personal responsibility has its place. It is even argued that the need for more personal responsibility is most urgent not necessarily in the lives of individuals, but in the world of African American entrepreneurs–entrepreneurs of color. Many of whom are tremendous and astute business leaders and serial entrepreneurs who are doing a lot of economic good for people of color, but who are in recent times being almost chastised for not doing enough.

Some of this ire has been directed toward African Americans and people of color who have total or at least a controlling interest in media companies, especially cable television networks, which are a tremendous asset for African Americans and all people of color. However, some argue that too many African American owned media companies are simply non-stop entertainment venues with very little news programming, very little teaching, or educational programming. In general, very little of the kinds of programming that African American scholars believe would serve not only African Americans, but all people of color. In a collective endeavor to progress as a nation within a nation. The logic behind the critique is explained by first acknowledging that media companies like this do make sure that there are African Americans and people of color working as directors, producers, artists, and designers behind the camera as well as the primary talent in front of the camera. However, the problem they interject is a seeming reluctance of some networks to consider retooling their programming to be more progressive. For lack of a better superlative, to be more pro-black in terms of really empowering African Americans and people of color by informing them with news and information vital to their futures. Programming that is more aggressive; more on the forefront–on the cutting-edge–in terms of educational and news programming. A little less *entertainment* per se and a bit more cultural, economic, and even political activism. But in light of all this, one might ask, What does the media have to do with economics?

Media psychologists have for decades understood the economic impact that different types of media, in particular cable or satellite television programming accessed through either traditional television screens or various smart devices with screens, have on societal economics. It is not just influencing economics in terms of transmitting stock prices and investor information, but also acting as a trade facilitator, a transmitter of both ideas and innovation.[33] Exposing people to information related to the importance of education, labor markets, and their underlying employment opportunities, to changes in tax laws, and spending money and saving money in general.[34] One example of the critical relationship between the media and economics can be seen by examining the lack of coverage by African American media outlets of the Tax Cuts and Jobs Act of 2017. The tax cuts, which were touted by the forty-fifth president of the United States through his social media accounts and cable news networks as being "So large and so meaningful . . ."[35] and purported to be the "Biggest Tax Bill and Tax Cuts in history"[36] and insisting that the cuts would encourage "Jobs, Jobs, Jobs!"[37] belied the fact that the cuts would actually be more profitable for or would be more inclined to cut taxes for Whites than for African Americans and people of color. With Whites seeing over two hundred billion dollars in tax cuts in 2018 and African Americans, grouped with Latino's, only receiving just over thirty billion dollars in tax cuts.[38,39]

Another example of the importance of media coverage with regard to economics is the gains in health coverage realized by African Americans under the health coverage legislation referred to as Obama Care (The federal statute is officially known as the Patient Protection and Affordable Care Act.). This downward trend of those without health coverage began to reverse for African Americans. In fact, it began ticking upward by half of a percentage point from 2016 to 2017.[40] And while half of a percentage point might seem like a small increase in the number without health coverage, it is by no means small to those millions of uninsured African Americans who have historically faced disparities in their struggles to find affordable health coverage. This increase is especially troubling in light of the fact that African Americans depend more on the benefits of Medicaid than Whites and are more likely to fall into the coverage gap if they live in specific southern states that are still refusing to expand Medicaid. This is just one example that makes a case for expanding news coverage by African American media companies and outlets.

Some economists concluded that while the economic policies of the forty-fifth president of the United States just happened to coincide with an unemployment rate that was already trending downward before he took office, his economic policies still hurt African Americans and people of color economically. And it was the implementation of those hurtful policies, systems, and practices which have the long-term potential to negatively and disproportionately affect African Americans and people of color the most. Take, for example, the actions of the United States Attorney General, Jeff Sessions, appointed by the forty-fifth president of the United States, rescinding a President Barack Obama led Justice Department letter. A letter that was written as a reminder to criminal courts across the country to be mindful of imposing unreasonable fees and fines on poor court defendants, many of whom were already deeply indebted and faced higher rates of recidivism quite often as it relates to their inability to pay court ordered fines and fees because of their existing debts.

The rescinded letter was also an admission that both President Obama's administration as well as the Justice Department under his leadership understood how excessive fees and fines bolster an accumulative effect. An effect that puts many of these individuals at risk of becoming ensnared in the vicious cycle of the criminal justice system even though they no longer pose any potential danger to their communities.[41] And the irony which is often played out in the criminal justice system is in some regard reminiscent of the emancipation of 3,953,761 enslaved Africans and African Americans who, although free, were in some regards still on parole as it were. Because at its core, "parole,"[42] is a conditional release from prison. The physical bars are quite often replaced by the invisible weight of unrealistic expectations by a society. The imagery of the relationship between enslavement and prison is what William Lloyd Garrison used to describe the condition from which America's greatest abolitionist, anti-slavery writer, and orator Frederick Douglass, had himself narrowly escaped from; the "prison-house of bondage;"[43] chattel slavery.

Historians and scholars believe that it is not farfetched to think that the African American media might have helped prevent the election of the candidate who became the forty-fifth president of the United States if viewers were presented with regularly occurring and consistent national election news and if other relevant news programming were in place. Some African American intelligentsia argue that the African American media could have encouraged the counter-culture necessary to not only disperse relevant information to the masses, but also as a way to take back and control the narrative of its people. Changing the way they see color as a social construct and transforming lives–long-term–by changing thought patterns. Not just hashing and rehashing the rhetoric of the typical American national news cycle. Their suggestion is that having a seriously noteworthy African American media presence might have played an important role in acting as a much needed filter against traditional media sources of national news reporting. Especially when mainstream media can on one end of the spectrum be flat-out false and on the other end partisan, unfair, lacking journalistic integrity or does not appear to have the best interests of African Americans and people of color at heart.

So, whether speaking of the roles of the African American media, African American corporations, or individual citizens, there is little argument about the validity of the role personal responsibility and self-help should play in the economic lives of people of color. The rub, say historians and scholars, is not personal responsibility, but the mechanisms that propagate a "racialized economic structure."[44,45,46] From the economics of the unpaid labor of enslaved Africans and African Americans; a number that would be in the trillions in today's United States dollars;[47] to the wage gap between African American men and White men; which was the same gap in 2014 that existed in 1950 under the Jim Crow laws;[48] to the lack of real support for the positive impacts of Affirmative Action concerning both education and employment,[49] to unconstitutional racialized gerrymandering, to algorithms which can predict the so-called race or ethnicity of voters based on their name[50] or address, to a company's human resource department performing online searches of the name of African American job candidates prior to interviews; candidates who often just happen to have names that some search engine algorithms recognize or interpret as possibly belonging to someone who is African American or Black. It then triggers advertising via personalized ads on the page or pages that may suggest an arrest record at first glance, due to the person's name being associated with the visual advertising of criminal background checking services being displayed on the page.[51,52]

So, the previously mentioned Black Codes of South Carolina and other states made it quite clear that it was not to be a secret that there was an important relationship between social, political, and economic equity.[53] Even with the right to earn wages and perhaps buy land it, was clear that a lack of social change as expressed through social relationships[54] between African Americans and Whites via community involvement, the dictation of social roles and norms, and the denial of social equity could be used as a tool to continue the subjugation of newly emancipated Africans and African Americans. However, while social inequities as a whole have become less overt in contemporary times, they still underscore the idea that access to community involvement and the dictation of social roles and norms is still controlled by hierarchy[55] and by those who self-identify as White. This is the case even when African Americans are part of the one-percenters, the wealthiest one percent of the American population.

A contemporary example of social stratification even when it comes to the wealthiest African Americans can be seen in statements made by Americans, such as the forty-fifth president of the United States. He said in a speech made before a sizeable audience of his followers and loyalists, "If an NFL player wants the privilege of making millions in the NFL, they should not be allowed to "[D]isrespect the flag."[56] To which his critics argued that the president's ire at the peaceful protests of NFL players and their sympathizers was simply a very common dog whistle. One that suggested that African Americans and people of color who have been able to arrive at the upper echelon of the economy have by default given up their right to speak out about racial inequity and oppression. Those who are adept at interpreting whistles such as this one were quick to explain that just because an African American's earned wealth has placed them at a higher rank than other African Americans; often creating a psychological distance within that group; does not nullify the fact that there is still an enduring inequity that exists between African Americans and those who self-identify as White.[57]

Another example of how racial hierarchy continues to remain deeply entrenched[58,59,60] in America, rearing its venomous head not only in resistance to social change but also embedded in the nation's economic psyche is the case of America's former Speaker of the United States House of Representatives, Newt Gingrich. Gingrich publicly claimed that because NFL players are rich, they need psychological therapy if they feel oppressed.[61] So, it is with heavy irony that an argument could be made that it is America who needs therapy for believing that freeing 3,953,761 enslaved Africans and African Americans and leaving them to live in the same general population with their former enslavers, overseers, drivers, and various other proponents of slavery would not in a best case scenario be tumultuous and in a worst case scenario a disaster. Gingrich's words were yet another whistle to be heard and deciphered. One that suggested that because some African Americans have achieved a higher status than other Americans, the notion of inequity no longer exists for them. This is because high African American achievers, because of their wealth or notoriety, have been ascribed the social identity and status as it were of Whiteness[62,63,64] as alluded to in the chapter on Social Change. Gingrich's whistle also suggested that the accomplishments of high achieving African Americans somehow shields them from having their rights and freedoms tested, which is a false assumption.

While Whiteness is not a racial identity, it nevertheless exclusively affords those who can self-identify as White a social status and hierarchy that exists irrespective of economic status.[65] Being able to claim the identity of Whiteness also shields the recipients from the three most pervasive forms of oppression common in contemporary America; marginalization, powerlessness, and violence.[66] Whenever public and derogatory statements are made by high-profile Americans who self-identify as White against high-profile African Americans and people of color, it simply underscores or reinforces the fact that economic resources are only part of the equation in which; social inclusion + plus economic resources + plus political influence = power. However, total power can only accurately be calculated after the assertion of status as a White American is entered into the equation as the most significant variable.

What many Americans do not realize is that through the use of false equivalency, people like the forty-fifth president of the United States, Newt Gingrich, and others have erroneously equated living daily within the midst of the racialized constraints of American culture with "free choice."[67] Not realizing that it is possible to live in an otherwise free society and still be oppressed. Free societies and cultures are more than capable of having oppressive constraints that are so ingrained in them that a large segment of their population is either not consciously aware of the restrictions or else they are the benefactors of the constraints. Usually, because they profit from the two other forms of oppression not mentioned previously; exploitation and cultural imperialism or cultural colonialism. So, public statements of the forty-fifth president of the United States and the Newt Gingrich's of the world encouraged the perpetuation of the notion that because some of America's one-percenters are African Americans, this must by false equivalency mean that racialized economic inequity no longer exists. Likewise, they also infer that everyone in America is operating under the auspices of unimpeded free choice. It is not unlike saying that an enslaved African or African American who did not try to escape or otherwise cry foul at their predicament must by default have desired to be enslaved of their own free choice; which is obviously absurd.

Psychologists suggest that it is a form of pluralistic ignorance, nescience, on the part of many who self-identify as White with regard to the notion that the oppressed must offer enough proof of their oppression in order to be taken seriously or to be seen as genuinely oppressed. And that they must also confront the oppressor face-to-face and make their grievances direct and clear. After all, how can the oppressor know they are oppressive unless they are told by the oppressed that they are oppressive? However, the problem with expecting the oppressed to confront the oppressor is that the oppressor's response is highly predictable, outright denial. The outright denial is typically followed by attempts to justify or legitimize wrong behavior through the guise of paternalism while denying having anything to do with hegemony.[68,69,70] The sad irony of this confrontational approach is that the accusations of the oppressed often only serve to provide a bit of breathing room for the oppressor as an exculpatory defense is being conjured up. And quite often, instead of preparing a justifiable defense, the oppressors time is spent strategizing even more ingenious ways to disguise acts of oppression and postpone any future similar accusations. Yet all the while, the oppressed, having already been scarred, now feels traumatized a second time by having to either confront the oppressor or explain in detail the oppressive acts to a third party. Perhaps it is this dysfunctional ritual of behavior which gave rise to the notion that in an oppressive regime, there are still two sides to every story, "she said-he said."[71] Evoking either a false equivalency or illogical use of causation psychology which is of course never true when it comes to the subjugation and oppression of people groups. Besides, the odds of any oppressive relationship being repairable are astronomically low, especially when one people group has a history of power and the other people group a history of powerlessness. So, psychologists theorize that it is as if those who self-identify as White cannot contradistinguish between personal or interpersonal oppression and institutional or cultural oppression.[72,73,74] Both of which are terrible, the latter of which is monstrous, and which some theologians lament is not unlike the text in Proverbs 14:31 (TPT), which states that oppression is an insult to "Creator-God" (Psalm 96:5 TPT).

Although the primary focus of this chapter is economics, inequity cannot be overly simplified; neither can it be compartmentalized. This is because racialized inequity, whether it concerns social change, economics, politics, religion, or sports as entertainment, is both interrelated and interdependent. It is the question of whether or not Americans who self-identify as White really believe that Dr. King's dream, his vision, was as simple as the right of people of African Americans and people of color to drink water from the same public water fountain as those who self-identify as White. That it was as simple as being able to sit at a racially segregated drug store lunch counter or simply the right to sit at the front– middle– side–or top, pun intended, of a racially segregated bus, just so long as African Americans; who are the descendants of enslaved Africans; were not by default relegated to the back of the vehicle. If Americans who self-identify as White think that this is what Dr. King's dream, his vision, was about then they do not really understand his dream, his vision, at all. Because his dream, his vision, was arguably the most grandiose, the most dramatic, the most futuristic, the most visionary document in American history. A case could be made that his dream makes the Preamble to the Declaration of Independence seem plain–ordinary and overly simplistic in comparison.

Born and raised in America's Jim Crowe South, Dr. King was an African American man, who had the unmitigated gall–the audacity–to say that he had a dream that America would "live out the true meaning of its creed."[75] That the sons of former enslaved Africans and African Americans and the sons of former enslavers would one day sit in brotherhood. Furthermore, he dreamt that even in the state of Alabama, which at that time was something akin to an apartheid state, but that African American children and White children would be able to join hands as sisters and brothers. Not only was it a grandiose vision, but a Herculean one as well because the year that his speech was given, 1963, African Americans had yet to acquire any meaningful civil rights legislation, nor did they possess the unencumbered right to vote. However, part of the problem then as it is now is that many Americans who self-identify as White see the 1950s-1960s Civil Rights Movement as petty and trite. As if the Movement, when broken down into its simplest form was just about the removal of signs which read "Whites Only" or simply about African Americans desiring a bigger share of America's economic pie through Affirmative Action. Likewise, King's grandiose, dramatic, futuristic, and visionary dream was never embraced as the blueprint for the multicultural Utopian nation that America had the potential to be, but was instead relentlessly persecuted and eventually assassinated.

Although those like Dr. King may have and many today still dream of America as an enlightened capitalist economy, it remains at its core a capitalist economy. And yet, while there is theoretically nothing inherently wrong with capitalism in and of itself, economic opportunity and equity are vitally important to both a people's survival as a group and their ability to thrive as individuals. One of the primary reasons why equity should be seen as a total package is because as important a component as economic progress is, focusing only on one aspect of equity often leads to false impressions. Take again, for example, the presumption by Americans who self-identify as White that if an African American professional athlete or entertainer can negotiate contracts that pay them millions of dollars per year, it must by default mean that social, political, even religious inequities no longer exist for African Americans as a collective, a nation within a nation, simply because economic inequity has been nullified for one particular African American individual. Perhaps this is why some historians and scholars have attempted to encourage a renewed focus on the idea that Dr. King's dream must not be narrowed down into only civil rights, it must remain about the broader issue of human rights. They argue that the narrative of civil rights has been condensed into economics alone. Thus, too often, many who self-identify as White find it difficult to see past the money into what the crux of the matter truly is; the humanity.

The idea of placing economic gain ahead of humanity is where many historians and scholars decry the frequent pomp and circumstance that touts America's Founding Fathers as godly men who were the progeny of generations of men and women who felt persecuted in Europe, as both sanctimonious and duplicitous. Because of this, contemporary historians and scholars have revalued past historical focus on the original colonists' motives being merely that of having this grand idea of coming to the New World to pray and worship as they saw fit and not as the British Monarchy told them to. In which case, it becomes more and more difficult to reconcile the eventual violent takeover of Native American lands by the colonists and later the union. The harshest critics argue that while freedom to worship may have been the dominant motive for some, their goals also included economics. Because, after all, they could have prayed in a closet in Europe, they could have worshipped in a small room in Europe. So, the impetus of religious freedom is being revalued by many historians and scholars. Especially in light of the introduction of something as brutal and inhumane as chattel slavery into a place that was supposed to be set aside for free worship. Thus, it becomes very difficult to dispute that the dream of wealth creation or prosperity was not on at least some of their minds, just as it has always been for many immigrants to America.

There is certainly no shortage of ideologues who contend that America's economic prosperity was and is a sign of Divine favor from the "God of Covenant" (Psalm 78:36-37 TPT), this in spite of

America's enslavement history. However, neither is there a shortage of historians and scholars who point to the fact that not unlike America with its chattel slave history, Egypt was also prosperous during the period in which it enslaved the Israelites. Thus, it is comparisons like this one between America and ancient Biblical nations that draw the ire of those who warn America's prosperity ideologues not to be so quick to equate the religiosity in the language and writings of America's so-called Founding Fathers to be unique to America. A lot of the same Biblical allusion and language was common around the globe during the time of America's formation as an independent nation. From the Geneva Bible of both the Mayflower Pilgrims and William Shakespeare[76] to The King James Bible of both George Washington[77] and Harriet Beecher Stowe,[78] historians and scholars proffer a reminder of what the rest of the world already knows, but that America may have forgotten, which is that America did not invent Protestantism neither did it invent evangelicalism.[79,80] Meaning that America never held any exclusive rights as it were to the "God of Covenant" nor to what is often depicted as Divine favor in the form of economic prosperity.

While America's economic prosperity was never dispersed equitably between emancipated Africans, African Americans, and those who self-identify as White, there was, however, a liberal acceptance of the tax dollars of emancipated African and African Americans. The Black codes of the Southern states essentially promised newly emancipated Africans and African Americans that they would not be afforded social equity and that their right to vote would be contested. However, the local, state and federal tax codes promised them that there would be absolutely no impediment, no encumbrance that might keep them from paying taxes with their newly found rights to earn wages and buy and sell land. And while paying taxes is patriotic, it is not always fair. For example, even before the Tax Cuts and Jobs Act of 2017 was signed into law, many economists were already predicting that the proposed act would primarily benefit the wealthy and those earning above a certain level of income, and they were right. Yes, America is a capitalist economy, but not all Americans are capitalists. Populist party Representative to the United States House of Representatives, Milford Wriarson Howard described America in 1895 not as a nation of capitalists, but as a nation of plutocrats,[81,82] a wealthy ruling class or what some might refer to in contemporary times as one-percenters. As opposed to a "wage-slave class,"[83,84,85] those Americans who have a total dependence upon employment with no financial independence, which might closely resemble a modern working-class.

> Here, on the soil enriched with the blood of the patriotic dead, is to be erected an aristocratic monarchy, with wealth as its God.[86]
>
> –Wendell Phillips c. 1884

The Civil War imagery depicted by abolitionist Wendell Phillips in the preceding quote paints a picture of America as a democratic republic built by a wealthy, privileged, ruling class. Thus America, as an aristocratic monarchy by any other name, democracy, republic, or united states, would smell just as sweet to those in power.[87]

Economics, not unlike social change, politics, religion, and sports as entertainment, has both positive and negative effects, advantages, and disadvantages, and offers assets and liabilities that can include both gains and losses. So, in all fairness to wealthy individuals, America is truly a land full of economic opportunity–a bonafide capitalist economy–but it is important to understand that money by itself is not a problem. After all, it has been said that it is better to have money and not need it than to need money and not have it.[88] It is, however, people's attitudes about money and what people do–or in some cases do not do–with money that causes most of the consternation regarding not just money in general but wealth in particular. And it is this idea of attitudes that suggests America's wage and wealth gaps can be attributed to the inequitable attitudes of the powers that be. In this case the powers are those in the positions that control America's economy, positions that control political discourse, positions that control so many of the narratives that can adversely impact America's underserved populations. It is not just African Americans who are economically marginalized but also Latino populations, American Indians, Alaska Natives, people with disabilities, new mothers and women with children, and refugees.[89] Groups with whom the powers that be have never shared the benefits they themselves reap from the trickle-down economics gambit; a theory which will be briefly explored in the chapter on Religion. But it is the historical ineffectiveness of this artifice, which is arguably why the vast majority of Americans, not just African Americas and people of color, are unable to escape the type of wage-slave economic status described earlier in this chapter. Because incentives such as tax cuts designed to entice large corporations, the wealthy, the plutocrats into spending their tax savings and extra wealth do not increase the demand for products and services as touted. Therefore, it does not, in turn, create new jobs or offer higher wages for existing jobs.

Again, in all fairness to wealthy individuals, a majority of whom, while they may not be too keen on investing in the economy in ways that might, in turn, benefit the other ninety nine percent of Americans, it can be argued that they do, however, represent a large percentage of America's philanthropic and charitable giving.

However, economic historians and scholars have questioned whether the motivation of the philanthropic and charitable giving of the one-percenters is not more closely tied to either their strategic public relations and brand building endeavors, tax deductions, or both. Also, in question is whether or not they do contribute a greater percentage of their incomes than those who are less wealthy than themselves. The same critique has even been aimed at those wealthy social and political activists—the enlightened capitalists—the one-percenters who at least on the surface appear to empathize with America's working class and its most vulnerable population; those living below the poverty line.

Yes, there are some wealthy Americans who appear to earnestly make concerted efforts to try to build bridges in spite of the parabolic chasm, that great seemingly unbridgeable gulf between the rich man and poor man (author's paraphrase Luke 16:26). However, some of the more captious economic historians and scholars suggest that in spite of projecting seemingly good intentions, many socially and politically active one-percenters only urge their fellow plutocrats or political party to become proactive in combatting economic inequity; that is the wealth gap that exists between America's top earners and the rest of America; when it is either economically or politically expedient for them.

Because the enlightened capitalists mentioned previously not only hold sway in economic matters because of their wealth, they often hold sway in the political arena as well. Their influence over political elections and even public policy can be felt by means of where they choose to contribute or not contribute their resources and what individuals, political parties, or policies they either decide to endorse or, very often, through their silence, oppose. One example of the sort of self-serving behavior of the empathizing one-percenters previously alluded to was the aftermath of Hurricane Maria, which devastated the United States island territory of Puerto Rico in 2017. And while the action or in this case, inaction of the socially conscious one-percenters may have gone virtually unnoticed by the majority of the American population, the United States government's action or in this case, inaction was heavily and openly criticized. Mostly, because there is a widely held belief that the United States government's slow response in the aftermath of the hurricane was motivated by the ethnicity of the island's inhabitants. And legitimate arguments were raised suggesting that history shows that when it comes to assisting large populations of those who self-identify as White, the powers that be; in this case, some combination of state or territory governors, the Federal Emergency Management Agency (FEMA), the president of the United States and the United States Congress appear more ready and willing to throw the full force and resources at their disposal at the crisis as opposed to helping communities of color. And it is not only the powers that be who have been accused of appearing more concerned and motivated to act quickly on behalf of predominately White communities than those composed predominantly of people of color, such as Puerto Rico. But many socially and politically active one-percenters have also been criticized for giving a proverbial whisper instead of a full-throated shout during this and other crises. Thus, the accusations of self-serving.

It is cases like Puerto Rico that embolden those who argue that when it comes to African Americas and other underserved populations such as the ethnic groups of people of Puerto Rico, racialized political body language often seems to imply that disaster victims are somehow to blame for at least a portion of the devastation simply because they live in poor or working-class communities. That there is quite often a cloaked narrative that arises to say that because of their poverty, people who find themselves the victims of natural disasters deserve to wallow in their misery as part of a misguided, inhumane and even cruel lesson aimed at inspiring the misfortunate to reassess their economic status. The teachers of these outlandish social experiments are the powers that be, in this case, quite often the president of the United States and the United States Congress. The powers, through either slow response or in some cases inept response to crises such as this, relay to those who know how to interpret such racialized political body language that helping the victims too quickly during this crisis could amount to a waste of resources. This is in opposition to the language, which often suggests that if the decimated community is predominantly White, then it is perfectly acceptable to write a theoretical check now and worry about how much is in the bank account later.

Their language and inaction suggest that the prudent thing to do is take a step back before rushing in to aid the crisis victims of color. It is as if their logic is implying that the middle of a life and death crisis is the right time to begin an investigation into the systemic poverty or lack of educational opportunities, infrastructure, and mismanagement by local or regional authorities felt by the people. In addition to this, the old adage of helping those who help themselves also comes into play. It is usually directed at African Americas and people of color and is not difficult to infer that it is an often-used dog whistle. On the surface, the powers are only pretending to be good stewards of the resources they are in charge of—as if they really have the long-term best interests of African Americas and people of color or those who are marginalized at heart. But historians and scholars argue that way too often; this is just a way to patronizingly admonish White social status and hierarchy over African Americas and people of color—those who are disenfranchised.

It has also been suggested that the instances where the powers want to take a step back in order to perform an in-depth analysis of a serious situation is when Black and Brown people need financial resources. However, this should not come as a surprise. Because the notions of either America's demonstrated or its perceived lack of good-will with regard to honoring treaties, pacts, acts, promises, and alliances with people of color have almost from the beginning involved a certain amount of incertitude. And this is regardless of whether the motive was driven by profit, benevolence, or paternal subjugation. And while these misgivings are most often directed at the government and the plutocratic membership, the motivation of Western colonial missionaries in general around the globe, whether purely benevolent or exploitive, have likewise been called into question. For example, concerning America's fiftieth state, Hawaii, it was said using various forms of wit concerning the so-called Christian missionaries who it was said, "came to the island to do good, and they did right well."[90] It has been interpreted by some historians and scholars to be a satirical way of questioning the economic gentrification of Hawaii. Or like the continent of Africa for which it has been said, "The missionaries taught Africans to pray with their eyes closed and when the Africans opened their eyes their land and its resources was [*sic*] gone."[91,92]

Yes, America is a capitalist economy, which is perhaps why most scholars would argue that wealth creation–prosperity will never take a back seat to so-called freedom and equity. It has even been posited that rarely if ever is America going to support an agenda or invest substantial resources in something; whether it be technology, education, agricultural commodities, or the like; simply because that agenda or thing is altruistically positive, beneficial to humanity at large, or just because it is the benevolent thing to do. The point is, after the exclusion of bonafide nonprofit–philanthropic–charitable endeavors, the individuals and organizations who invent, design, and manufacture products and services that will benefit humanity greatly are overwhelmingly profit-driven. Take, for example, the revelation that South Korea had faster internet speeds than the United States. America at the time had 4G (fourth generation) cellular network technology, but South Korea at the time was already into 5G territory. This perplexed many Americans who struggled to understand how and why a nation like America that leads the world in technological advancement, fell behind in this type of technology. One theory as to why America lagged behind South Korea is that America, in spite of its often international persona of being the land of freedom, democracy, and boasting of a mixed economy, is at its core a profit–first capitalist economy. And its profit–first ideology is so simplistic that even an animated American television character like Homer Simpson, who after stealing sugar from an overturned sugar truck muttered, "In America, first you get the sugar, then you get the power."[93] He understands how Anglo patriarchal power works in America. The number one question is always going to be: Is it profitable? And the number two question is typically: Will it either save money or else prevent loss? The horrible irony of the simplicity of America's profit motives belies the imitation of life through art expressed via a cartoon character because if slavery had not been so profitable, there would not have been so much resistance to its abolition.

Again, as previously alluded to in this chapter, capitalism in and of itself is neither the main topic of discussion nor is it meant to play the villain because there is nothing inherently sinful about profit. It takes money to be generous as individuals and as a nation–it takes money for faith-based missions and benevolence–it takes money to perform humanitarian work around the globe–it takes money to be able to provide charity to fellow Americans. So, the prevailing question was and still is, Have things gotten better, worse, or remained the same in the nation as a whole since South Carolina implemented its Reconstruction era Black Codes? Well, the answer to that question depends upon the answer to yet another question, and that is, Do little African American boys still grow up to earn less than little White boys even when the parents of those African American boys are wealthy? It bears repeating that one of the overarching themes of this book is that the eradication of tribalism or changing the condition of the human spirit of Americans will not be done using statistics and comprehensive research reports. However, while economic progress can be seen in relationship to the upward mobility of intergenerational income for Hispanics and Asians, both African Americans and American Indian income levels have either plateaued or decreased. Economic data suggests that the earnings gap between African Americans and American Indians and Whites is intergenerational. African Americans and American Indians are the only two minority groups in which environment or class is not necessarily a predictable success indicator. This is the case even among African American children whose parents are top one-percent earners. There is still a twelve to thirteen percentage point earnings gap between African American and White children. And reducing this gap is going to take more than merely seeing a surge in African Americans moving from working class neighborhoods to middle or upper-middle class neighborhoods. It would undoubtedly take socioeconomic policies capable of crossing even class lines.[94]

The moral to the story is about the big picture–the totality of what civil rights and human rights encompass. It is about more than money. Money quite often can be relegated to a written, binding, enforceable contract of sorts. Treating people who happen to look different than oneself with basic human dignity should also be a binding contract. Is this not the golden rule, treating others the way you want to be treated? This is much more powerful than mere man-made legislation. It is where high minded spirituality–the proverbial rubber–meets the proverbial road.

Another moral to the story is the truth that Black and Brown lives matter cannot be reduced to or limited to police brutality and the broken criminal justice system. It extends to the idea that people of color are more than worthy of not just the same equitable rights and privileges, but the same presumption of humanness, such as the same resources that those who self-identify as White are readily afforded access to during a crisis. Historians and scholars have proclaimed that since the Emancipation Proclamation, African Americans; who are the descendants of enslaved Africans; have consistently voiced the idea that while they may be extended rights and privileges on paper–vis-à-vis legislation–there are times where those rights and privileges are not expressed as everyday reality.

Like the truths of humanity, whether presented as civil rights or human rights, are self-evident, the success of government is, in turn, foundational. Because it was George Washington, who said, "To form a new Government required infinite care and unbounded attention." "[F]or if the foundation is badly laid, the superstructure must be bad."[95] Words that, of course, in retrospect appear blatantly hypocritical after centuries of legal review and thorough analysis of the United States Constitution.[96] Perhaps it is because of statements like this one by Washington, strongly suggest that he and presumably the other Founders were not nescient about the importance of the document, which incites some of the most Aristarchian historians and scholars to pillory both the document and Washington. Often refusing to mince words, with some even calling the United States Constitution a "coup,"[97] as in coup d'état. They point to the fact that the "Constitution is undemocratic [because] it protects the wealthy"[98,99] by transferring "power from the many to the few."[100,101] Even Washington's contemporaries like his close friend and delegate to the Continental Congress, Edward Carrington, who admitted in a letter which Carrington wrote to Thomas Jefferson, in which Carrington admitted that he was genuinely frightened by the authoritarianism of the Constitution, even before it was ratified.[102] Carrington also acknowledged to Jefferson that after the war, the Americans most interested in running the nation were the "[D]emagogues of desperate fortunes mere adventurers in fraud."[103]

The moral to the story is also that even though for the most part America was egalitarian, the majority of its Revolutionary leaders still "clung tightly to the concept of a ruling elite, presumably based on merit, but an elite nonetheless–a natural aristocracy . . ."[104] This aristocratic leaning was in spite of the fact that incomes were, in reality, more equitably distributed in Colonial America,[105] and poverty was less pervasive in America than in Europe. Even after taking into consideration the fact that after the Revolutionary War, money was, of course, tight, individual state constitutions were, in fact, very democratic. Before the ratification of the Constitution, common people had more power; thus, it is argued that the Constitution was the wealthy's way of controlling power.

One of the ways in particular that power was maintained was by ensuring the continuation of America's chattel economy through Article I, Section 2, Clause 3,[106] of the Constitution known as the three-fifths rule or three-fifths compromise. And despite the fact that the Constitution's defenders insist the motivation of the three-fifths rule was for the division of representative political power, the

Constitution's complainants believe that the accurate interpretation of the three-fifths rule is that it equated enslaved Africans and African Americas to three-fifths of a human being. However, the chattel economy was later bolstered through Article IV, Section 2, Clause 3,[107] known as the Fugitive Slave Clause, which meant that the so-called free states could not become a safe haven for Africans and African Americas who were able to successfully escape their captors. Historians and scholars think that Washington's statement about the "infinite care and unbounded" attention required in the formation of a new government must have been either naïvely credulous or else purposefully duplicitous in light of how worthy of criticism the constitution has always been. However, there is a strong possibility that Washington's remarks were neither naïve nor duplicitous. Because to the one-percenters, the plutocrats, the proverbial powers that be; whether it was the slaveholders, large planters, or merchants in 1787 or the modern contemporary elite; their eyes beheld then and behold now that the foundation was good. Thus, the Constitutions planners, architects, and its author knew exactly what they were building. Every article, section, and clause, whether the three-fifths rule or the Fugitive Slave Clause was laid out and prepared just as they had planned. Eminent historians and scholars suggest that because the foundation was not properly laid, the American experiment is a fissile society; capable of splitting or dividing along natural planes.[108]

The problem is that while the original unamended document left ample room to deal with enslaved Africans and African Americans, wage-slaves, the working class, and the poor, it was not designed to deal with free Africans and African Americans. This premise is not unlike the perceived motivations behind the Black Codes of the former enslaving states. For example, the previously mentioned state of South Carolina for example that openly acknowledged the rights of African Americans to earn wages and buy and sell land, but also openly acknowledged that those same African Americans are "Not entitled to social or political equity with White persons."[109] Thus, the pointed argument can be made that while the letter of the law, the constitution, does attempt to make room for free Africans and African Americans through the Thirteenth, Fourteenth, and Fifteenth Amendments to the Constitution; it is the spirit, or lack thereof, of the constitution that America has been grappling with for centuries. For if the spirit of the constitution encapsulates or cloaks social barriers, then an acknowledgement not just of common humanity but of a common American identity foundation would have to be established before generational economic and political barriers might be torn down.

The true spirit of the Constitution is just below the surface, but still in plain sight, not unlike the temporal artery, located in the head, which may represent the best location to check America's metaphorical pulse as it relates to economics. The temporal artery, also known as the superficial temporal artery, is the smaller of the two branches of the carotid.[110] Metaphorically speaking, it is the superficiality of this human artery that sutures it together nicely with the often-debated idea about the importance of not just money but wealth in particular, and whether it is, in and of itself, superficial. Furthermore, because the temporal is visible under the skin,[111] it adds a visual cue to its superficiality. And when used as a metaphor, it further highlights the superficial and temporary material objects that money affords while allegorically lending credence to an illusory idea, such as the idea that the head or intellectual capacity and the heart or the nature of the soul are often disconnected.

So, perhaps it is this disconnect between America's intellectual capacity and its conscience that has throughout history led many Americans to take what was a sustained period of economic prosperity and interpret it as a sign of Divine will. Because it can be argued that since the average life span of the long-lived West, East, and Holy Roman Empires of antiquity was roughly 800 years,[112,113] America, by comparison, is still in its theoretical infancy, which means that its capitalist economy's future is unsure. While on the other hand, in comparison to the Spanish, French, and British empires that only lasted around 300 years,[114,115] America is fast approaching its latter years. Perhaps its capitalist economy is on borrowed time.

Now while there is no shortage of those who would quickly point out that empires no longer exist in theory, yet the frequently even if reluctantly do admit that imperialism still exists in practice. They should perhaps be more open to the idea that when nations in practice look, behave and speak like empires, never mind that they may lack some of the physiological-taxonomic traits of the species they are accused of resembling, they are not ducks; they are empires. Furthermore, it is not only sociologists and anthropologists who warn America not to discount the supposition that it too could have a venerable expiration date in terms of being able to sustain its empire. But it is theologians who are quick to remind America that while the most apparent sign that individuals or nations were walking in lockstep with Divine destiny; as told in the stories of the Old Testament; may have very well been the manifestation of prosperity; flocks, herds, wine, oil, milk, and honey; however, the leading indicator of this destiny based upon precepts in the New Testament is quite arguably not the prosperity of, but the persecution of, the saints.

Perhaps the ultimate moral is not the moral to the story, but the moral to the moral. Because philosophers and ethicists suggest that it is possible to "infer the moral status of an action . . . from its nonmoral properties."[116] And, in this case, the moral being America's philanthropic and charitable giving, whether real or perceived and the nonmoral being its cultivation of an unenlightened capitalist economy, whether real or perceived. The point also to be made through the testimonies of some of the writers noted in this book is that a common moral to the moral theme of sorts can be interpreted as an admonishment of America's ideologues. In particular, the ones who, as previously mentioned, contend, through language couched in morality, that America's economic prosperity was and is a sign of Divine favor from the "God of Covenant" (Psalm 78:36-37 TPT), this in spite of America's enslavement history. So, the moral to the moral is perhaps most importantly this: Since there are claims made about the nation's economic prosperity being tied directly to a Divine alliance and that the nation was founded based upon moral principles, then based upon those moral principles should not the nation be willing to ascribe to the equitable distribution of wealth or at least the equitable opportunity to create such wealth? Or based upon those moral principles, be willing to admit that it is in a state of rebellion against those same moral principles by either creating or by default allowing, an aristocratic ruling elite to deny the equitable distribution of wealth to the nation's wage-slave class and its poor?

It is this idea of the poorly laid foundation, socioeconomically speaking, upon which America sits which writers argue has led to accusations of hypocrisy with considerable ire directed at those American's who: (1) have an apparent aversion to the so-called entitlements which help the poor and the disabled; an aversion which writers say contradicts the Bible, (2) needlessly mourn over the writing of censorious news articles by their critics about the preaching of or the support of financial prosperity and so-called conservative social or fiscal conservatism, (3) revel not in telling a lost and dying world about Christ the Redeemer, but instead find comfort in landmark court decisions regarding the Establishment Clause; the First Amendment of the United States Constitution prohibiting Congress from either establishing religion or prohibiting the free exercise of religion,[117] (4) seem to possess an almost incessant need to compare America's contemporary Evangelical Church to the first-century church of believers. First-century believers who theologians note were not persecuted because they were protesting something as farcical as "taxation without representation"[118] as was the case of the American Colonist's.

Some writers even refer to America's contemporary Evangelical Church comparing itself to the first-century church of believers as the creation of an "evangelical persecution complex"[119,120] or playing the victim role to the "nth degree." The first-century church was not relentlessly persecuted for being fiscally conservative but for preaching the Gospel. And the Disciples and other followers were not figuratively martyred by means of a critical social media post, a print article, or a broadcast news story referring to a thin skinned and vindictive preacher being accused of preaching sermons chocked full of omissions, exaggerations, and unscriptural anecdotes.[121] No, the Disciples were instead literally martyred. Killed not because of their political party affiliation and being strident believers in a capitalist economy, but for being recognized as believers in, and followers of Christ.[122,123]

CHAPTER 3

POLITICS

This tyranny is just that arbitrary power of an individual
which is responsible to no one . . . No freeman, if he can
escape from it, will endure such a government.[1]

–Aristotle 350 B.C.E

W hat was America thinking when it emancipated 3,953,761 enslaved Africans and African Americans and then left them to live in the same general population with their former enslavers, overseers, drivers, and various other proponents of slavery? Yes, What was America thinking? Did it not know that once 3,953,761 emancipated Africans and African Americans were given citizenship and the right to participate in the political process, they would undoubtedly vote to secure and protect their own self-interests as a group of people? Of course, America must have anticipated this. Still, it was primarily the former enslaving Southern states, forced to relinquish the political power of Southern planters into the hands of the industrial-merchants of the North.[2] They saw the unabridged right of the formerly enslaved to vote as a stumbling block to any hopes they had of regaining political power lost due to their military defeat during the Civil War. And this is arguably one of, if not the, most important reason why the Black Codes were created. Take, for example, the State of Texas, which in 1866 presented African

Americans and people of color with what amounted to a statutory carrot and stick.

> That all laws and parts of laws relating to persons lately held as slaves, or free persons of color, contrary to, or in conflict with, the provisions of this act, be and the same are [hereby] repealed; Provided, nevertheless, that nothing herein shall be so construed as to repeal any law to permit any other than White men to serve on juries, hold office, vote at any election, State, county, or municipal...[3]

The statutory carrot being the fact that Africans and African Americans were to no longer be governed by slave laws. And the statutory stick being the "nevertheless" fact that Africans and African Americans, while now free, are still not White men and only White men serve on juries, hold public office, and of course vote. Perhaps this is why it has been said that voting and participating in America's political process is a privilege. At first glance, it looks and sounds like a very reasonable, and some might even contend a grand or lofty assertion, unless that privilege pertains to African Americans and people of color and is to be doled out primarily at the hands of those who self-identify as White. And as the previous chapters have pointed to red-flag warnings that the experiment was laying a foundation for failure, another red-flag was not only the issue of suffrage but the United States Supreme Court's ruling that the Civil Rights Act of 1875 was unconstitutional. This should have together with suffrage brought on some degree of trepidation in the minds of African Americans and people of color. Especially, when the highest court in the land ruled that neither the highest court nor the United States Congress had the right to protect African Americans from racialized segregation when it involved private acts at the hands of private actors:

> When a man has emerged from slavery, and, by the aid of beneficent legislation, has shaken off the inseparable concomitants of that state, there must be some stage in the progress of his elevation when he takes the rank of a mere citizen and ceases to be the special favorite of the laws...[4]
>
> –Associate Justice of the Supreme Court
> of the United States Joseph P. Bradley 1883

This "constitutional nod"[5] given to racialized segregation as it related to whether or not African Americans and people of color should ride or sit in the rear of a train or the back of a bus or be forced to stand in the back alley of a restaurant to place an order so as to keep them separated from White patrons, however, in a separate but equitable fashion was in truth, not the most glaring issue. The glaring issue was not the equitableness of public accommodations. The real problem was and still is: Why is the separation of people based upon the quantity of melanin possessed in a human being's skin necessary in the first place? The real crux of the matter presented as a question was and still is, What was the real motivation behind the desire to be separate? In hindsight, this was a red-flag that suggested that if the melting pot[6] experiment were to continue past this point, people of color would be expected to essentially accede to the idea that their civil rights would look like an oasis in the middle of a dry and thirsty land. Sometimes the water is real, and other times, it is just a mirage (author's paraphrase PSALM 63:1). Surely African Americans must have been thinking that it was as if the "unalienable" rights that the Declaration of Independence spoke so highly of had no provision or remedy for a group of people who had already for more than a century including the time frame in which the Declaration was created been alienated from "life, liberty and the pursuit of happiness" (US 1776). And while some argue that it is disingenuous to measure unalienable rights using the hindsight of contemporary historians and scholars to judge an antiquated word, others suggest that perhaps the definition of the word meant something totally different in 1776 than what the contemporary rendition, "inalienable," does in modern times. Nevertheless, Declaration apologists of all ilks suggest that surely there is a way to somehow justify what appears to be hypocrisy at first glance. However, it is the unapologetic who declare that the spirit of the Declaration was always intended to represent the rights of White men only, which is what a majority of contemporary historians and scholars concur.

This quandary lends itself to this book's oft-repeated refrain, What was America thinking? And to be more exact, what were the Founders thinking? Yes, what did America's christened Founding Fathers; men like George Washington, John Adams, Thomas Jefferson, and Benjamin Franklin; themselves products of a monarchy; what did they really know about democracy? Because like a perfidious Judas kiss (author's paraphrase Luke 22:47-48) or like the two natures that beat within the breast of human beings, the Founders discovered inspiration in the Judeo-Christian thinking and sacred text that promote the ideas of life and liberty. While at the same time they were politically appropriating, exploiting, and at times even abusing that same Judeo-Christian thinking and text.[7,8] This difficulty alone has inspired many essays, articles, and a plethora of books to been written about the subject. And while some writers charge, and others beggingly ask. The question is always, How were the Founders able to reconcile their own quest for freedom from the monarchy with the continued enslavement of Africans and African Americans in the New World? Contemporary theological writers have also asked, How could these same Founders; men on the venerable list for sainthood; men who, as it were, singlehandedly made sure that America was contrived as a Christian nation, justify rebelling against the authority of both Great Britain's Prime Minister and King George III? The point writers often make is that the foundation for this purported great nation of faith was an act of refusing to submit to–be subject to–authority. The 1611 King James Version of the Bible, which is what the Founders might have perused, would have spoken to them in passages using now obsolete word spellings, but would have still been very clear concerning revelations such as being subject to authority:

> Let euery soule bee subiect vnto the higher powers: For there is no power but of God. The powers that be, are ordeined of God (Romans 13:1).

Rendered in the Contemporary English Version as:

> Obey the rulers who have authority over you. Only God can give authority to anyone, and he puts these rulers in their places of power (CEV).

While some have, in defense of the Founders, remarked that it is acceptable to disobey authority if that authority is immoral or unjust, which in turn has led to the begging of the question, Was the enslavement of Africans and African Americans moral or just? To which one can only speculate that the Founders either made a purposeful decision to act counter to this admonition to obey rulers and those in authority or else they found an alternative interpretation of passages such as this one in such a way as to absolve themselves from responsibility. Some historians and scholars have argued that Washington, Jefferson and their fellow enslaving peers may have not only taken Biblical passages related to the word slave or slavery out of context which is most often translated as servant. But they also encouraged the normalization of the ownership of enslaved Africans by those who self-identify as White. Thus, the misappropriation of words, titles, and classifications meant that an enslaved person was always exclusively African or African American, while a so-called servant could be either Black or White. This is further evidenced by the fact that these men must have during that time either possessed a working knowledge of the concept known as "convict servants" or were perhaps even proficient with the machinations of the institution of convict servants in the American colonies.[9] Historians and scholars hypothesize that the reason why many non-historians have quite often overlooked the fact that Great Britain via Britain's Transportation Act of 1717 routinely sent convicted felons to the New World[10] is not because the enslavement of Africans and African Americans was always so dastardly. But it was arguably laying the foundation for the idea of race as a social construct as well as the creation of the color line–a demarcation between a slave which meant Black and a servant which meant White.

Although the politics of American slavery was not birthed out of Great Britain's Transportation Act, the Act did, in some regard, set a precedent for nation-building. It was the precedent that the majority of the heavy lifting required to build a new nation would be, just like it is with all empire building, provided by those relegated to the bottom of that society. And once those bottom resources are completely exhausted, it is imperative that the definition of the bottom must be expanded as quickly as possible. Most Americans are unable to associate or put into proper context the social, economic, political, and cultural elements introduced into America through the passing of Britain's Act. An act that sent felons, the vast majority of them White Europeans, to either the colonies of Virginia or Maryland to be used as convict labor in the colonies. Also known as indentured servants, an estimated 50,000 convicted criminals we forced to leave Britain and enter the New World[11] from 1717 until well after the Revolutionary War's end when Britain eventually shifted the flow of its convicts to Australia. Some historians and scholars even question whether Britain's busyness colonizing and expanding its empire around the world distracted it from taking full advantage of its position of military superiority in the American Revolutionary War. In 1775 its empire was made up of approximately forty-two territories and countries[12] in addition to the American Colonies and its heavily vested interest in India."[13] Great Britain's numerous conquests have never been in dispute, with contemporary accounts of the history of the British Empire suggesting that it has at some time in history invaded one hundred and seventy-one of approximately two hundred United Nations member states.[14]

So, directing some of its 1783 military resources to its "Jewel in the crown;"[15,16] India; months before the official conclusion of the Revolutionary War at the Battle of Cuddalore (which was technically the final battle of the Revolutionary War;[17] not Yorktown) probably contributed to why Britain was unable to subdue the Americans. Historians and scholars conclude concerning Britain that in the end, "their hearts were not in [a] war"[18] being waged over grievances that many now believe could have been reasonably settled in parliament by mere legislation instead of on the battlefields.[19] So, was Britain's Act of 1717 America's fork in the road? Where the choice was whether America would go left at the fork and build the new nation by any means necessary, on the backs of convicted White criminals and reducing Africans to chattel to obtain America's desired or expected economic gains. This, to prove not only its self-sufficiency to the monarchy but also its value. Or would it go right at this fork and concede that although the great experiment was not a total failure, it was much less grand than it might have otherwise been?

Although the faults and shortcomings of the Founders are often explained away in terms of them simply being "men of their times"[20] who were in a sense trapped in the flawed socioeconomic and political thinking of their era. Some unapologetic historians and scholars do not shy away from pointing out the fact that while these men are frequently lauded for being courageous enough to start a war with a powerful king across the Atlantic, they were not courageous enough to oppose the prevailing views of their peers. Peers who are often portrayed as unpretentious and pious farmers, printers, editors, brewers, smugglers, a lawyer, and the like. Many historians and scholars believe that America should not esteem its so-called Founding Fathers more highly than they should, thus avoiding the creation of a "false image of . . . importance" (Romans 12:3 TPT). Yes, give them honor, but real wisdom would suggest allowing the "Mighty God of All the Earth" (Isaiah 54:5 TPT) to provide them with halos if deemed worthy of such an honor. It is, however, easy to understand how, throughout the centuries, many Americans have equated the perceived religiosity of those men with spirituality. So, the question is not whether or not they should be put up on manmade pedestals or their images carved by men into the sides of mountains which are made by "Creator-God," (Psalm 96:5 TPT) for doing what was common. For doing what was tradition. For doing what was customary for "men of their times." The question then, posed to so-called believers in, and followers of Christ should be, Is it the so-called Christian nation, the state church, or the Holy Spirit that possess the genuine power to redeem humanity?

It may simply be representative of the lengths some apologetic American historians, religious scholars, and theologians go through in order to prove that America is a so-called Christian nation by propping up its Founders, due to a real or perceived threat of atheism or agnosticism. Perhaps it was simply just part of the American evangelical tradition of preaching that everyone should become a Christian because after all, the Founders were Christians. So, there was a counterpoise and even an overcompensation by both clergy and laity which deified the Founders. Many historians and scholars believe that propping up the Founders was unnecessary and that pointing out the mistakes made by the Founders is not correcting history or revising it based upon newly discovered historical documents. It would simply be uncovering history that has been hidden, most of it in-plain-sight, and begging not the question of how much of the truth has been hidden, but why? The argument can be made that if much of the hidden history was in-plain-sight, the motive must have also existed in-plain-sight. Once the generation of historians tasked with documenting America's foundation was finished with their work, probably after the death of the last of the Founders, President James Madison, who died in 1836, they had the epiphany that America's nuanced empire was not won simply because of its grandiose ideas about freedom and liberty. Nor could the success be attributed to its so-called moral values or even its religion, but it was because of "its superiority in applying organized violence."[21]

This revelation must have been a Grand Canyon-sized fork in the road. This realization would also have been in such vigorous opposition to both the nation's freedom and liberty narrative as well as the patriarchal power structure that redactions would have been deemed necessary. And embellishment of the truth, even if it more closely resembled hyper romanticized heroic folklore as opposed to "the whole truth, and nothing but the truth,"[22] would not have been challenged. The choice was to either go left at the fork and be forced to almost immediately begin rewriting the history of an otherwise illustrious demonstration of how to shift a nuanced empire narrative. For example, divide and conquer would be transformed into explore and establish trade, hegemony would be redefined as peace treaties, and cultural assimilation, treason and rebellion against George III would morph into a righteous revolution, and treason and rebellion against the United States would be known merely as the battle for states' rights. And of course, America chose to go left. Perhaps the idea of going right and of behaving like a guilty person who throws themselves at the mercy of the court or like the sinner who beat his breast and pleaded for mercy in the presence of a just God (author's paraphrase Luke 18:13), was simply unbearable. It would not only be acknowledging not just that the foundation was created in error, but that the foundation was irreparable as it stands, and needed to be reconstructed virtually from scratch.

Political historians do not dispute that the political appropriation of Judeo-Christian ideas about Divine providence leaves little doubt that the Founders were all on some level religious men. Take, for example, how through much of the eighteenth-century, Americans, in general, were routinely fined for breaking the sabbath."[23] However, what historians and scholars do often quibble with is the mystique created by apologists of the Founders who suggest that the political theology of the Founders was especially uncommon for the age in which they lived. In light of the religious and political climate of the eighteenth and nineteenth centuries, one would have quite naturally been hard-pressed to find a bonafide self-professing atheist or agnostic. Because not only was the Anglican Church or Church of England the state Church of Virginia until 1776, of which both United States presidents George Washington and Thomas Jefferson were members, but the Founders would have been the progeny of generation after generation of religiousness.

Not only did their ancestors; thanks to the advent of the printing press and translation of the Bible into English; read or hear the reading of the Bible on Sunday's exposing them to Biblical text, but Biblical imagery was very commonplace. Not only was Biblical imagery common in popular music, but even the alehouses back in Europe might have had enough Biblical texts displayed via artistic expressions such as wall hangings of painted sacred texts or imagery. It provided patrons with some level of familiarity with Bible stories and ideas and was quite prevalent in the seventeenth-century.[24,25] So, even for Founders such as George Washington, who was noted as attending church service on average about one Sunday per month,[26] any religiosity that might be attributed to him was arguably not only part of a church upbringing, but also part of the culture in which he lived.

Comparing American politics to the carotid artery–the strongest pulse point–is a very fitting metaphor. Just as the carotid carries oxygenated blood from the heart to the brain,[27] politics has the ability to take a nation's desires for social, economic, and political change and translate those desires into meaningful legislation. If politics really is a vessel capable of transporting the often intangible desires of the human heart to a place capable of melding them into something tangible; and if politics is the tool that people who live in democratic societies can band together and use to enact socioeconomic and sociopolitical revolution; then why does it seem so rare? Take, for instance, the question of, Why is it that African Americans–Latinos–Asians–Native Americans and people of color, in general, have not united together politically to fight socioeconomic injustice, racism, and White privilege? The answer to which might beg the question, Is it because a zero-sum game is being played? A game which is based on political inclusion and economic opportunities regarding underserved populations. And yet another question would be, Is it because of the various studies and surveys related to the idea of a purported "unspoken conflict"[28] between these groups? Conflict which some historians and scholars dismiss as merely hypothetical tinder which is easy to ignite, very short-lived, and rarely backed by any kindling or substantial fuel. Perhaps the primary reason why African American and Latino communities in particular, at times appear to be at odds is because one of the groups is as alluded to in the chapter on Social Change, a voluntary immigrant, while the other group is a forced immigrant.

This is not unlike the idea that African Americans and American Indians, in spite of common political concerns and some shared interests have never on a grand scale been able to partner together and devise a stratagem; not just against oppressive overseers and labor camps more commonly known as plantations; against White subterfuge, tyrannical courts and government bureaucracy. Because beginning from the initial European attempts to control the New World in the late fifteenth-century after Christopher Columbus landed at Hispaniola in 1492, to the first Massachusetts Bay Colony slave law in 1641, and on past the emancipation of Africans and African Americans in 1865, American Indians had themselves quite often been captured and enslaved in both the colonies as well as the West Indies.[29,30,31] And while they were not captured in as large a number as Africans and African Americans were captured, they were nonetheless captured and enslaved. However, perhaps one of the reasons why there has historically been a lack of partnerships between these groups is because of the chicanery of Whites through the executive branch and legislative branch policies that proactively discouraged underserved populations from developing stronger communal relationships. Examples of this range from the United States' hegemony over American Indians who in turn enslaved African Americans as an act of the oppressed wanting to become more like the oppressor,[32] to the Fugitive Slave Laws prohibiting Indians from providing refuge to escaped African Americans, to the skullduggery and loss of tens of millions of acres[33] of Indian land to Whites. With much of the land loss being an act retaliation on the part of Whites for the Seminoles providing refuge for escaped Africans and African Americans. In addition to this, it has been made evident that it was America's guile and double-dealing that led to its involvement in the Seminole Wars. The war was subterfuge used in retrieving escaped Africans and African Americans, disrupting any alliances between American Indians and African Americans, as well as the elimination of alleged free territories that African Americans might find refuge in.[34] This suggests that the "American Indian wars, were in some regard, also Negro wars."[35] With the irony of it all being the idea that while many of the Europeans who came to the New World were themselves fleeing persecution, yet the offspring of the oppressed became oppressors.

The greatest collaboration between African Americans and those who self-identify as White was obviously during the Abolitionist Movement. However, although there were very few true loyalists of Africans and African Americans post Reconstruction, there were occasions of alliances and even unions of considerable cooperation between what was essentially African American agrarian and related labor and equitable or similar White labor post Reconstruction. For example, after both the Republican Party and the Democratic Party essentially turned their backs on both African Americans and poor Whites, African Americans and poor Whites formed strategic economic alliances aligned along class lines rather than the social construct of race. In which case, they pooled their labor and buying power, a coalition of about three million individuals.[36] The groups even aligned themselves with Southern populist politicians who were not afraid to admit that many African Americans and many poor Whites could set aside their socially constructed racial differences in order to advance their economic agendas.[37] Their agrarian movement was even instrumental in the formation of America's most successful third political party in history, the People's Party (Populist Party), founded in 1892.[38] In addition to these, another noteworthy alliance between African Americans and those who self-identify as White took place in the 1930's known as the Southern Tenant Farmers Union (STFU). In which mostly Southern African American and Southern White sharecroppers recognized that one of the things they had most in common, almost above all else, was their need to get fair agreements as well as fair prices for the crops that they produced.[39,40]

Historically, there have always been people who would align themselves socioeconomically or sociopolitically with African Americans and people of color; potential allies. Even sociopolitical conservatives and professing evangelicals who self-identify as White have at different times and for different causes aligned themselves with African Americans and people of color. However, they, meaning those who self-identify as White are afraid of a nonsensical bogeyman-hobgoblin-superstition, arguably an irrational fear, which they refer to as a slippery slope. They view aligning themselves with civil rights issues—the rights of immigrants—gender rights and other causes as a reason to fear that what may start out as simple, common-sense rights might be taken for granted or may become uncontrollable. Their fear is that, for example, if all fifty states in America were to allow same-gender couples to marry, then eventually the country might see ridiculous things like much older adults wanting to marry underage children, humans wanting to marry animals, people wanting to marry their pet goldfish or their automobile. They basically fear the unknown. It is not unlike like the words President Jimmy Carter articulated regarding the opposing political party when he surmised that they are, "[M]en of narrow vision, who are afraid of the future."[41]

The coming together of different groups of Americans who have either common or at least similar reasons to collectively align themselves in hopes of being able to affect real social, political, or economic change is not easy. It can take years of grassroots activism, and in the case of White evangelicals, it has been argued that both sleight of hand and misdirection have been used to advance their sociopolitical causes. Take, for example, some historians and scholars have said that it was not the United States Supreme Court's 1973 Roe v. Wade decision; which by the way legal scholars point out did not, in and of itself, legalize a woman's right to terminate a pregnancy. But instead simply concluded that "the right of personal privacy includes the abortion decision . . . ;"[42] that galvanized or better yet politicized the so-called Religious Right or New Religious Right. The Religious Right was a socially conservative religious movement that began in the 1970s which was later associated with a politically active religious group called the Moral Majority; a group which was founded by Jerry Falwell in 1979.[43] No, what appears to have woken the Religious Right up from the neutral, nonpolitical slumber they appeared to be in for the duration of the Jim Crow laws era, as well as during the Civil

Rights Movement, was the federal mandate that Christian schools either integrate racially or lose their tax-exempt status.[44,45]

The federal mandate was a move supported by then President Jimmy Carter, who ironically was himself an evangelical Sunday school teacher.[46] As a matter of fact, the so-called Evangelical Church's initial response to the Roe v. Wade ruling was that the ruling was just another reason why the church should *not* become more involved in the things of the *world*, but should in opposition become less involved and become more isolated.[47,48] The so-called leader of the so-called Religious Right himself, Jerry Falwell, was quoted in 1965 as essentially saying that preaching the gospel precluded him from doing anything else, "[I]ncluding fighting Communism, or participating in civil-rights reforms."[49,50] Falwell even took a thinly-veiled swipe at Dr. Martin Luther King, Jr.; himself an ordained minister and civil rights activist; to whom Falwell exclaimed that "We are not told to wage war against bootleggers, liquor stores, gamblers, murderers, prostitutes, racketeers, prejudiced persons or institutions, or any other existing evil as such."[51] Going further Falwell added, "Preachers, are not called to be politicians, but soul winners."[52] To which at least some of his critics could have facetiously asked whether or not it is possible for those who believe in creationism and those who oppose evolution to have evolved. Because in the late 1970s Falwell appeared to have himself evolved, having become a very vocal proponent of both ministers and laity involving themselves in politics. How convenient that his *come to politics* epiphany took place not at the announcement of United States Supreme Court's Roe v. Wade decision in 1973, no, the year was in fact 1976. This was after the fundamentalist college, Bob Jones University; whose founder believed that racial segregation or apartheid was Biblical; had its tax-exemption rescinded after years of warnings from the United States Internal

Revenue Service for not racially integrating the school.[53,54] This was also after Pat Robertson, founder and chairman of the Christian Broadcasting Network (CBN) is reported by one writer to have exclaimed in 1975 that "Abortion is not a legal matter. It is strictly a theological matter not subject to judicial interpretation."[55]

Critics of America's pro-life movement have repeatedly pointed to the hypocrisy of those who take staunch pro-life positions with regard to the unborn, yet ignore the lives lost because of capital punishment, unjust global wars, a lack of access to or affordable healthcare both domestically and globally, and [u]ndernutrition. Undernutrition, happening not in poor countries but rich countries, contributes to the deaths of more than three million children under the age of five annually.[56] Facts which arguably expose America's pro-life movement to criticism based upon Jesus's sermon warning about hypocrisy in which he used two very stern words, "hypercritical and a hypocrite" (Matt 7:5 TPT) to admonish the sanctimonious, pious, religious imposters and pretenders in that day. An ever growing-number of not only secular political scholars, but contemporary religious thinkers as well acknowledge that the real reason behind the rise of the Religious Right, the Moral Majority, and in more contemporary times political evangelicalism is demonstrated to have been only speciously tied to the moral causes that its leaders proclaimed. But that it was instead more about political machination and duplicity with regard to the right of Bob Jones University to deny the admission of African Americans, and other students of color into its student body. It is because of these and other related issues that the Republican Party; the party of the forty-fifth president of the United States; was accused by both political scientists as well as theologians of using its party platform ideals; specifically the ones which deal with a woman's right to choose whether or not to terminate a pregnancy and same-sex marriage; as a way of essentially blackmailing the consciences of so-called evangelicals. Blackmailing them into voting for and supporting even the vilest of political leaders, all in the name of a greater good. Then frequently finding themselves being forced to go down metaphorical rabbit holes in order to defend the often indefensible[57] actions of their chosen candidate.

Perhaps, the fear–the reservation–the reticence–of those who self-identify as White; those who could potentially align themselves with African Americans and people of color; is based upon a misunderstanding of the timeline of sociopolitical change in America. They forget that the seeds of Black and Brown struggle take a long time to come to fruition in America. As a matter of fact, if those who self-identify as White would simply look at history, they would realize that the rights that African American people fought for have taken centuries to come to pass. And based upon this history there are some who fear that it may literally take centuries for African Americans; who are the descendants of enslaved Africans and African Americans; to witness the introduction of any new landmark legislation. It is also believed that the collective time, effort, and resources of African Americans and people of color that could be spent pushing for new legislation is instead spent fighting to hold onto the gains of the 1960s Civil Rights Movement. From the time that the initial first enslaved African people arrived in Jamestown, to the time of the Emancipation Proclamation was centuries. But the irony is that if this were a movement for rights by those who self-identify as White–if this were people who self-identify as White wanting, demanding, asserting their rights, then meaningful changes could very well happen much quicker. So, it is conceivable that those reluctant White allies could, in reality, have something to fear if of course, this were primarily a movement by those who self-identify as White–but it is not.

So, what happens when the previously mentioned bogeyman-hobgoblin-superstition; arguably an irrational fear; the great White psychological fear; manifests itself in the form of a great White hope, a savior? In that case, America received number forty-five, as in the forty-fifth president of the United States. The same forty-fifth president of the United States who seemed to revel in defaming a war hero like the late American Republican Senator John McCain. Not only defaming McCain while he was alive but even posthumously. And while not everyone agreed with Senator McCain's policies, most Americans, even African Americans and people of color did not find it beyond reason to garner at least the minimum amount of respect due to a war hero and a United States Senator. As a matter of fact, even though McCain, for reasons unknown other than arguably pure jealousy and pettiness was subjected to the venom of the forty-fifth president of the United States, the late Senator saw numerous African American politicians, as well as numerous African American political pundits, come to his defense. This is because it is believed that he had earned a new level of respect from many African Americans and people of color who could never forget a noteworthy and memorable incident which took place in 2008 when he was campaigning to become president of the United States. He was running against fellow Senator Barack Obama, who would later defeat him and become president.

The incident in question took place at a Republican town hall meeting filled with McCain's supporters. At this meeting; during an open mic question and answer session; an older White woman was given the opportunity to ask McCain a question or else make a comment. This woman commented to both the audience and McCain that she could not trust Barack Obama because she believed Barack Obama was an Arab. Senator McCain simply shook his head in disagreement and said, "No ma'am, Barack Obama is a decent family guy and a fellow American and not an Arab."[58] It can be debated whether or not McCain is worthy of being placed upon a pedestal based upon his civil rights record. But his simple act of taking the moral high ground in the middle of a hotly contested election campaign; even if it meant defending his opponent; projected to African Americans and people of color that he was willing to extend some respect to his African American opponent. A simple act of civility and decorum that some political science scholars note may have been the last of its kind. The irony being that a genuinely bipartisan gesture by one man may have been the unintended precursor to the total collapse of his party with regard to any semblance of political bipartisanship or the notion of moral high ground. Two attributes that were already at historical lows in American politics.

Of course, American politics has always had the capacity to show glimpses of just how grisly, squalid, and even how noxious it could be. However, that was before the cataclysm of tribal politics became indelibly stamped on the electoral process. The beginning of a new age. Not at all like the previous age when Americans in spite of partisanship; whether politician, war hero or someone trapped in intergenerational poverty; instinctively knew that they should never acknowledge criticism from the kind of person whose advice they would never be interested in seeking advice from in the first place. Even if said critic was the forty-fifth president of the United States, who by the way applied for and received five draft deferments which exempted him from serving in the Vietnam War.

On the other hand, John McCain, who the forty-fifth president of the United States slandered for being a military POW (prisoner of war), was a highly decorated and awarded Vietnam War pilot. So, it was viewed as nothing short of extreme hypocrisy when the same forty-fifth president of the United States accused professional athletes of color and their supporters who kneel during the playing of the national anthem at various professional and amateur sporting events of being disrespectful of the military. Him being a military draft dodger as well as publicly showing a sort of jealous disdain for the military service of John McCain. This was, of course, the same self-righteous president who told a group of his followers at a political rally in Alabama, "Wouldn't you love to see one of these NFL owners fire players who disrespect the flag!" Then in an unrepentant manner, as mentioned in the chapter on Economics, he later doubled down on this sentiment tweeting that NFL players who choose to kneel as opposed to standing during the national anthem should be fired or find something else to do.[59] This is the hypocritically patriotic president who in 2013 tweeted that then President Barack Obama should not be, "[T]elling the Washington Redskins to change their name."[60] The hypocrisy is that he was attempting to tell the then forty-fourth president of the United States, President Obama, that a president's priority should be on solving the nation's problems and not weighing in on pop culture or social issues. Something that critics of the forty-fifth president of the United States say he was to the nth degree far more guilty of.

Some of the harshest critics of not only the forty-fifth president of the United States but also the party which chose to nominate him noted that the outspoken woman from the previously mentioned story about the John McCain rally was no mere fluke. And that whether she was suffering from senility, whether she was simply biased or prejudiced based upon misinformation, or whether she was an outright, bonafide, unadulterated, unapologetic, and unrepentant racist, her racialized and ethnocentric world view is nothing new. If anything, it merely represents a reminder of what the political landscape of the experiment looked like prior to and during the Civil Rights Movement. So, it should, therefore, come as no surprise that not just speech such as hers, but her attitude as well, is a primary source of motivation for people of color to vote against even the most moderate and even liberal of America's Republican Party candidates.

If such is the ideology of voting within the experiment, then how disheartening it must be for those on the outside of the experiment looking in to see the image of African Americans fighting on the same side of freedom and democracy as Whites in military conflicts? But then essentially being forced to vote in opposition to the majority of those same Whites at the voting polls. Another perspective of that same image is that of African American men and women giving–risking–everything in championing American democracy as part of the same forces as men and women who self-identify as White, but each with their own definition of both freedom and liberty. One group fighting for their right to experience a genuine taste of life and liberty and the other group essentially fighting for their right to deny or at least prohibit that taste. This image is both ironic and enduring when it could be easily argued that the approximate number of Africans and African Americans who were emancipated, 3,953,761, is roughly the number of Africans and African Americans who have fought in America's major military conflicts both domestic and abroad starting with the Revolutionary War. Millions of African Americans in addition to both free and enslaved Africans, since first arriving in either the Americas (North and South America) or the Caribbean, fighting on the same side of democracy as Whites. They gave–sacrificed–their lives. Not only so that they could participate in the political process, but also their posterity could participate unincumbered in the political process. So, what a strange sight it must be for outsiders to see Americans act with such unity on the battlefields but then immediately scatter into their respective nations within a nation after the battle has ended.

It is not just examples like the ones previously discussed, but also the psychology of voting; passive or passive-aggressive attitudes or ironic detachment; along with changing demographics. They have brought to light a truth about voting that was perhaps once widely known and felt but was perhaps at some point lost in translation from one generation to the next. Which is that voting, if it is really worth fighting for, even dying for, it must be much more than just a privilege. In fact, an easy argument could be made that it is a mandate. And perhaps it was the election of the man who would become the forty-fifth president of the United States which awakened a large segment of the American population from what may have been viewed as a season of indifference with regard to voting, because voting is now being viewed as an imperative to exhort with renewed vim and vigor voting. With metaphors abounding that describe voting as that proverbial sharp double–edged sword, able to slice and dice through hatred and bigotry, able to accurately cut up and more equitably distribute pieces of the capitalist economy pie. And when wielded as a show of force can obligate those who are elected or placed in positions of power to actually do what is expected of them, which is to make a positive difference in the lives of their constituents.

However, demanding that elected or appointed officials do their job of, for lack of a better term, pastoring, their constituents is not easy. It is not easy even when those officials are sociopolitical conservatives and professing evangelicals who claim that their professions of faith mandate that they act and behave virtuously in decision making and the general fulfillment of their duties. To which their detractors ask the question, If ethics and morals are a faith mandate, then why are those same ethical and moral standards not clearly visible in decision making and actions taken? Perhaps it is such claims of hypocrisy as well as inaction by politicians and those in public authority, which paint the picture of voting as the sword needed to poke or prod the powers that be, in this case, elected officials. It pricks them, making sure they do not allow their biases or what many critics call laziness, to keep them from making a positive difference in the lives of their constituents. Voting rights advocates exclaim that no longer can African Americans; who are the descendants of enslaved Africans; and people of color say things like, "voting is an option" or that "voting only gives individuals the right to complain." They argue that voting is so much more than merely a right to complain, interjecting that voting is not an option; it is mandatory! Going further, they contend that voting is literally a matter of life; Black Lives, no pun intended; melanin life. Voting is life for people of color; those who live their lives in continued marginality; those whose lives are quite often lived rehashing the same sociopolitical trials and tribulations that their parents, grandparents, and great-grandparents dealt with.

However, because the political stakes are vastly different for those who self-identify as White than they are for African Americans and people of color, this difference is communicated in both the language used by those who self-identify as White as well as in their actions. For example, even the rhetoric of those who self-identify as White; those who may even be philosophically labeled sociopolitically as either progressives or liberals; can come across as patronizing or disingenuous to African Americans and people of color when publicly speaking about the infamous United States Presidential Election of 2016. Even though what those who self-identify as White may be saying in regard to the Election of 2016 is not wrong. It is, however, somewhat patronizing when it manifests itself in the form of a hypothetical trove of "could have–would have–should have" sentiments spewed from the lips of those who self-identify as White because they are themselves the very beneficiaries of White privilege. And to be fair, yes, of course, many who self-identify as White were also genuinely surprised by the forty-fifth president of the United States' election. And likewise, many of them also feel a sense hurt or betrayal caused by a flawed system which allowed the election of the candidate who became the forty-fifth president of the United States. And yes, many of them are adversely affected by his election. Still, at the end of the day, their White privilege maintains its ability to shield them from being totally overwhelmed by the reality of having to live under the authority of the candidate who became the forty-fifth president of the United States. A commander in chief who many Americans believed did not have the tiniest clue about civility or decorum. Someone who his detractors claim has always gotten the proverbial "richest guy in the room" exemption his entire life. This is perhaps why it is not surprising that even well-meaning, well-intentioned Americans who self-identify as White can irk readers or listeners with their rhetoric, even though African Americans and people of color do still see them as allies. This seemingly empathetic rhetoric about how the forty-fifth president of the United States stole the election when regurgitated ad nauseum, creates a mood that irks many African Americans and people of color in such a way that it is seen as both patronizing and disingenuous. Because no matter how narcissistic, incorrigible, and xenophobic, a politician or public leader is, those who self-identify as White will arguably always be granted a certain amount of mercy or leniency within the experiment. Historically speaking, these politically moderate or perhaps even liberal Whites are more likely to be treated with a larger portion of humanity than African Americans and people of color. They are much more likely to be extended a certain amount of residual brotherhood based on their Whiteness.

Historically speaking, if people who self-identify as White make a mistake, there is far more likely to be an automatic presumption of innocence until proven guilty. Historians and scholars contend that, if a crime is committed by a person who self-identifies as White, the White public at large will have a much greater desire to find out what the "backstory"[61] is or what the background and context of the perpetrator's life as a whole was. It is as if someone who self-identifies as White making foolish and ill-advised mistakes or committing flagrant acts of criminality is so unheard of that they must get to the bottom of why this one individual was not perfect like the collective. Furthermore, this implies that no matter how oppressed Whites may feel, they will continue to have some reasonable semblance of a voice. It is kind of like the infamous meme that depicts an image of a male figure with a seemingly light brown skin complexion holding a rifle and the caption read: "Terrorist." The same meme also shows the image of a male figure holding a rifle whose skin complexion appeared to be a darker shade of brown than the first, yet the captioned labeled him as: "Thug." Then lastly, there was an image in the meme of a White male holding a rifle–whose caption read: "He is a complex individual, with specific mental health issues, who was kind to his neighbors, etc." Satirical whit notwithstanding, memes such as this one arguably represents the pervasiveness of racialized bias in America usually acted out in the form of racialized profiling.

However, if the followers and loyalists of the forty-fifth president of the United States are entrenched on one side and the patronizing-disingenuous haters of the forty-fifth president of the

United States are on the other side, then to what or whom is the attribution due to the small statistical minority of African Americans and people of color who critics describe as having the unmitigated gall to vote for the forty-fifth president of the United States? Not only did they vote for him, but they also continued to have an almost obsequious support for him. A strange phenomenon which begs the question, What happens when a splinter group of people of color, such as those who voted for the forty-fifth president of the United States, create a moral dilemma for the rest of the group, who staunchly oppose the forty-fifth president of the United States? It creates more than just a bit of a quandary, a quagmire, perhaps even a schism, when a splinter group supports a president who appears to be in direct opposition to the major goals of African Americans and people of color as a collective body. This issue becomes even more perplexing if any of these political defectors have now, finally, been awakened, able to clearly see the rise of White Nationalist ideology in America. Including the blatant denial of the existence of systematic racism in America, racialized bias and microaggression in private sector American jobs, xenophobia, misogyny, and what many Americans referred to as just blistering political invective by the president. So, the presumptive idea that the African Americans and people of color who endorsed the election of the forty-fifth president of the United States are often viewed as traitors who cannot be trusted, which is not a totally unreasonable presumption.

Furthermore, what some believe is even more horrendous than the fear of there being spies or double agents; those who may only be pretending to be able to see that they had a lapse in judgment in voting for and supporting the forty-fifth president of the United States. But that there are still those African Americans and people of color who still may not have a clear understanding of why what they did was a mistake in the eyes of the broader African American and communities of color. It suggests that perhaps there was something deep down within the psyche of followers and loyalists of the forty-fifth president of the United States. Something that simply would not allow them to see that his pre-election and post-election words, behavior, and the majority of his policies are diametrically opposed to the language, behavior, and policies that a large majority of African Americans and people of color believe is in their own best socioeconomic interests as a group.

Many African Americans and people of color who resisted the election of the forty-fifth president of the United States believe that while it is possible to explain to those who got the election wrong exactly why it is they got it wrong, they cannot, however, make them comprehend it.[62] Their stance is that if they have to decode the old Southern Strategy as well as the contemporary Othering Strategy[63] for their brothers and sisters in order to rouse them as it were from a state of unconsciousness, then it is, therefore, this seeming naïvety which raises doubts about the sincerity of their repentance. However, even though this divide, this chasm, which separates those who oppose the forty-fifth president of the United States from those who supported him appears to have no bridge that can be constructed to reconcile the two sides. It does not, however, mean they necessarily now see each other as the enemy. It has been made very clear by those who resisted the election of the forty-fifth president of the United States, that those who had the unmitigated gall to vote for the forty-fifth president of the United States should be emphatically reminded that African Americans and people of color are not operating on an even playing field with those who self-identify as White. Many of whom are followers, loyalists, and sycophants of the forty-fifth president of the United States. This means that African Americans and people of color cannot afford to be a narrowly focused one or two political issues voter group. The reason why they cannot afford to be a one or two political issues voter group is that it is imperative that all Americans have a big picture view of politics and lawmaking. And even more imperative for African Americans and people of color, for whom the socioeconomic stakes have historically been higher than it has been for those who self-identify as White. It may seem inconsequential, even trivial, that a small statistical minority of African Americans and people of color sided with those who self-identify as White in support of the forty-fifth president of the United States based on one or two political party platform issues. But when it comes to the other dozens of issues, issues that the forty-fifth president of the United States and his party platform stand for–time and time again, those issues have undermined the best socioeconomic interests of African Americans and people of color. Political pundits suggest that African Americans and people of color who supported the forty-fifth president of the United States may have ill-advisedly believed that they would be getting plaudits for introducing this minute counterculture into the African American electorate. Although who they were expecting to appease by this act of political treason is not entirely clear. Unfortunately, this type of symbolism appears to have been all for naught because this small splinter group of African Americans and people of color who voted for the candidate who became the forty-fifth president of the United States served only to increase the resolve of the remainder of African American electorate in attempting to make him a one-and-done president. Meaning they would do everything in their power see to it that he was not elected for a second term.

Political scientists believe that it is reasonable to assume that it was political expediency that drove the Republican party to support

and elect a candidate whom many, both in America and around the
globe, viewed as lacking good character, as being immoral, obviously
never having held any public office, being unprepared, ill-equipped,
and being generally unfit to hold the office of the president of the
United States. It is that same often dangerous political expediency
which is what Dr. Martin Luther King, Jr. warned of five decades
prior when he articulated that expediency may ask the question, "is it
politic?" But conscience asks the question, 'is it right?'"[64] And it is this
same subject of political expediency that goes back to antiquity
predating even President Abraham Lincoln's dilemma of political
expediency. Unlike the contemporary political idea of making
America great again, Lincoln was actually attempting to make America
a more perfect Union.[65] As such, political expediency even predates
the great Roman statesman and philosopher Marcus Tullius Cicero,
who "dabbled"[66] in the philosophy of the Greeks. But whose true
allegiance was not to his lofty ideas and grand orations, which he was
indeed famous for, but was at his core a "Roman of Romans."[67] So,
perhaps not unlike like Cicero, Lincoln too was only dabbling with
the idea that all men are created equal. And also, like Cicero, Lincoln,
in spite of his own "political faith,"[68] himself full of lofty ideas and
grand orations; which he was indeed famous for; but was at his core
a Republican of Republicans. Whose true allegiance was not to the
abolition of slavery but his desire to preserve the United States, more
commonly referred to as the Union, at all costs with what was perhaps
just the hints of an evolving abolitionist bent. It had the makings of
the very sort of quagmire that Swedish post World War II avant-garde
writer Friedrich Dürrenmatt was speaking of when he said, "Religion
and political expediency go beautifully hand in hand."[69] Therefore,
Lincoln, not unlike Cicero, was at his core not just a member of the
Republican Party, and not just a Union conservationist, but he was a

guardian of it. So, the theory which suggests that it was this idea of expediency as being the catalyst behind a movement which allowed someone like the candidate who became the forty-fifth president of the United States to garner the support of the overwhelming majority of the Republican party, has historical precedent on its side.

The moral to the story is that racialized politics are not dead. Even though the Black Codes no longer exist in letter, sociocultural anthropology suggests that they are still very much alive in spirit. And while the Voting Rights Act of 1965 may have dismantled the obstacles, which were in place for almost a century, hindering and preventing African Americans from voting, it did not completely destroy those obstacles. They can be reassembled. So, while African Americans may never statistically have the electorate numbers which would be necessary to launch a successful political coup, they do, however, have the numbers to sway elections and influence public policy. In addition to this, their massive economic spending power as consumers can steer the civic responsibilities of some of America's largest publicly and privately held corporations not in the direction of diversity, but of inclusion. Because the truth is that even America's largest and most powerful ships are steered by just one man or woman using the smallest of rudders; a part which is only a tiny fraction of the size of the overall vessel itself (author's paraphrase James 3:4). However, the stratagems of the opposition abound. They are the people and policies that political scientists suggest are systematically attempting to make America great again through the time machine of revisionist history. Desiring to return the nation back to a time when White people knew their place in America and African Americans knew theirs. Superior and subordinate, respectively. Historians, scholars, and political scientists alike are quick to point out the fact that when people refer to making America great again, they never indicate a past specific time reference. They never say what century or what decades they wish to transport the nation back to. No doubt they would probably prefer not to revert back to those centuries that included the chattel enslavement of millions of Africans and African Americans, or the periods before, during, or after the Civil War. They probably want to forget, if possible, the Black Code years, and the Jim Crow Law decades are also probably off the table. As are any of the decades that witnessed the regular lynching of African American men, women, and children by White vigilante groups. Perhaps making America great again simply means going back to the so-called good old days of the twentieth-century when America had:[70,71]

- Coal miners' strike of 1902
- Springfield, Illinois race riots in 1908
- World War I from 1914 to 1918
- Race riots around the nation in 1919
- Boston police strike in 1919
- Steel workers strike of 1919
- Prohibition of alcohol starting in 1920 and lasting for over a decade
- Tulsa, Oklahoma race riots in 1921
- Rosewood, Florida massacre and race riots in 1923
- The biggest financial crisis in United States history; the Stock Market Crash of 1929
- Followed by the Great Depression which lasted for a decade, and a full recovery was not complete until full twenty-five years after the original crash
- Taxes were raised across the board in 1932

- The largest strike in nations history in 1934; involving textile workers
- Flint Michigan autoworkers strike in 1937
- World War II started in 1939
- The Japanese bombed Pearl Harbor in 1941
- Race riots in 1943
- South Carolina executed the youngest person in United States history in 1944; a fourteen-year-old African American boy
- World War II ended in 1945
- In 1948 President Harry Truman issued an executive order ending segregation in the military
- Anacostia pool riots in 1949; protests against African Americans being allowed to swim in a pool
- The Korean War started in 1950
- The United State Supreme Court ruled that segregated schools were unconstitutional in 1954
- Montgomery Bus Boycott in 1955; protest by African Americans against segregation on public transportation
- The nation fell into a recession in 1957
- The Little Rock Nine in 1957: nine African American high school students enter racially segregated public school
- In 1963 Martin Luther King, Jr. gives famous "I Have A Dream" speech during the march on Washington against segregation in America
- Civil Rights Act of 1964 is passed outlawing racialized and other forms of discrimination
- The United States entered the Vietnam War in 1965

- Voting Rights Act of 1965 is passed dismantling the racialized barriers to voting

So, instead of seeking to pick a particular point in America's storied past to return to, an effort to recapture some romanticized notion of former greatness, perhaps they should start by clearly defining what great or greatness means. If the criteria for making America great again is making it obvious that every aspect of society no matter how important or how seemingly inconsequential, is overtly and domineeringly White again, then all speculation about whether the melting pot experiment is alive or deceased must stop. Because in such a case the Coup de grâce will have been delivered. However, if the platitude of making America great again has anything to do with sincerely striving to make that union, which is the United States; states that are united; a more perfect union, then it should be explored. However, the making of a more perfect union entails possession of a clear goal which seeks to end the denial psychology and the constant attempts to explain away racism, White privilege, as well as "white fragility."[72] In addition, it must also seek to end the ironic detachment with regard to the oppression of people of color in America, in particular, African Americans and American Indians. This would be a great place to start and prove that even though the character of the pulse of the experiment might still be extremely faint, nevertheless, the heart of America still beats. So, any future political gains to be made by African Americans and people of color, just as it has always been, will be much more difficult to achieve than it seems–not impossible–but difficult to say the least. However, in spite of the difficulty, there remains a large segment of the African population that believes that not trying is not an option. Because in the words of the

1980's American television crime drama series character Hawk in *Spenser for Hire*, "Can't– is a luxury a Black man cannot afford."[73]

It seems apparent to most but not all Americans, and for that matter, the rest of the free world that the candidate who became the forty-fifth president of the United States was not supposed to win. At least, not according to almost all of the pre-election polls and the rhetoric of political pundits, and especially after he lost the popular vote. However, contrary to popular belief, American presidents are not elected based upon the national popular vote. It is the Electoral College which elects the president. And the people who get to be part of the Electoral College; the electors; are hand-picked prior to the election by the political parties in each state.[74] Thus, America has a system in which for only the fifth time in the nation's history, a president was elected without winning the popular vote. So, it is not only the election of a man like the forty-fifth president of the United States, whom many African Americans claim fits the profile that either their parents or grandparents warned them about. The profile of the rich White millionaire or billionaire who lies, steals, and cheats his way to the top of the business world, but who they were taught to never publicly ridicule for fear of being labeled as being envious of the hard work and dedication of someone else. Or be accused of playing the idiomatic race card; using minority status as an advantage or as a display of power; by assuming that it was the benefits of White privilege which helped secure this perceived success. No, African Americans and people of color are also dismayed with the election system in America. Many feel as though their votes were essentially wasted when they voted overwhelmingly against the candidate who became the forty-fifth president of the United States. Yet, he, through the electoral college, won the election anyway.

Even though some political scientists warn African Americans and people of color not to abandon the voting system, others warn that the system is flawed and that egregious disappointments such as the election of the forty-fifth president of the United States could very well happen again because of it, and sooner rather than later. And it is this idea that the bar was raised to elect President Barack Obama but was dramatically lowered in order to elect the forty-fifth president of the United States that is sparking serious debate. Debate as to whether or not emigration, fleeing the system, is smarter than trying to change the system or perhaps expecting record-breaking electorate turnout for every single election. Another way to frame America's new political status quo is to say that a new benchmark has been established because the bar appears to have been lowered so low that it was eventually simply just discarded. So, political scientists warn African Americans that going forward when looking at candidates they must ask themselves: Does the candidate have the potential even if they are not showing it now to be at the higher end of the spectrum, like take, for instance, a President Barack Obama, or do they have the potential to end up at the lowest end of the spectrum, like say the forty-fifth president of the United States?

It has been said that fairness in a post-truth, hypertribalized, and politically toxic America is next to impossible, however, to be fair, it must be noted that persecution and oppression in America do happen to those who self-identify as White. However, typically the persecution in those instances is individual based, meaning that it is typically personal and is on a case by case basis. It is not systemic and rarely if ever is it long-term or lifelong. But this does not mean that there are no Americans who self-identify as White, even if they are small in numbers, who are not afraid to admit that they too are exhausted living in such a racialized nation. A place where White supremacy ideology and prejudice based on color or ethnicity seems to be lurking around every corner. So, if significant numbers of Americans are tired of the nation's social, economic, and political trajectory, then the question becomes, What, if anything, is being done to change its course? Some scholars insist that this question can really only be answered by those who self-identify as White because they are the group with the power; they are the majority. And it is predominantly that majority who are doing most, if not all, of the political filibustering, road-blocking, and premature dismissal of socioeconomic ideas and policies that are specifically designed to benefit people of color. So, scholars believe that most of the movement and good-will has to come from that White majority, it has to start with them. No, that White majority did not have a hand in the enslavement of Africans and African Americans. It is a given that no one alive today was an enslaved African or African American. So, likewise, no one alive today was an enslaver, overseer, driver, or various other proponent of the enslavement of Africans and African Americans. However, systemic racism and racial bias still exist, and many scholars would argue that it is increasing.

Have the attitudes, core values, and belief systems of the vast majority of politicians who self-identify as White changed appreciably since President Warren G. Harding's 1921 speech, given in front of what was at the time an amazingly large segregated Alabama crowd? A speech in which he did not mince words in exclaiming his disapproval of miscegenation, which he referred to as "racial amalgamation?"[75] This question cannot be answered without having a clear understanding that systemic racism and racial bias could be described as a vicious cycle. But a cycle would suggest that things get better and then they get worse again, and then it repeats itself.

However, this question instead reveals a cruel and arguably inhumane stagnation caused by a nation whose capitalist economy ideals and acumen have never been questioned, but whose people skills lack something to be desired. Because it is still stuck on diversity, which means it is unable to even fathom the philosophy of inclusion. Likewise, many political scientists suggest that the same spirit behind America's Black Codes and Jim Crow laws is driving the strict voter identification (ID) laws in states such as Georgia, Indiana, Kansas, Mississippi, North Carolina, Tennessee, Virginia, and Wisconsin. And while it is less strict in states such as Arkansas, Alabama, Florida, Hawaii, Idaho, Louisiana, Michigan, Rhode Island, South Dakota, and Texas, it is still prohibitive.[76] Again, just to be clear, the eradication of tribalism or changing the condition of the human spirit of Americans will not be done using statistics and comprehensive research reports. However, it seems clear that in states that have less strict voter ID requirements, the gap between African American or Black voter and White voter turnout is roughly three points. And the gap between Latino voter and White voter turnout is around five points in general elections. While at first glance, these numbers may not be jarring, it should be noted that those numbers more than double in primaries. So, the gap between African American or Black voter and White voter turnout spikes to between eleven and twelve points and the gap between Latino voter and White voter turnout jumps to just over thirteen points in primary elections.[77]

Perhaps it would be reasonable to now answer the question of whether or not the attitudes, core values, and belief systems of the vast majority of politicians who self-identify as White have changed appreciably since 1921. So, while suffrage must have experienced an evolution of sorts through the Voting Rights Act of 1965, the spirit of President Harding's ideas about racial amalgamation and a then segregated electorate, a spirit which is arguably still alive today, has not evolved. In fact, the contemporary political strategies such as America's voter ID laws, not only reflect the abhorrent spirit which Harding spoke of but they also arguably resemble something that could be likened to the de-evolution of an electorate. An electorate which took nearly a century to desegregate; devolving into a segregated electorate in half that amount of time.

CHAPTER 4

RELIGION

*Erroneous exhibitions of Christianity do more than
[anything] else to create and strengthen her enemies.*[1]
                                                    –John Sayre 1821

W hat was America thinking when it emancipated 3,953,761
enslaved Africans and African Americans and left them
to live in the same general population with their former
enslavers, overseers, drivers, and various other proponents of slavery?
Yes, What was America thinking if the early American colonists and
later the general population of those who self-identified as White;
those who claimed to be believers in, and followers of Christ; really
believed that Africans or enslaved Africans were subhuman? Or as
the Nazis would say, "Untermensch," referring to any non-Aryan
inferior people;[2] then why did they bother to proselytize them? Why
evangelize them? Because the fact is that in the first-century AD,
Christianity actually spread through the northern parts of Africa
before it made its way to the most northern parts of Europe.[3-8] The
Bible, through the Apostle Luke in the Acts of the Apostles, even
presents evidence of the presence of the first-century church in Africa
by noting that the Apostle Apollos was born in the north African city
of Alexandria, Egypt (Ref. Acts 18:24). In addition to this, Luke also
tells the story of a book of Isaiah reading, chariot riding Ethiopian
official, who had traveled to Jerusalem and was later baptized by

Philip before returning home (Ref. Acts 8:26-40). The Apostle Paul also mentions that Clement, quite possibly Clement of Rome or Clement of Alexandria, taught in Alexandria (Ref. Phillipians 4:3). So, Christianity already had enough seed planted on the continent of Africa that it did not require the enslavement of millions of Africans and their subsequent transport to the New World to justify pursuing Africa's infamous "Slave Coast"[9,10] as a new mission field for European and American missionaries. And even Israel's King David predicted that Africa would by its own free will embrace Christ, not as a result of kidnapping and enslavement when he wrote, "Africa will send her noble envoys to you, O God. They will come running, stretching out their hands in love to you" (Psalm 68:31 TPT).

During the centuries that Africans and African Americans were enslaved in America, the major issue within the so-called Christian church and its church or religious culture, with regard to the enslavement of Africans and African Americans was about both the moral dilemma and hypocrisy of slavery. Take miscegenation, for example, if those who self-identified as White; those who claimed to be believers in, and followers of Christ; really believed that enslaved Africans were subhuman and that intermarriage and romantic liaisons between the two groups should be forbidden, then why was there so much adultery and fornication perpetrated by White enslavers, their sons, brothers, grandfathers, and any random White field hand with enslaved as well as free Black women? Having said this, and with fear of being accused of repeating a phrase ad nauseam, nonetheless it bears repeating that the eradication of tribalism or changing the condition of the human spirit of Americans will not be done using statistics and comprehensive research reports. However, it is ironic, and many historians and scholars argue that in addition to being ironic, it is also hypocritical that the population of children fathered by White enslavers with enslaved Africans or African American mothers increased by nearly seventy percent between 1850 and 1860. Yet the population of children fathered by enslaved Africans or African American fathers grew by only twenty percent during that same time.[11] Of course, this is just one example of the moral dilemma and hypocrisy prevalent during a time when adultery routinely disqualified White men from holding positions of church leadership. Yet, sexual liaisons with enslaved African and African American women, committed by those same men, typically found both the church's leadership, the congregation, and quite often even the offended spouses of the adulterers, all suffering from blind eyes and deaf ears.

Ethicists suggest that in a typical moral dilemma, there must exist a conflict between two choices, both of which are moral. And typically, the person who has the dilemma is viewed as the protagonist, someone who is expressing their moral duty or moral obligation through choice. However, because admitting that Whites and Africans share a common humanity and thus a common Creator-God (Psalm 96:5 TPT) would mean that a White man who assaults an enslaved African or African American woman is guilty of the same sin of adultery as if he had been in an adulterous relationship with or assaulted a free White woman. So, this is not technically a real moral dilemma because to enslave or to keep enslaving Africans and African Americans was not a moral choice to be made, and the true nature of the protagonist would have been uncovered as being the antagonist.[12]

This is why historians and scholars contend that when it comes to so-called Christians, the notion that the emancipation of enslaved Africans and African Americans was a moral dilemma is clearly a false dichotomy. Instead, they charge that emancipation was not a moral choice but a moral obligation. So much so that it has even been suggested that emancipation, which is simply the removal of restraints, was not a strong enough word to describe the calamitous predicament that imprisoned Africans and African Americans. This reasoning goes on to imply that when it came to the enslavement of Africans and African Americans, a bonafide believer in and follower of Christ would have had the spiritual unction necessary to discern that these captives should be extricated; immediately removed or rescued; from their present condition. And as for any theological argument of whether or not enslavers, overseers, drivers, and various other proponents of slavery who professed to be Christians were indeed genuine Christians, it has been said that while only God has the authority to judge, believers in, and followers of Christ, on the other hand, are not prohibited from acting as inspectors of spiritual fruit.[13] This simply asks whether looking at an individual's lifestyle reveals religious teaching that is being "put into practice" (Luke 6:46 TPT), or simply used as a mask that hides hypocrisy (author's paraphrase Proverbs 26:25-26 TPT).

Furthermore, theologians warn that ideas that mislead believers into thinking that some semblance of changed behavior in the life of a convert is not an expected by-product of a redeemed spirit border on heresy. Because faith without examples of action is phony (author's paraphrase James 2:17 TPT). However, there are those who counterargue that since the domestic enslavement of Africans and African Americans was legal in fifteen of America's states at the onset of the Civil War,[14,15] it was therefore technically not immoral for so-called Christians who lived in said chattel states to participate in chattel slavery. And of course, this counterargument is quite often met with strong rebuttal from those who scathe at the hypocrisy of those who claim that chattel slavery was not immoral simply because it was legal.

Further rebuttal adds the contrasting idea of how a woman's right to terminate an unwanted pregnancy is legal in a large number of America's states, yet the opponents of that law believe that it is immoral to participate in it. In which case, an analogy such as this one is meant to point out that the same principle of moral or natural law, which holds that the enslavement of Africans and African Americans is just because it is legal, must conversely hold that a woman's freedom of choice is likewise just. Not only because it is legal, but because of the venerable Latin phrase *"Lex iniusta non est lex"* (an unjust law is no law at all).[16] And while this rebuttal is not an attempt to present moral equivalence, it is an attempt to apply deductive reasoning with regard to the question of whether enslavers, overseers, drivers, and various other proponents of slavery could have been authentic believers in, and followers of Christ. Could they have possessed a genuine faith in God and, at the same time, been participants in chattel slavery without having their consciences seared to such a degree that they would once and for all cleanse themselves from the dirty business of chattel slavery?

To keep slaves as chattel meant to believe that Africans and African Americans were naturally inferior to Whites. Thereby making them perfectly suited for servitude, or else that they were not human at all, but belonging to some animal kingdom lower order of non-homo sapiens. The irony of such a belief system is that it would, by default, suggest an intermingling of Christian creationism and Darwinism for this belief to have been proven true. Furthermore, it would also imply that millions of Americans who self-identify as White today can trace their ancestry back to a White man who essentially mated with an animal, which in and of itself to believers is a sin separate and arguably more disgusting than even adultery. And likewise, millions of African Americans would not only be able to trace their ancestry back to sinful White men with an affinity for intimate relations with animal kingdom lower order non-homo sapiens.

Furthermore, for a Christian to view sex with an enslaved person as not being the same as committing the sin of either adultery or fornication is to believe, again, that Africans and African Americans were naturally inferior to Whites. Thereby making them perfectly suited for servitude, in this case, adultery or fornication, or in this case, the belief that they were not human–homo sapiens–at all. This would imply that although they, African and African American women, possessed anatomically correct and thus compatible body parts for White men, an African or African American woman was not really a "woman;" but an "other."

Without a real moral dilemma, without a real choice between two moral or two good outcomes, the antagonist is stripped of the ability to be the moral hero because only one of the two choices is moral. The other choice, the status quo, is, in fact, immoral. And if the antagonist chooses the status quo over morality, then it would appear as though that act would be comparable to living in a perpetual state of willful rebellion. Rebellion that cannot be explained away. Any deontic logic is quite difficult to fathom, especially if purely economic motives are removed from the equation. For example, if the moral dilemma is replaced with a moral obligation, a moral obligation that does not involve the extrication or manumission of the enslaved, then the moral duty or moral obligation of so-called Christian enslavers would have been to simply increase their wealth. So, getting rich as the owners of and wardens of labor camps, commonly referred to as plantations, would be the obligation or duty. Or perhaps at the other extreme, the moral duty or moral obligation would have been to simply eke out a subsistence living. As ludicrous as this argument sounds, and putting circular reasoning aside, both of these scenarios, whether wealth creation or abject poverty avoidance, should have begged a question to bonafide believers. One question should have been, Is participating in such an ugly business worth more than my soul (author's paraphrase Mark 8:37 NLT)? And even then, the best attempts to justify the chattel enslavement of Africans and African Americans would have just as it does today, required descending metaphorical rabbit holes. Metaphorical rabbit holes that lead so-called people of faith into antithetical philosophies such as Darwinism and evolution, the practice of bestiality, and the willful misinterpretation of scripture in order to defend the morally indefensible.[17] This, in addition to various other irreconcilable and illogical actions not unlike the nonsensical rabbit hole, mentioned both here and in the previous chapter on Politics.

Some of America's Founding Fathers may have studied the classics such as the Greek philosopher Socrates' ideas regarding the meaning of justice, such as whether or not it is right to give or return to someone what is owed to them if that act, in turn, may harm another person.[18] Or the question of whether an unjust individual is representative of the larger collective, such as a city, state, or perhaps even a nation. However, the average American would not have needed a formal education in philosophy in order to understand that moral dilemmas quite often give people the ability to protect humanity. So, the concepts, precepts, and other instructions on morality could have been understood even without the Bible or literacy. This would have been through songs, paintings, and even the stained-glass windows of churches, and of course, through oral storytelling. Oral storytelling was not unlike the way contemporary cinema is used to tell stories of honor, valor, and moral heroism, even if the hero is himself a thief as in the cult classic American film *Gone*

In 60 Seconds, not the original film (1974), but the more contemporary version (2000). In this film, both the protagonist, as well as the antagonist, are presented with moral dilemmas. The film's protagonist, a former automobile thief, has to decide whether to continue down the righteous path that he is on, with his criminal past long behind him or to begin stealing automobiles again in order to save the life of his younger brother, who has also become an automobile thief. And while his moral dilemma; his choice; to attempt to save his brother's life is made clear early in the film, the film's antagonist, a veteran police detective, whose moral dilemma does not appear until the second to the last scene of the film. This second to the last scene is one in which the detective, having finally apprehended the unretired car thief after a high speed car chase, explains to the protagonist, "Here I am smack dab in the middle of a moral dilemma . . . You've ripped this city to shreds with that little escapade of yours . . . But I understand what brought you back here. A brother's love—is—a brother's love."[19] However, unlike this post climatic fan favorite scene depicting the culmination of the love an older brother has for his wayward younger brother, even before the Civil War ripped the nation to shreds, America's major church denominations had already been torn in two. As early as 1844, the Methodist Church passed a resolution stating that: "Resolved, that we believe an immediate division of the Methodist Episcopal Church is indispensable to the peace, prosperity, and honor of the Southern portion thereof, if not essential to her continued existence..."[20] and that, "We regard the officious, and unwarranted interference of the Northern portion of the church with the subject of slavery alone, a sufficient cause for a division of our Church."[21] Furthermore, just as Southern states would secede from the United States in support of the enslavement of Africans and African Americans, Baptists in the Southern states

separated from the rest of the denomination in 1845 forming the
Southern Baptist Convention.[22] Likewise, just a few years prior to the
Civil War, battle lines within the Presbyterian denomination had
already been drawn on the issue of the enslavement of Africans and
African Americans, which eventually spawned a short-lived new pro-
enslavement denomination called the United Synod of the
Presbyterian Church.[23]

So, the so-called church's moral dilemma over the
enslavement of millions of Africans and African Americans, as well
as the deaths of and charges of attempted genocide of millions of
Africans during the arduous Middle Passage, apparently was not
resolved by a mere executive order and the passage of a constitutional
amendment. The Black Codes and the Jim Crow laws reveal the image
of two brothers whose anti-climactic behavior exposes the fact that
the two continue to be at odds with one another in perpetuity. After
having ripped the nation apart with the Civil War, they go through the
motions of trying to put the pieces back together again. However,
they begin to question their legitimacy–their paternity–their
nationhood. This raises questions such as, Was the Declaration of
Independence really the seed from which the nation was planted? Was
the United States Constitution really the womb from which both the
Northern as well as Southern states sprang? And with no official
treaty being signed to end the war, no heartfelt truce, was this simply
a case of one combatant forcing the other combatant to submit? So,
perhaps the last one hundred and fifty plus years have been little more
than a ceasefire. Maybe there was really no letting bygones be bygones
as this book's title implies.

In the 1990s, the acronym "WWJD" was a way to help young
followers of Christ, mostly teens and young adults, handle any moral
dilemmas they might find themselves facing by simply asking the

question, What would Jesus do? or WWJD? It became a worldwide phenomenon.[24] Simple yet profound, it spoke volumes to faith or a faith-based community and the trendy WWJD? bracelets and other novelty items spoke volumes to those on the outside of the faith looking in. Wearing a WWJD? bracelet or T-shirt meant identification with Christ. And while mottos or catchphrases like WWJD? the four-letter acronym, which seemed to flow ever so smoothly when spoken, only come along ever so often; perhaps it is time to churn up the phraseology. Instead of four letters, try five. ITITB? "Is–That–In–The–Bible?" No, it does not roll right off the tongue like WWJD? but it asks the very important question, How does the social, economic, or political discourse, which may be dominating America's twenty-four-hour news cycle, line up with what the Bible has to say about society? And not just, What does it say about money, but about wealth in particular, and those in positions of power or authority–leadership? A follow up question might ask, Why choose to use the Bible as a reference? Especially since some historians facetiously ask whether or not those who self-identify as White thought that there was a White god for Whites and a Black god for Africans and African Americans. This, in light of the fact that as late as the 1960s, it was common practice for courtrooms to have two separate Bibles for White and African Americans to swear on before testifying in court.[25,26,27] But quite frankly, the Bible is used as a point of reference because a great deal of America's social, economic, and political discourse is purported to be or is quite often tied to the idea of Judeo-Christian values.

This relationship between politics and religion is relevant in spite of the fact that world renowned, beloved, and influential evangelical minister, Billy Graham in 1981, was quoted as saying that the only real interest the "political right"[28] or "hard right has in religion is to manipulate it."[29] Perhaps there lies some irony in the fact that not all, but many, of the kidnapped and then enslaved Africans who were brought to the New World and forced to forget their family names, languages, culture, and their religious practices were introduced to the faith of their Protestant or Catholic enslavers for the first time. This was arguably in spite of the fact that many of the enslavers themselves did not have a thorough knowledge of the very faith that they forced upon enslaved Africans and African Americans. The remainder of the irony is that this very same Judeo-Christian faith incorporates justice, vengeance, and deliverance from one's enemies. And it is the idea of deliverance that Harriet Tubman, known as the great conductor of the Underground Railroad, a secret network of individuals and groups that aided in the liberation of enslaved Africans and African Americans, believed wholeheartedly. Tubman herself, an escaped enslaved African American, said that she knew that God, whom one modern Bible translation refers to as the Mighty Defender (Isaiah 51:22 TPT), had a plan for her life. She also said that she had dreams and visions she believed came to her from God, whom one modern translation refers to as the Guardian-God (Psalm 121:4 TPT). These dreams and visions inspired her to successfully guide as many as seventy enslaved Africans and African Americas to freedom—[30] to deliverance. It is stories such as this one that historians and scholars note only serve to reinforce the hypocrisy of slavery. Because a system that bought and sold other human beings as if they were cattle, yet felt obligated to introduce many of those enslaved Africans and African Americans to the same "Creator-God" (Psalm 96:5 TPT) who delivered over two million[31] enslaved Israelites out of the hands of their enslavers is the ultimate hypocrisy.

Harriet Tubman used her faith, the seeds of which may have been ironically planted in her and her ancestors either directly or indirectly by their enslavers, as a way to access Divine deliverance. So, it comes as no surprise that many of the revolts led by enslaved Africans and African Americas have often historically been downplayed through a type of psychological minimization. Minimization almost to the point of belittling the revolts, especially when the faith of an individual or a collective body of enslaved people, was reported to be the primary inspiration for the revolt. A great example of Biblical passages or concepts inspiring uprisings among the enslaved is Nat Turner's Rebellion. This was a violent uprising of the enslaved against their enslavers, overseers, drivers, and various other proponents of enslavement in the pursuit of not just vengeance but Divine justice. And in an attempt to thwart rebellions of any kind, it has been proven that some sacrilegious American enslavers even went so far as to create their own version of the Judeo-Christian Bible, which excluded key passages of scripture from the King James Version of the Bible that might be related to the ideas of freedom.[32]

It is also ironic that many contemporary theologians lament how the Biblical ideas of freedom were perverted into what has been called the "religious heritage" of White Supremacy ideology. An ideology through which so-called Christian enslavers moved from using the word Christian as a designation of freedom to using the word White as a representation of freedom. This was deemed necessary by the proponents of enslavement in order to exclude baptized enslaved and free Africans and African Americans from the notion that Christianity was a faith of inherent freedom. And instead subjugating them to the idea that any inherent freedom Christianity offered was reserved for Whiteness.[33,34] In addition, many so-called Christian enslavers, overseers, drivers, and various other proponents of the enslavement of Africans and African Americans attempted to use the Bible as a tool to help bolster and defend the institution of the enslavement of Africans and African Americans through flawed or self-serving interpretations of the Bible. Because while scripture may have given instructions on how believers in, and followers of Christ should operate within societies and economies where enslavement was permitted, it never specifically endorses it.[35]

However, while the act of chopping the Bible into bits and pieces during America's Antebellum Period to help promote an immoral agenda was sacrilegious, to say the least, it was just as common throughout most of America's history for individuals to take a single Biblical idea out of proper context to create dogmas and doctrines. Take, for instance, the so-called Protestant work ethic and other erroneous ideas, teachings, and Biblical misinterpretations about the concept of self-sufficiency or relying on oneself. The concept was promoted as a virtue instead of a vice which many theologians suggest fits the philosophy of men and not that of a Divine creator. The previously mentioned so-called Protestant work ethic is where the idiomatic idea of pulling oneself up by one's bootstraps, also known as bootstrapping, comes from. It is unfortunate that the fictitious ITITB? "Is–That–In–The–Bible?" acronym and phrase mentioned in this book was not around during German sociologist Max Weber's time. Because it may have just sparked the question as to whether or not the so-called Protestant work ethic is specifically noted in the Bible. Weber's 1905 book *The Protestant Ethic and the Spirit of Capitalism* helped introduce the phrase Protestant work ethic into common usage in America.[36] It was not Weber, but many prior generations of the proponents of Calvinism that were at the heart of the Protestant work ethic ideology. And they were not as concerned about people being industrious and hardworking, as indicated in the various chapters of the book of Proverbs and verses from various New Testament letters, as they were about wanting to judge people's salvation based upon their outward level of prosperity. Wealth to them was a likely sign that a person had received the salvation given by the grace of the "Creator-God" (Psalm 96:5 TPT). Likewise, poverty was a sign that a person could be judged as being spiritually or eternally lost.[37]

This was yet another red-flag suggesting that if the melting pot[38] experiment were to continue past this point, people of color would have to ask themselves the question, If the system is built to favor those who self-identify as White, then who can become wealthy, and likewise if a person is not White, then who can be saved (author's paraphrase Luke 1826)? Although steeped heavily in theological legalism vis-a-vis works; the eisegesis idea that works or good deeds lead to salvation as opposed to the exegesis idea that works or good deeds follow salvation;[39] it can be posited that this idea of works is one of the core elements of what many Americans believe makes America the so-called greatest Western nation on the planet. It is inferences to qualities such as sixty to eighty-hour work weeks that they believe somehow makes them more godly than other less industrious nations. To which many theologians rhetorically ask, Is the "Mighty God of All the Earth" (Isiah 54:5 TPT) more interested in building a relationship with his creation or in building empires and in heretical "Christendom?"[40] And their resounding rhetorical answer is that one would be hard pressed to find a Biblical precedent that would lead one to believe that relationship is not more important than empire or Christendom.

Now, while it is very difficult to argue against the inspirational and motivational qualities of the Great American success story, it nonetheless seems as though the stories of how yet another person, who happens to self-identifies as White, pulled her or himself up by their own bootstraps is wearing thin on African Americans and people of color. Some African Americans maintain that as long as White privilege and systemic racial inequity exist; privileges and systems that studies have shown provide a racialized advantage to Whites over African Americans; then those who self-identify as White should strongly consider toning down any self-made person rhetoric. A term which not unlike the ideas of freedom and liberty for which each American has their own individual definition of. But it is a term that when broken down into its most rudimentary form, is meant to refer to people who either self-identify as being self-made or are commonly referred to as such by either their peers or their admirers because they are said to possess "a drive to make money and become important."[41] Perhaps the backlash over the term is a result of America for over a century placing too much social capital and emphasis on the economic capitalist idea or theory of bootstrapping when it is quite clear that America's socioeconomic system discriminates based upon racialization. And in the ears of African Americans and people of color, bootstrapping is a repetitive story told ad nauseum about the mythical self-made White woman or White man, which historians and scholars assert are almost all based upon misread or misinterpreted scripture viewed through Western eyes. Again, a lot of the so-called bootstrap misconception is derived from the flawed ideology of the so-called Protestant work ethic and other erroneous ideas, teachings, and misinterpretations about the Biblical concept of self-sufficiency, which is promoted as a virtue instead of the vice that it technically is. In addition, take a look at the book of Deuteronomy that, for instance, says, "God... gives you the ability to produce wealth..." (Deut. 8:18 NIV). This is an idea that even to a layperson seems to clearly stress or focus on God as the ultimate source of wealth, not on the individual's abilities per se. Take, for example, another translation of the same verse says that "God gives you the strength to make a living . . . " (Deut. 8:18 CEV), a passage along with other similar passages begging the question, From what Biblical concept or precept do America's self-made women or men infer the right to self-aggrandizement? Which, then begs the question, Do the bootstrappers really believe that everyone with intestinal fortitude and a strong work ethic will automatically become a millionaire or billionaire? To which theologians suggest that it should be noted that there is a difference between an individual's right to be successful and an individual's destiny or pre-destined lot in life. Otherwise they could be accused of being little more than just social Darwinists in disguise.

Now, for the sake of clarity, this book does not seek to in any way, shape, or form encourage the swinging of the pendulum from one end of philosophical extremism; self-made women and men; to the other; self-defeated women and men. Besides, it is difficult at best to argue against America being a land of opportunity–prima facie. However, at the same time, it is like the analogy that every American cannot be the fictional American superhero Superman; however, every American can be Superman's alter ego Clark Kent. And from a purely statistical point of view, America is made up of mostly Clark Kent's when the richest one percent in the United States have more wealth than the bottom ninety percent. So, this bootstrap mythos, also known as rugged individualism ethos or the Horatio Alger myth, is based upon particularly noted fallacies. One fallacy is the presumption that individuals are judged solely based upon individual merit. Another fallacy is that each and every individual has fair opportunities. Then, of course, there is the cumulative notion that individual merit always succeeds regardless of the social construct of race, ethnicity, gender, class, or education level. Critics also argue that those who love the bootstrap mythos often forget about specific American institutions that have historically favored those who self-identify as White, such as:

- Labor markets
- Housing markets
- Civil courts
- Criminal courts
- Law enforcement
- The free press

In addition to this list of institutions and systems that assisted in the building of and the perpetuation of the bootstrap mythos there was America's history of free land or cheap land for those who self-identified as White. These, as well as other ideas, were the manifestation of the belief that Europeans and the early American Settler Colonists conquering American Indian lands was justified because Pope Alexander VI issued the 1493 decree, "Inter Caetera,"[42] also known as the Doctrine of Discovery.[43,44,45] This gave European Catholics the right to colonize newly discovered lands. Likewise, it was protestant John Winthrop's 1630 "Modell of Christian Charity,"[46] which essentially compared the Anglo-Saxon; a mythical heritage to say the least;[47] conquests of America to Israel's Promised Land edict from God noted in Deuteronomy chapter thirty.[48] This, in spite of the fact that the gentile church did not possess a land covenant with God as Israel did.[49,50] Theologians point out that as a matter of fact, Deuteronomy makes it quite clear that out of all the nations on earth, the "God of Covenant" (Psalm 78:36-37 TPT) only chose Israel to be his very own (author's paraphrase Deut. 7:6 CEV). So, once again, had the fictitious ITITB? acronym and phrase mentioned in this book existed around the time when John L. O'Sullivan was coining the phrase "Manifest Destiny" in his 1845 essay "Annexation,"[51] it may not have curtailed this or any other divide and conquer ideology but it may have at least challenged the status quo. It may have perhaps even helped answer the question that has been posed by believers, agnostics, and even atheists, centuries later and that is, Did America's so-called 'Men of God' simply look the other way at such injustices? And the rhetorical answer is that although the Bible admonishes a nation's leadership, the king, to be the voice that speaks "on behalf of the disenfranchised and pleads for the legal rights of the defenseless and those who are dying" (Proverbs 31:8 TPT); not many, whether nobility or commoner, answered the question or the call to either speak or act.

However, there were a few who refused to let their voices be tamed, take, for instance, the congregational minister Daniel Butrick, who in 1838 witnessed firsthand America's infamous Trail of Tears. This was the infamous forced removal and relocation of American Indians from their native lands. To which Butrick stated vehemently that the American Indians had "[D]one no wrong to merit any parts of this evil . . . "[52] Another example was the Welsh missionary John B. Jones, another eyewitness to the Trail of Tears, who lamented that he would not be able to see the faces of those American Indians who had perished along the trail until, "[T]he great day when the oppressor and the oppressed shall appear before the tribunal of the righteous judge."[53] And it was not just men of God, but even men of war who witnessed the aftermath of the forced removal of American Indians from their indigenous lands, who found the whole business appalling such as Private John G. Burnett. Still haunted at the age of eighty by the scenes he witnessed in his late twenties, he exclaimed, "Somebody must explain the 4,000 silent graves that mark the trail of the Cherokees to their exile."[54]

In addition to American magazines and newspapers, many of which glorified and romanticized the ideology of Manifest Destiny through both words and imagery,[55,56,57] the bootstrap mythos was further aided by other extremely important tools of the free press, which were radio and television broadcasting media, respectively. Although these were tools of the later part of the nineteenth-century and the early part of the twentieth-century, respectively, they we not only able to extend the life of the bootstrap mythos but aided in romanticizing its ideology. However, aside from the free press, one of the most important institutions in a capitalist economy or society, its banking institutions, had been present almost since the nation's founding. Take, for example, the home of America's New York Stock Exchange, the iconic, world-renowned financial district known as Wall Street. Whose original physical wall was in fact erected by enslaved Africans and African Americans in 1653. And Wall Street was later a location where enslaved Africans and African Americas were bought and sold as early as 1709,[58,59] and was by 1789 already established as a financier to the slave trade.[60] Yes, America's famous Wall Street along with various banks played a central role in the brokering of loans to build enslavement ships and the insurance for both the ships and their human cargo. In addition to loans that were directly tied to chattel slavery such as the construction of sailing ships, land, the human capital of Africans and African Americans, seed, domesticated farm animals, working capital, and all of the various other agrarian tools and implements necessary to produce agricultural commodities, Wall Street also supported businesses indirectly tied to chattel slavery. Businesses such as the massive textile industry, the numerous merchants involved in the marketing and export of slave-produced agricultural commodities, and even the smallest of rural general merchandise stores.

However, it takes more than just financial resources to build a nation, and, in this case, it took forced labor, which was, of course, mostly African and African American. And not to gloss over or minimize the contributions of Hispanic and Asian labor which were also utilized to varying degrees in the making of America, but the metaphorical icing on the cake was, without any argument, the centuries of enslaving Africans and African Americans in labor camps, more commonly known as plantations. This human capital which not only provided centuries of free agrarian labor and laid the foundation for America's robust economy, but it also helped lay the foundation for America's industrial revolution. It was instrumental in the building of its infrastructure from railroad construction to the White House and even the United States Capitol building.[61,62,63] This human capital provided the economic advantage which put America many years if not several decades ahead of other nations that had either already banned the importation of enslaved peoples or the domestic trading of enslaved peoples. Therefore, contemporary scholars base their assessment of America's socioreligious climate not on feel good slogans and empty platitudes about freedom and democracy, but on America's raw and unfiltered history. An assessment that is rooted in the reality that even one hundred and fifty plus years after emancipation the core belief of the Manifest Destiny, that America is the Promised Land for those who self-identify as White, is still very much alive and well. The proof that scholars offer for this assessment is: (1) the election of an autocratic ideolog like the forty-fifth president of the United States; (2) the deteriorating state of relations between the followers and loyalists of the forty-fifth president and African Americans; (3) the disdain that followers and loyalists of the forty-fifth president who self-identify as White have toward individuals or groups that they view as "other" or outside of the social construct of Whiteness, whether the notion of race, gender, class, or religion; (4) how they marginalize the poor in general.

Concerning the marginalization of the poor, What does the Bible infer, if anything, about how the wealthiest nation on the planet should treat its poor? How should they, the haves and the have-nots, co-exist? Can they co-exist? These questions about the difficulty of two very distinct groups learning to co-exist are reminiscent of a famous scene about peace from the epic American science fiction film *Independence Day*. In this particular scene about peace, the actor playing the role of the president of the United States says to a creature from outer space who just crash landed on earth, "I know there is much we can learn from each other–if we can make a truce." The fictitious president goes on to say, "Can we find a way to co-exist? Can there be a peace between us?" To which the creature replies, "Peace? no peace!"[64] So, the analogy to be made, aside from art imitating life, even if that life is extraterrestrial, is that perhaps one way to think of how to close the wealth gap in America is for some type of peace treaty to exist between the economic classes. But what does the Bible say, if anything, about the rights and responsibilities of the haves; the wealthy in America, commonly referred to as the one-percenters?

Furthermore, what does the Bible have to say to the majority of those who self-identify as White, those who are not only espoused to the bootstrap mythos but also believe that much of what is going on regarding socioeconomic and racialized economic disparities in America are isolated incidents as opposed to systemic problems? Well, it does not take a Bible scholar to recognize that there are numerous Bible passages that actually scold people for being rich, but that it is mostly void of passages that might seem to scold or chastise people for being poor or having a disability. Indeed, the Bible is chocked full of passages that seem to be speaking directly to those who have a lot of material possessions:

Do not be proud . . . (1 Tim. 6:17 CEV).

Be generous and share . . . (1 Tim. 6:18 CEV).

The poor man Lazarus went to heaven, but the rich guy, he went to the "other" place (author's paraphrase Luke 16:19-28).

The rich seldom get a good night's sleep (author's paraphrase Ecclesiastes 5:10-13).

The wicked do not care about the rights of the poor, but good people do (author's paraphrase Proverbs 29:7).

While these are all good examples, most of which caution or perhaps even reprimand the wealthy, there is, however, one passage that some readers may find especially harsh or disturbing. And that is the warning to rich people which states, "Your money has rusted, and the rust will be evidence against you" (James 5:1-3 CEV). Which one commentator suggests is a warning against the hoarding of wealth.[65]

Perhaps it is passages such as this that lead some opponents of politicized theology to ask, Why do so many so-called evangelicals in America, who self-identify as White, support the narrative that so-called entitlements for seniors, people with disabilities, veterans, women, children, and families that live below the poverty line should be scolded or chastised for needing financial or medical assistance? These opponents also ask, Do White evangelicals understand that the majority of those who qualify for America's Social Security and other benefits have lifelong histories of paying into both the Social Security insurance program and America's Medicare health insurance program by way of payroll tax deductions? With the irony of it all being that the same so-called evangelicals often portray the forty-fifth president of the United States' greed, narcissism, and his abuse of tax, housing and bankruptcy laws as a narrative of shrewd business practices, strategic thinking, and even virtuous stewardship.

Scholars contend that the philosophy of wealth and financial stewardship as it applies to so-called American evangelicals who self-identify as White, and in particular, the followers and loyalists of the forty-fifth president of the United States, at best only vaguely resembles anything Biblical. At worst, it very closely resembles the trickle-down economic theory touted for decades by staunch fiscal conservatives. It is an economic proposition purported to be rooted in a fiscal responsibility strategy that is supposed to benefit all Americans. In actuality, it bears closer resemblance to arbitrarily cutting tax rates for the wealthiest Americans and rolling the proverbial dice, hoping that the strategy will help grow the American economy overall, increase individual income and wages specifically, and ultimately lead to quantifiable job creation. However, there is another aspect to this proposition, which many of its most ardent believers reveal, is the root of their economic philosophy for the reduction of poverty in America. And to boil their philosophy down into its simplest form, they use a very humanistic proverb, an idiom whose figurative meaning probably has some type of translation in almost every major culture and language in the world. It says that giving a man a fish only feeds him for a day, but if taught the skill of fishing he can eat for a lifetime.[66] An idea almost all would agree is a very heartfelt, proverbial, and pragmatic sentiment except for the fact that as alluded to in the previous chapter on Economics, while there is no shortage of scholarly research and an abundance of books written on the subjects of personal responsibility and self-help, the truth of the matter is that not everyone can fish. Not all of America's senior citizens, not all of its veterans, not all of the individuals with disabilities, not all of the single parents with children, not all of those who at first glance may appear to be able bodied are actually able bodied.

While the sentiment is indeed heartfelt, proverbial, and even pragmatic, political economists argue that this oversimplification of a complex issue begs a flurry of follow up questions such as, Who or what agency is going to be responsible for teaching and training these future catchers of fish? Who is going to be responsible for any tuition, books, or other required educational fees? Who is going to supply the teaching and training equipment and any necessary resources? Will there be public transportation available to transport the students to and from the fishing location? Will daycare be provided for students who have non-school aged children? Will after school care be provided for students who have school aged children? Will the students be required to possess a license to fish in local, state, or federally controlled waters? Will the fish they catch be taxable? The point of this exhaustive set of questions is not that personal responsibility and self-help are not important. Neither is it that the poor do not deserve immediate help, basic food, and shelter, even if they were to fail some seemingly arbitrary litmus test for eligibility to learn how to fish. Because those who are believers in, and followers of Christ and those who do not adhere to a politicized theology believe that the Bible contains some of the most compassionate language regarding how to treat not just those who are obviously poor or those who it is plain to see have a disability, but those who in general simply have less:

Every time you give to the poor you make a loan to the Lord (Proverbs 19:17 TPT).

If any of your people become poor and unable to support themselves, you must help them . . . (Leviticus 25:35 CEV).

Giving brings a far greater blessing than receiving (Acts 20:35 TPT).

[I]f you're heartless, stingy, and selfish, you invite curses upon yourself (Proverbs 28:27 TPT).

Out of generosity they even sold their assets to distribute the proceeds to those who were in need among them (Acts 2:44-46 TPT).

Theologians; the ones who do not adhere to a politicized theology; acknowledge that there will always be individuals who exaggerate or falsify their indigent status—those who contrive nefarious stratagems to improperly use the existing system which is set up to assist those in need—who accept more than what is fair or more than what they really need for daily living. However, likewise, there will always be wealthy Americans and American corporations that operate in gray areas or those quasi-legal areas. These are individuals and corporations that fabricate profits and losses, those who inflate or distort the truth to make a sale, and those who operate under the guise that just because a business practice may be legal, it must be moral.

On the contrary, it was Christ, the head of the Church, who told the wealthy nobleman to sell all of his possessions and give the proceeds to the poor (author's paraphrase Luke 18:22 TPT). The point of which was not to condemn this wealthy man or rich people in general. But at least one commentator suggests that while the point was not an attempt to introduce a new commandment in which all should take vows of poverty or should necessarily engage in communal living arrangements in which every cent an individual owns belongs to the group. It was, however, a special warning to the wealthy that they should be both ready as well as willing to share their wealth.[67] This is in light of the fact that as previously mentioned in this chapter, it is difficult at best to argue against America being a land of opportunity–prima facie. This means that it is rather difficult to live in and benefit from living in a capitalist economy or country like America yet truly–wholeheartedly be against prosperity. Because as mentioned in the previous chapter on Economics, 'it is better to have money and not need it than to need money and not have it.'[68] Yet it should also be clearly understood that while the goal should never be to make martyrs out of every single person who relies upon government subsidies for financial or medical assistance, neither should they be demoralized or marginalized.

Ethicists maintain that if character and integrity is what matters most to White so-called evangelicals in America how did they reconcile that belief with not only the election of the forty-fifth president of the United States but the continued staunch support of him by his base? Some scholars had even implied that if comparing the character and integrity of the forty-fifth president of the United States before he was elected; who by the way had the unequivocal support of so-called White evangelicals; to his opponent Secretary of State Hillary Clinton, she appeared to possess a more positive character and more integrity than the future forty-fifth president of the United States. But instead of relying upon people's opinions, why not find out what the Bible has to say, if anything, about character and integrity in general and the character and integrity of leaders in particular? So, did the forty-fifth president prior to or after his election express any of these fruits of the spirit or character qualities based upon Galatians 5:22-23 (TPT)?

> Joy that overflows
>
> Peace that subdues
>
> Patience that endures
>
> Kindness in action
>
> A life full of virtue
>
> Faith that prevails
>
> Gentleness of heart
>
> Strength of spirit

After reviewing this list, theologians; the ones who do not adhere to a politicized theology; believe that even a layperson could make a sound argument based upon both the private and public statements of the forty-fifth president of the United States that the verses mentioned above line up more with the character of Secretary of State Hillary Clinton than they do the forty-fifth president of the United States before he was elected to office. And from this, another sound argument could be made that the Bible's warning for believers to "[N]ot repay evil with evil or insult with insult" was never practiced by the forty-fifth president of the United States. Instead, he was perhaps best known for often vengefully striking back at his opponents using social media, press conferences, and even lawsuits. And this was both before and after he was elected to office.

In addition to this, the forty-fifth president of the United States appeared to have never been made aware of the idea that believers in, and followers of Christ should not "[S]teal anything or cheat anyone, and don't fail to pay your workers" as mentioned in Leviticus 19:13 (CEV). A passage which some argued must have fallen on deaf ears since it was reported that the forty-fifth president of the United States, whose different business ventures filed for bankruptcy protection six times,[69,70] was also accused of being notorious for not paying the fully negotiated price to suppliers and contractors who provided goods and services to his real estate businesses.[71] Furthermore, it was because of both character and integrity flaws such as these which suggested that the Biblical exhortation to "repay evil with blessing ... " (1 Peter 3:9 NIV) was probably not in the repertoire of the forty-fifth president of the United States either before his election to office or after.

But what does the Bible say about the qualifications for leadership? Was the Bible even consulted by those White so-called evangelical followers and loyalists who have been accused of giving their unequivocal support to the forty-fifth president? Or did they perhaps simply push past the forty-fifth president's propensity to hurl insults at anyone he deemed as a threat to his election? Insults which were not only hurled upon contenders in the opposing party, personal and political antagonists, news media outlets who dared to print or post unflattering stories about him, individual reporters who dared to ask him pressing and difficult questions, but also contenders in his own party? It is questions like these that lead theologians; the ones who do not adhere to a politicized theology; to suggest that there was perhaps some confusion within both the leadership of White so-called evangelicals and within the congregations of so-called believers during the one to two year time frame that led up to the actual election of the forty-fifth president.

There was confusion as to why it was paramount for so-called evangelicals to stand firm on the Biblical principles with regard to a woman's right to choose whether or not to terminate a pregnancy and same-sex marriage. Yet it would be acceptable for those same so-called evangelicals to vacillate on Biblical principles regarding how to treat and care for the poor, the same poor mentioned in the previous chapter on Politics who are children under the age of five, millions of whom die due to undernutrition.[72] It is crises such as poverty and a lack of access to affordable healthcare that draw the ire of evangelicals; the ones who do not adhere to a politicized theology; who scathe at the hypocrisy of those so-called evangelicals who claim to be champions of unborn life, but turn a blind eye to the pain and suffering of the children who are already born. Furthermore, there was also confusion as to whether it would be acceptable to vacillate on Biblical principles regarding how to treat and care for strangers and foreigners, how to treat and care for recent immigrants, refugees, and asylum seekers. Unsure whether or not to embrace the men, women, and children, many of whom are often fleeing war torn nations, severely underdeveloped economies, despotic political systems, and histories of internal violence.[73] And of course, there was confusion as to whether it would be acceptable to vacillate on Biblical principles regarding how to treat and care for one's neighbors. Neighbors being the forty-two million[74] African Americans as well as millions of people of color still suffering from intergenerational racialized socioeconomic oppression one hundred and fifty plus years after emancipation in 1865 and a little over fifty years since the Civil Rights Act of 1964.

There was also past confusion among evangelicals as far back as 2007; a period of time that has been described as argumentative regarding the pros and cons of coal use in Texas. It was fractious concerning drilling for oil and gas in Alaska. And it was quarrelsome with regard to whether the evangelical political agenda was capable of broadening its scope beyond women's reproductive rights, judicial appointments, and same-sex marriage. In order to include, for example, discussions about what, if anything, global warming, which is simply one facet of climate change, had to do with the "core Christian duties to spread the faith and protect the unborn?"[75] Which is both a great question as well as one that is difficult to answer succinctly except for the fact that Christ's commands were not to "spread the faith and protect the unborn," but he instead summed up[76] the ten commandments into two: (1) love God; and (2) love your neighbor (author's paraphrase Mark 12:29-31). And His Great Commission; an "active imperative command;"[77] was for His followers to make Disciples, which is a concept that infers teaching, training, and relationship with both God and fellow believers. However, the point ethicists and theologians; the ones who do not adhere to a politicized theology; have attempted to insert into the evangelical confusion, as a bit of a buffer, is the idea that it is not that African Americans and people of color are asking the White evangelical laity to denounce what they claim are their core values. But to simply be aware that an unwavering focus on a limited set of issues has for decades led to a general refusal among White evangelical leaders, organizations, and their members to combat one of America's gravest and most abiding ills, which is racism.

At least one scholar has warned that cults and radical religious movements of the past did not survive and many were "mocked and remembered as being on the wrong side of history."[78] In addition to this, at least one evangelical leader has admitted that not only were people confused about whether or not they should support the candidate who would eventually become the forty-fifth president. But that he had never seen such bitter division amongst evangelicals than that expressed because of the candidacy of the candidate who would eventually become the forty-fifth president.[79] Another lamented that evangelicals who were supporting the candidate, who would eventually become the forty-fifth president, were "tossing aside everything that evangelicals have previously said about character matters and about human dignity."[80,81] While yet another remarked that for evangelicals to ally themselves with someone like the candidate, who would eventually become the forty-fifth president, was akin to the violation of the sacred in exchange for "vain hope."[82,83] Hope that an untruthful candidate with a "record of betrayal"[84,85] could save them. Not only were evangelicals confused, but at least one pundit posited a reminder that evangelicals were also being threatened by the candidate, who would eventually become the forty-fifth president, who ran as a Republican but also threatened to drop the party and run instead as an independent if he was not "treated with respect."[86] A move that would have more than likely handed the election to the Democratic Party nominee, former Secretary of State Hillary Clinton.

However, in spite of all of this confusion, whether real or imagined, historians, scholars, and theologians; the ones who do not adhere to a politicized theology; point out that judgments concerning the character of anyone campaigning to become president of the United States of America should have been of vital importance. It may be argued that the New Testament speaks more about formal church leadership than it does about so-called secular endeavors such as business, community, or political leadership. But it does, however, set a precedent of standards that have historically been used when critiquing America's aspiring political candidates. And while it has been applied less frequently to those in positions of power in for-profit business endeavors, 1 Timothy 3 (TPT) is recognized by many as the Biblical standard for the qualifications for leadership:

He should be one whose heart is for his wife alone and not another woman (3:2).

He should be recognized as one who is sensible, and well-behaved . . . (3:2).

He cannot be . . . someone who lashes out at others . . . argumentative . . . craves more money . . . (3:3).

He should not be a new disciple who would be vulnerable to living in the clouds of conceit and fall into pride . . . (3:6).

He should be respected by . . . unbelievers . . . [have] a beautiful testimony among them so that he will not fall into the traps of Satan and be disgraced (3:7).

Just as the goal of the previous chapter on Politics was not to argue against the lack of natural qualifications of the man who took office as the forty-fifth president of the United States, neither is the goal of this chapter to argue against his lack of spiritual qualifications. This chapter simply seeks to ask the questions, If character and integrity are no longer a prerequisite to leadership in America, why not simply say so? Why wear the facade of sanctimonious piety every year except election year? If the endorsement and election of a candidate is really about a candidate's contribution to society as a whole, meaning if the contribution to society is big enough–valuable enough–is this not the same as saying that not unlike a big corporation–this individual is too big to fail? This last question has led some to surmise that perhaps this is one of the many reasons why the forty-fifth president of the United States and those like him were allowed to flourish in America instead of being ostracized or marginalized for their lack of character and integrity.

Perhaps this is also why the forty-fifth president of the United States said that he would ask for forgiveness only if he ever did anything wrong. And again, it may be argued that the New Testament speaks more about formal church leadership than it does about so-called secular endeavors such as political leadership. However, some historians and scholars would argue that it is not the detractors of evangelicals but evangelicals themselves who have historically chosen to use the Bible as a moral standard for the qualifications of holding public office. This leaves them open to criticism when they choose to publicly endorse a candidate who has an obviously flawed moral character. It becomes even worse if they continue to support an elected official even after it has been revealed that the official has committed unethical or immoral acts while in office. So, just as this book describes different red-flag moments for either African Americans or those on the outside looking in at America as pivotal moments in the history of the melting pot experiment, there were numerous warning signs that the candidate, who would eventually become the forty-fifth president, would be a source of consternation to nearly the entire world. With the exception being White evangelical Americans and perhaps the Russian government that was found guilty of interfering in the election in order to help the candidate who would eventually become the forty-fifth president win the 2016 election.[87-90]

Again, historians and scholars argue that it is not the detractors of evangelicals but evangelicals themselves who have historically chosen to use the Bible as a moral standard for the qualifications of holding public office. Likewise, the candidate himself, who would eventually become the forty-fifth president, publicly acknowledged that he is a Protestant Presbyterian.[91] And just like the evangelicals who supported him, he left himself open to criticism when he sought the endorsement of evangelicals in spite of his obviously flawed moral character. One example that the qualifications for evangelical leadership during the one to two year time frame that led up to the actual election of the forty-fifth president were "evolving" is when the candidate, who would eventually become the forty-fifth president, was asked on two separate occasions during the same televised interview whether or not he had ever asked God for forgiveness. The first time the question was asked, the candidate attempted to skirt the question by mentioning that he was a Presbyterian who goes to church and loves God. But when pressed further and asked the same direct question, "Have you ever asked God for forgiveness," to which he answered, "I'm not sure I have . . . I just go and try and do a better job from there . . . I don't think so . . . I think if I do something wrong . . . I think I just try and make it right . . . I don't bring God into that picture . . . I don't."[92] And it was statements like this that raised the spiritual antennae of not just theologians, but believers in, and followers of Christ in America; the ones who do not adhere to a politicized theology. The general sentiment emanating from that answer seemed to suggest that it was as if the candidate had never read the Bible verse, which says God corrects his "children." If he does not correct you, then you are not his child (author's paraphrase Hebrews 12:8 CEV).

Historians and scholars contend that Americans, and the entire world, for that matter, should bear in mind that the candidate, who would eventually become the forty-fifth president, was not the first candidate for president to be heavily scrutinized for the appearance of a lack of morality during his election campaign. However, he was one of the few to have made it through the process in spite of having such an obviously flawed moral character. For instance, it has been said that one of the reasons New York Governor Nelson Rockefeller was denied the 1964 Republican nomination for president is because he had divorced his wife.[93] Something which was still very taboo even through the 1960s. And it should be noted that both Alfred E. Smith, the 1928 Democratic Party nominee for president who was ultimately defeated by Herbert Hoover;[94] and John F. Kennedy in 1960 were heavily criticized for being Catholic. However, Kennedy was still able to win the presidency. So, the idea is that evangelical Protestants have historically, in some fashion, although often vague and subjective, always had to sign off on candidates for public office through the vetting of the character and integrity of candidates. Whether it was the requirement in the seventeenth and eighteenth centuries that any holder of public office in colonial America be affiliated with Virginia's Church of England.[95] Or the Southern Baptist Convention's prohibition of alcohol litmus test for political candidates seeking their endorsement.[96] Or the general consensus although often vague, that one of the prerequisites for public leadership should be moral qualifications. That is until the candidate who would eventually become the forty-fifth president came along and did what at least one religion research institute calls the bending of evangelical ethics[97] in order to elect the preferable or more electable candidate.

So, it is quite clear that the Bible both admonishes the rich and provides the blueprint on how to treat or care for the poor and those with disabilities. It even gives clues as to how to spot a Biblical leader. But what does it say, if anything, about the social construct of race and racism as they relate to religion? And so perhaps it is this introduction of the social construct of race and its offspring; racism; into this chapter on Religion which presents itself as the perfect segue into a peek into clear, tinted, or even stained glass windows of American houses of worship on Sunday mornings. Something which Dr. Martin Luther King, Jr. called, "[O]ne of the most segregated hours . . . in Christian America."[98] However, before plunging straightway into scripture as it relates to the notion of race, racism, and the segregation of believers, there is a question being begged in scholarly writing with regard to what is being referred to as a racial divide.[99,100,101] Not just in the so-called secular world, but also within the Church in America. And the question which is being begged is, In light of the legacy of Dr. Martin Luther King, Jr., an ordained minister and one of America's greatest moral philosophers, why do American churches headed by African Americans and people of color have so few parishioners who self-identify as White? Take, for example, the fact that there is a mega-church in America's Atlanta Georgia area, which is led by an African American man. A man who is of course, like the majority of African Americans, a descendant of enslaved Africans, but who is also a household name in many African American religious circles. However, a casual observation of any of his television broadcasts would, on average, reveal only ten regular attendees or members who probably would self-identify as White. Another example can be taken from America's west coast, where there is a legendary preacher–teacher known worldwide. But according to a visual survey of his television broadcasts, he has perhaps, on average, around seven regular attendees or members who probably would self-identify as White. Finally, there is a bishop in the state of Texas who many high profile African American entertainers, athletes, and various other high-profile people of color often publicly refer to as their spiritual mentor. However, even he may only average around twenty regular attendees or members who probably would self-identify as White. Unfortunately, all of these examples are unable to unearth an unequivocal reason why there appears to be a shortage of parishioners who self-identify as White attending American churches headed by African Americans and people of color. Instead, examples like these only beg more questions such as, Could it be that one hundred and fifty plus years after emancipation, that those who self-identify as White are still incapable of submitting to the leadership and tutelage of an African American pastor or pastor of color?

The moral to this story contains four parts. The first part is a recommendation that the mythos of America's self-made man or woman and the mythomania that it often encourages should be officially put to rest. Because the truth is that each American, each individual, is not self-made but is actually made up of "thousands . . . of other people."[102] Furthermore, it has been said that any American "who has ever done a kind deed"[103] for another American "or even simply spoken one word of encouragement"[104] has actually helped to make up the character, integrity, thoughts, and success of their fellow Americans.[105] However, making a case for removing the term self-made from American or United States English will not be easy. It has grown to become more than just a term, not unlike the reference to the word love in the scene from the American film *The Matrix Revolutions* mentioned in the chapter on Social Change. It was stated that love was just a word, but what really mattered the most was "the connection that the word love implies."[106]

So, the term self-made is much-much more than just a word; it is a connection to an ideal. It has not only become more than just a term. It has in fact birthed a myriad of nodding acquaintances such as the phrase that 1960s pop culture author John Cawelti used called the "success ideal."[107] A term he used when referring to Founders such as Thomas Jefferson and Benjamin Franklin regarding how they and men like them helped lay the foundation for the phrase, "self-made man."[108] A term which was later officially coined by Kentucky Senator Henry Clay in 1832. However, it was in the distant past, just as it is in more modern times, an adjective that not every American believes is authentic. A term which many believe is disingenuous and embellishes and even romanticizes the successes of protagonists who are predominantly White. It only serves to perpetuate the denial psychology ingrained within the ideas of White privilege and "white fragility"[109] as they relate to the perpetuation of the bootstrap mythos mentioned earlier in this chapter. Take, for instance, Francis Lieber, a German born American who not only sided with the United States, more commonly referred to as the Union, during the Civil War but also helped establish the United States' "formal guidelines for its army's conduct toward its enemies."[110] However, perhaps anthropologically speaking, he is more renowned for having challenged a man who claimed to be a self-made man by wittingly replying, "what a pity I was not present! I have long wished to be present when a man was making himself."[111] Another antagonist of the term self-made was Horace Greeley, founder, and editor of the New York Tribune newspaper. Who, when confronted by a man who pompously beat his own chest and exclaimed, "I am a self-made man." To which Greeley quipped, "Sir, I am glad to know that; it takes a terrible responsibility off the Almighty God!" [c. 1872][112,113]

Perhaps America's Founding Fathers simply mischaracterized or misinterpreted their roles in the great American melting pot drama. Just as the Pilgrim-Puritans who proceeded them may not have fully understood, not only the true power of their words but the consequences of their words (author's paraphrase Proverbs 18:21 Proverbs 18:21 GNT), when using Biblical passages or even abstract language. Unfortunately, assessing blame for any false or misleading narratives with regard to America being the Promised Land, the bootstrap mythos, or the aggrandizement of the self-made person, whether charged to the Founders themselves or to the hyperbolists who have historically trumpeted them as lay theologians, may be untraceable. And in all fairness, even some of the harshest of critics of the bootstrap mythos understand that it is arguably unfair to accuse the Founders of purposefully attempting to supplant Israel as the recipients of the Promised Land. However, apologists of the Founders refuse the extension of this type of olive branch as it were. Instead, they prefer to argue that antagonists who suggest that the predominantly Protestant Christian Founders where knowingly exclaiming parity with Israel are misinterpreting the motives of great men. Not only that, but that any errors to be laid at the feet of the Founders were simply the result of their nescience and unfledged sacrilegiousness. However, there are those who counterargue that while neither the motives of the Pilgrim-Puritans nor the Founders can be demonstrated, without doubt, they did nevertheless create an allegorical Biblical narrative. And regardless of whether or not their deeds can be proven to be acts of omission or commission, they did, as a result of both word and deed, add both a second undisclosed allegorical prophecy and an undocumented Promised Land to the traditional Judeo-Christian narrative. With the irony of it all being that in this new perquisite Promised Land, not a single signer of its Declaration of Independence was Jewish. Neither were there any Jewish among the legislators who voted to ratify the United States Constitution in 1788.[114] All of this was done in spite of the Pilgrim-Puritan and Founders' gravitas of the eisegetical Deuteronomy 30 Promised Land.

The best way to describe or explain the second part of the moral to the story is by asking the question, Why is it that White evangelicals refuse to clearly and unequivocally repudiate narratives that paint poverty as vile and sinful and wealth as virtuous or righteous? And while there is no definitive answer, it can be argued that too often their silence not only runs counterclockwise to what the Bible says, but it also allows the poor or those with disabilities to be painted with the same broad-brush strokes of resentment by complete strangers. Strangers who stereotype them as a group. Strangers that do not have a clue as to what their backstory and unfortunate circumstances look like. When not challenged, that narrative also gives those who oppose people of Protestant faith in general, or who simply oppose evangelicals in particular, supportive evidence with which to accuse them of being hypocritical. In addition to this, theologians; the ones who do not adhere to a politicized theology; believe that the fact that neither America nor the United States is clearly mentioned in the Bible[115] is reason enough to once and for all do away with the narrative of America as the Promised Land and to call America to repentance. Repentance for the enslavement of Africans and African Americans and the "extirpation,"[116] of American Indians under the auspices of the Doctrine of Discovery.[117,118,119]

Yet contemporary narratives still abound suggesting that the Pilgrim-Puritans saw themselves in the position of the Israelites crossing the Jordan River, and the Founders saw themselves in the position of the Biblical followers of Christ, who were in a sense rebelling against religious rulers. However, the prevailing narrative strongly suggests that the actions of the Founders who rebelled against King George most closely resembled, not the Biblical followers of Christ; the Disciples; but that of the religious rulers; the Pharisees. The same religious sect that Christ often criticized for their hypocrisy, a sort of "theocratic party,"[120] who not only opposed the secular government, but also the personhood of Christ the King—Messiah. After all, most of Christ's displeasure was not with a secular government but with the hypocrisy and refusal of the religious leaders of the time to recognize him as Messiah. And while evidence may support the argument that the majority of America's Founders did not deny the personhood of Christ, they did little or nothing to repudiate narratives that paint poverty as vile and sinful. Take, for example, Benjamin Franklin, who erupted in a scathing editorial rebuke of *The London Chronicle* concerning reports of how well England took care of its poor. He snarkily accused England of de facto enabling its poor by taking such good care of them. His editorial rebuke articulated a vicious circle; a concatenation of events concerning the economy, foreign trade, and farmers; which was at its core about Franklin's desire to receive a higher price for his corn in addition to his belief that being generous to the poor only served to make them poorer and dependent. The editorial also captures Franklin sarcastically admitting that he knew that if corn prices were raised, the poor could not afford the increase. Yet, he desired the increase anyway, citing the notion that he could not afford to raise the wages of his laborers unless he could get a higher price for his corn.[121,122]

However, historians and scholars contend that the real irony was not the fluctuating price of corn or some other commodity but was instead the fact that America's first President, George Washington, referred to the Western United States as the "second land of promise."[123] Therefore, inferring that the rest of America was the "land of promise"[124] containing "milk and honey"[125] reminiscent Israel's Promised Land. It was America painted as Utopia, heaven on earth, and Shangri-la for the elite, but as mentioned in the chapter on Politics was just a mirage not only for its people of color but apparently also to its poor. And it was not just the lack of tangible compassion for the poor living in a land purported to be flowing with milk and honey which raised the ire of some Protestants, those who possessed courage enough to openly rebuke their own. It was an overall lack of not just tangible compassion, and basic human decency, but of the subjective quality of the Founders, which the apologists of the Founders arguably seem to relish touting the most, that is they were predominantly Protestant and Christian and therefore men of moral conscience. Which, in turn, exposes both the Founders and the church to accusations of hypocrisy.

> If there were a drunken orgy somewhere, I would bet ten to one a church member was not in it . . . But if there were a lynching I would bet ten to one a church member was in it.[126]
> –Reinhold Niebuhr 1923

> Surely Satan exalted sat as mobs hung, shot, burned, gouged, flogged, drowned, impaled, dismembered, garroted, and blowtorched to death almost 550 individuals, including aged cripples, young boys, and pregnant mothers, in American lynchings, 1919-1939. Surely, also, the Protestant Churches should not have remained silent in the face of this shameful record . . .[127]
> –Robert Moats Miller c. 1957

Not afraid of being labeled as iconoclastic, some of the harshest critics of America's Founders argue with impugnability that if the new nation was going to be founded upon Biblical ideas and principles, then perhaps its Founders and its leaders should: (1) be able to interpret the Bible correctly, as in an understanding of the difference between exegesis, which is a thorough evaluation of the text–letting the text speak for itself, and eisegesis, which is leading the text in a direction based upon a person's personal views[128,129] instead of those of the book's author; (2) be wise enough to know that having "A public faith is not an attempt to set up a theocracy."[130] And although many of them attended universities like Harvard, King's College (Columbia), and Yale, just to name a few, how many of them, if any, had any meaningful advanced Biblical studies? However, to be fair, while there were Bible study tools such as concordances written in English in the sixteenth-century, the more contemporary and popular Young's, Strong's, and Walker's Concordances, respectively, did not arrive on the scene until the later part of the nineteenth-century. Likewise, unfortunately, many of the contemporary English versions of the Bible, such as the Passion Translation, which might have expounded the meanings of key passages of the Bible, were not available to the Founders. Take, for example, the thoughtful Passion Translation rendering of 1 John 3:6, which was an ongoing idea regarding character, suggesting the importance of seeing the Messiah with discernment and knowing him by intimate experience (author's paraphrase). Again, to be fair, it should be noted that the narratives which compare the founding of America as a nation to the Israelites crossing the Jordan River to enter into their "Creator-God" (Psalm 96:5 TPT) given Promised Land were not only entrenched in the minds of the Founders. They were also pervasive throughout America as a whole. And as was mentioned in the previous chapter on Politics, Biblical imagery, in general, would have been very commonplace. Take, for example, political cartoonist Thomas Nast's 1865 illustration titled "Palm Sunday," although a post Antebellum piece showed the triumphal entry of Jesus Christ into Jerusalem on the left side of the illustration. And on the right side of the illustration was the General of the United States Army, Ulysses S. Grant, accepting the surrender from former United States Colonel Robert E. Lee. Colonel, of course, being the rank of Lee in the United States Army before he resigned in order to become the military leader of the Confederacy.[131]

The third moral to the story is to make it clear that the goal of any criticism directed toward the Founders in this book is not an attempt to diminish the idea that Americans should not be thankful and grateful for the accomplishments of the Founders. Instead, the goal is simply to point out the fact that America's history should be one of full disclosure in combination with an appropriate amount of humility in terms of honest historical acuity. Because while there is no denying that the Founders did set in motion the possibilities of the construction of a more perfect union. However, some of the deficiencies that they either purposefully incorporated into both the Declaration of Independence and the Constitution or simply allowed them to persist were not just insignificant byproducts of the trial and error of a laboratory experiment involving mice. On the contrary, when millions of the lives of human beings are part of the experiment, the good deeds of the Pilgrim-Puritans and of the Founders outweighing their bad deeds or the efficacy of risk–benefit ratios are rendered meaningless in light of the enslavement of Africans and African Americans and the calculated "extirpation"[132] of the American Indians. However, what complainants of the Constitution often protest the most is its transfer of "power from the many to the few."[133,134] This is the Pandora's box to authoritarianism,[135] which, as mentioned in the chapter on Economics, elicited fear in men like Edward Carrington, delegate to the Continental Congress, and one of George Washington's close friends.

Furthermore, not only is the Constitution critiqued, but also the notions of empire, Christendom, Divine destiny, and Manifest Destiny that almost wiped an entire people group off the Northern Hemisphere. Leaving unhealed wounds, not unlike the "slavery scars"[136] that American poet Langston Hughes spoke of. It has also been argued that it is the flaws in the Founders as men and in the flawed documents they created that helped create exactly the kind of deficiencies that would allow a candidate, who would eventually become the forty-fifth president, to amass a cult-like following. A following of devoted to a fault loyalists who defiantly exclaim that because his mission was considered so big and so important to their White Evangelical agenda, his character and integrity did not matter because the ends justify the means.

Along the way to some of its most grand successes, the melting pot experiment created a very large population of wounded people. And it is the idea of attempting to understand what it means to be wounded, which is a great way to characterize some of the amazing work of psychologists and sociologists from around the world in the particular area of psychological trauma. Because there is now no disputing the fact that the progeny of enslaved Africans and African Americans, as well as other persecuted and marginalized ethnic groups, are the legacy recipients of transgenerational trauma.[137] Just like the progeny of former enslavers, overseers, drivers, and various other proponents of slavery or racial segregation, inherited at best some level of generational wealth and at least some level of societal privilege. And of course, as previously mentioned in the chapter on Politics, no one alive today was an enslaved African or African American. Likewise, no one alive today was an enslaver, overseer, driver, or various other proponent of the enslavement of Africans and African Americans. However, the multigenerational feelings of insecurity, the everyday societal acculturation, assimilation stresses, and the trauma of the descendants of enslaved Africans and African Americans can now be quantified in what is known as complex post-traumatic stress disorder (CPTSD).[138,139] Likewise, the progeny of former enslavers, overseers, drivers, and various other proponents of earlier slavery or the later racial segregation, even if they did not inherit anything even closely resembling wealth, they did inherit inclusion into the social construct of Whiteness. But in addition to this inheritance, psychologists and sociologists believe that they are also the legacy recipients of their own transgenerational trauma.[140] Although perpetrators or antagonists are not victims; they do however possess their own distinct set of symptoms, triggers, and responses, some of which sociologist and psychologist Rachel MacNair refers to as perpetration induced traumatic stress (PITS)[141,142] in her study titled, "The Effects of Violence on Perpetrators."[143,144] So, whether it is the theoretical values of the great philosopher of education Paulo Freire, imbibed in the idea that oppression in some capacity dehumanizes the oppressor as well as the oppressed;[145] an idea which was previously mentioned in the chapter on Politics. Or the arguably analogous experimental values of the transgenerational legacy of trauma. America nevertheless has endured its share of both centuries of the sharing of grief and grievance through the descendants of enslaved Africans and African Americans, as well as the shock and denial of those who self-identify as White.

Finally, the moral to the story is the question of, Why do White American evangelicals, so-called "values voters;" those who choose to affiliate themselves with political candidates and parties based upon the perceived moral, religious, and philosophical principles of candidates and parties;[146] allow themselves to be so closely associated with far-right extremists and hate groups? Groups such as the Ku Klux Klan, neo-Nazi groups, the skinheads, Proud Boys, the so-called alternative right or alt-right, and any other group that "embraces [W]hite ethno-nationalism as a fundamental value."[147] And just like there is no definitive answer to why White American evangelicals will not unequivocally repudiate narratives that paint poverty as vile and sinful and wealth as virtuous or righteous, there is no definitive answer to why White evangelicals refuse to unequivocally denounce far-right White extremists and hate groups. This might logically assist in proving that they themselves are not racist. However, critics insist that White American evangelicals should be willing to go even further and proactively identify as being "antiracist."[148] Because it is often these same White evangelicals who are labeled as hypocrites for refusing to openly denounce racism. Yet they have denounced innocent Muslims for not more openly condemning acts of terror by so-called radical Islamic groups. All of which some theological historians; the ones who do not adhere to a politicized theology; say begs the question, How can White American evangelicals embrace groups such as these and yet claim to share the same faith with African Americans, people of color, and even Messianic Jews?[149] Especially in light of Bible verses that exclaim that, "Ethnic hatred has been dissolved by the crucifixion of his precious body on the cross" and that "His triune essence has made peace between us by starting over—forming one new race of humanity . . . " (Ephesians 2:15 TPT). So, if White evangelicals who are part of what has been described as a civic religion purporting to worship God, guns, and the military,[150] are spiritually related to African American evangelicals, then perhaps White evangelicals should submit to spiritual DNA testing. This is because the Bible compares hating someone to taking a life (author's paraphrase 1 John 3:15 TPT).

Perhaps it is this intriguing duality of White American evangelicals supposedly identifying with the Biblical belief that there is "one faith, one baptism, and one Father" (author's paraphrase Ephesians 4:5-6 TPT), yet being fully engrossed in the denial that the majority of the enslavers, overseers, drivers, and various other proponents of America's history of enslaving Africans and African Americans were self-professing protestants and evangelicals. Perhaps it was the recognition of this dualistic propensity to hypocrisy that led to Republican Barry Goldwater's 1994 prophetic prediction that when "preachers get control of the party," referring to the Republican Party, "it's going to be a terrible [darned] problem." He even went so far as to admit that the so-called religious right frightened him, insisting that "politics and governing demand compromise."[151] To put this into historical context, most of the Founders were orthodoxical conformists, and at least a few of them were deists. However, there is no real way of deciphering what may have been mere religiosity in the Founders, a kind of "sociocultural Christianity,"[152] or a Christian heritage, that was prevalent during the time in which they lived. This in contrast to an authentic relationship with "Creator-God" (Psalm 96:5 TPT). Perhaps this ambiguity is why some apologetic American historians and scholars, by default, paint a picture of America as a Christian nation, not because it follows the practices and teachings of Christ, but merely because of tradition and cultural indoctrination.

However, if the Founders were "men of their time" with regard to their stances on the enslavement of Africans and African Americans, then it would stand to reason that they must have also been "men of their time" with regard to the role played by state churches in the everyday lives of not just the Founders, but all men, women, and children in the colonies. This means that it would be disingenuous to stretch the religious knowledge and beliefs of the Founders "beyond reasonable historical limits."[153] Just like it would also be disingenuous to redact America's inhumane and tyrannical deeds from the history books. But, it is the unapologetic historians and scholars who argue that ideologues may choose to deify the Founders, fitting them with halos, a King James Bible in one hand and a copy of the Constitution in the other. Still, both their mortal humanity and the atrocities inflicted upon American Indians and the enslavement of Africans and African Americans will always be the skeletons in their closets. The third rail of American politics, or Harper Lee's "polite fiction."[154]

It has been suggested in this book that America's pulse can be taken at any of five strategic points and that the radial artery–wrist pulse, described in the chapter on Social Change, is the most common location for taking the pulse and the easiest to read. However, this is often considered a rather casual indicator of a being's true health or strength, and even small children are taught how to take the pulse there. Religion, on the other hand, perhaps most closely resembles the brachial artery because this is where the seriousness, the longevity, and the quality of humanity is revealed. It also requires intense listening while restricting and then releasing the flood of life-giving blood as it splits or divides into the radial and ulnar arteries. This is not unlike some of the previous splits or divisions in American church denominations, which were centered around the argument for or against the enslavement of Africans and African Americans. However, the contemporary split was between staunch followers and loyalists of the forty-fifth president of the United States and evangelicals of either color or conscience.

The Abolitionist Movement attempted to force the American people into a moment of conscience. However, it may have very well been what philosophers refer to as the "evil of violence"[155-158] and the future threat of the use of more violence that played the most weighty role in opening the eyes of at least some Americans prior to the Civil War to the evil of enslavement through the evil of violence. This paradigm is not unlike the topic of the Problem of Evil[159] argument "Why is there evil?" which is often part of a typical introduction to philosophy learning module or course. With the answers often begging both questions as to the existence and nature of God and the defense of the existence and nature of God to which it has been said that "One often has to see evil before they are willing to turn to God."[160]

It is this idea of when, if ever, is violence the right tool to use to demand justice, that spurs some who read the account of John Brown's 1859 raid on Harpers Ferry, Virginia (now West Virginia) to label him as a murderer, while others read the exact same account and label him as slavery's first White martyr. Nevertheless, Brown was an abolitionist who believed that the emancipation of enslaved Africans and African Americans was not something that could be done by simply naming and shaming Southern slaveholders or in the words of a poem, "His name and shame equal his disgrace."[161] No, Brown believed that using carefully articulated words written in mainstream or abolitionist newspapers or posted on flyers would never truly pierce the hearts of enslavers, overseers, drivers, and various other proponents of slavery and lead to the extrication or manumission of the enslaved. Nor could it even be negotiated in the halls of congress. No, Brown believed that freedom, at least in the case of enslaved Africans and African Americans, must be both demanded and ultimately taken by force.

Furthermore, it has been argued that John Brown turned the raid on Harpers Ferry into a "dress rehearsal" for the Civil War. Again, he was arguably the one and only White man out of millions in the pre-Civil War history of America whose position on slavery was unequivocal because of his actions. Unlike Thomas Jefferson, who chose only to write about manumission and emancipation while never lifting a finger to act on behalf of it. No, Brown's reasons for war were unambiguous. Unlike President Abraham Lincoln whose call to arms many historians and scholars believe was purposed more in political expediency than in an altruistic belief that all men are truly created equal.

Nevertheless, Brown, along with a small group of men, launched an unsuccessful offensive at the United States Armory at Harpers Ferry in an effort to secure arms, which he hoped would spark an armed revolution against the continued enslavement of Africans and African Americans.[162,163,164] After this failed attempt at sparking a revolution, Brown was tried and hung for treason and murder. However, his declaration left in a note to a jail guard right before his execution revealed his belief that "[T]he crimes of this guilty land will never be purged away but with blood."[165] Words which were not just eerily prophetic, but which permanently endeared Brown to the hearts and minds of both free and enslaved Africans and African Americans as a martyr. It also provided a plethora of consternation to enslavers, overseers, drivers, and various other proponents of slavery. Because pacifist abolitionist's attempts to end chattel slavery by appealing to the so-called morality of the Christian South proved to be futile.[166] Likewise, so were petitions and rally's that espoused William Lloyd Garrison's ideas that America's constitution was both flawed and corrupt since its very inception. This is because of the belief that the Constitution's language incorporated the system of chattel slavery in it and needed to be reinvented.[167] After all, while the framers of the Constitution could have quite simply ended the chattel enslavement of Africans while it was being drafted in 1787, they instead chose to perpetuate it, if not bolster it. This was accomplished through the use of language that made clear their positions on the issue of the enslavement of Africans and African Americans. And as mentioned in the chapter on Economics, the use of the phrase, "[T]hree fifths of all other Persons,"[168] and the constraining of Congress from acting to prohibit the import of enslaved Africans until "the [y]ear one thousand eight hundred and eight,[169] left no doubt as to their beliefs about chattel slavery. Besides, historians and scholars note that America's first fugitive slave law was not the Act of 1850, but the Ordinance of 1787, which stated that "any person escaping . . . from whom labor or service is lawfully claimed . . . may be lawfully reclaimed and conveyed to the person claiming his or her labor or service . . . "[170,171] All of these are examples which many of the unapologetic historians and scholars believe leaves the Founders and the framers without excuse for failing to emancipate enslaved Africans and African Americans in 1787.

Contemporary historians and scholars not only criticize the Founders, but they also cringe at the ever vacillating, ever wavering positions on emancipation of the so-called great emancipator, President Abraham Lincoln, even after the Civil War started in 1861. Lincoln's inaction was, in a sense, stubbornly pharaoh–like and excruciating[172] as he conjured up ideas of how to save the United States, more commonly referred to as the Union, without expressly saving or destroying enslavement. But then in his Gettysburg Address, two and a half years into the Civil War, promising, "That we here highly resolve these dead shall not have died in vain; that the nation, shall have a new birth of freedom."[173] One moment, he was promising to emancipate all of the enslaved while the next moment planning to allow the South to keep enslavement to continue for another 40-years. The next moment he was hedging his bets with a plan that would relocate the enslaved to other nations or colonies. An idea which will be explored briefly in the chapter on Emigration or Immigration. As a matter of fact, up until the last minute on January 1, 1863, abolition groups were still not certain Lincoln would keep his word and emancipate enslaved Africans and African Americans. Thank God that he did![174]

From the initial locution of the phrase, Founding Fathers, to the neologism of a Utopian Promised Land, the melting pot experiment has seemingly been fraught with error.[175] And the very same harsh criticism that John Sayre, in the opening quote of this chapter, directed at the Reverend Nathanael Emmons in 1821, charging that some of the enmity between the secular world and the church is the church's own failing. With its "absurd doctrines, intolerance, tyranny, and impiety."[176] A stern Antebellum scolding, which is not at all unlike the contemporary criticism of so-called evangelicals nearly two hundred years later. Take, for instance, the presumptuous narrative circulating that only the candidate, who would eventually become the forty-fifth president of the United States in 2016, had the shrewdness and perspicacity to implement the so-called moral agenda of White American evangelicals. When the truth is that regardless of the Republican Party nominee, the party's overall agenda would have still progressed unabated through the control of the Executive Branch and the Senate. So, the issue for those who oppose the character of the forty-fifth president of the United States, who often ridicule him through the use of the dishonest used car salesman trope; a trope most often used to lambaste former President Richard Nixon; go beyond his personal character flaws and instead take a look deep into the ideology of his followers and loyalists. As a matter of fact, the supporters of the forty-fifth president are believed by eminent psychiatrists to have been suffering from what is known as a shared psychosis.[177,178] Which is essentially the pathological sharing of a delusion in much the same way that some physical illnesses can be communicable.

It was the French political philosopher Montesquieu, the father of the theory of the separation of powers, who whether through literary paradox or revelation of foolish wisdom spoke so eloquently about the idea of self-righteous delusion and dehumanizing others into spiritless unrighteous beasts. He said, "It is impossible for us to suppose these creatures [Africans] to be men, because, allowing them to be men, a suspicion would follow that we ourselves are not Christians."[179,180] It is this suspicion that Montesquieu is referring to, of early modern period so-called Christians not being true Christians. It is arguably what is plagues contemporary White self-professing evangelical followers and loyalists of the forty-fifth president of the United States. Montesquieu's suspicion also begs the question that many may find frightening or even terrifying and that is, Is eternity where all of the horrors of history do finally settle into a meaningful pattern?[181,182] Where meek–longsuffering–nonviolent–formerly oppressed and oft brutalized people will forever reside in the same eternal paradise as their unyielding, intolerant, brutal saved-by-grace enslavers?

CHAPTER 5

SPORTS

Race rioting broke out like prickly heat all over the country
late today between Whites, angry and sore because Jeffries had
lost the fight at Reno, and Negroes, jubilant that Johnson had
won.[1]

–Los Angeles Herald 1910

What was America thinking when it emancipated 3,953,761 enslaved Africans and African Americans and left them to live in the same general population with their former enslavers, overseers, drivers, and various other proponents of slavery? Yes, What was America thinking? Did it really think that everyone could all just let bygones be bygones? Take, for example, the racially motivated bias and racism of the Black Codes, such as those of the state of Georgia, that seemed to infiltrate every nook and cranny of society, including America's Great American Pastime.

It shall be unlawful for any amateur [W]hite baseball team to play baseball on any vacant lot or baseball diamond within two blocks of a playground devoted to the Negro race, and it shall be unlawful for any amateur colored baseball team to play baseball in any vacant lot or baseball diamond within two blocks of any playground devoted to the [W]hite race.[2]

Again, it was this type of codification which would have been an obvious red-flag moment. One which made it abundantly clear that if the melting pot[3] experiment were to continue past this point, people of color would have to contemplate the rationale of continuing to reside in America. In a nation where their mere presence was considered so appalling by those who self-identify as White that they could not even play games in close proximity to them. Yes, even playing baseball was strictly regulated and allowed only when and where the powers that be, in this case, the state of Georgia, said it could take place. This type of implicit control wielded by those who self-identify as White over Africans and African Americans had a long and demeaning historical beginning. It started with the objectifying of Africans and African Americans who were forced to sing and dance while still embarking on the deadly Middle Passage by their enslavers in what was known as "[D]ancing the slaves."[4] The practice of enslaved Africans being forced to dance for their captors or else be flogged was not really a choice but a dilemma. It was enslaved Africans having to decide whether they would allow yet another thread of their dignity to be stretched to its limits or else endure physical punishment. This barbarous ritual was a technique employed to force Africans to exercise while on board enslavement ships because it was thought to help to maintain the health of the enslaved. Of course, throughout world history, the oppressors requiring the oppressed to perform is nothing new. Take, for example, the Prophet Jeremiah,[5] who lamented about Babylonian captivity, "Our captors tormented us, saying, "Make music for us and sing one of your happy Zion-songs!" (Psalm 137:3 TPT). And for enslaved Africans, being forced to perform or entertain continued even after their arrival to the New World. Dancing was quite often as much a part of survival as it was entertainment. It was either assimilate or die trying to retain some semblance of freedom. So there should be no surprise that modern American music, dancing, and public displays of athleticism owe a fair share of their history to the influential plethora of styles that the enslaved Africans retained from the tribal culture and customs of their native homelands.

As for sports, it was not until much later that enslaved Africans and African Americans began learning about American or European sports and excelling at them. History documents the fact that sports and entertainment were, as they are today, not merely pastimes but a reflection of society at large. This book begs questions regarding the societal role of sports as entertainment, such as, How intimate is the relationship between sports as entertainment and social change? How closely coupled together are sports as entertainment with economics? What is the nature of the kinship between sports as entertainment and politics? Do sports have a religion of their own, or are sports a religion? While there may be no definitive answers to these questions, it can be surmised that sports as entertainment does enter into a philosophical covenant with social change. This takes place whenever African American NFL players are allowed to, in the words of American comedian D.L. Hughley, "[B]e on the field with a concussion, but not be on the field with a conscience."[6] This covenant is considered consummated by the fact that NFL players are in many instances sacrificing both their present and future physical and mental well-being in order to maintain an intimate relationship with the NFL. With the NFL being the metaphorical body known to have thousands of potential suitors, but only desires to have the best of the best. As a matter of fact, the odds of an American teenager or young adult becoming a professional American styled football player are extremely rare. Take, for example, the fact that out of the over one million who play the game at the amateur high school or secondary school level, the NFL selects only about two hundred and fifty new individuals to play professionally each year.[7] To solidify the argument that the NFL is a picky suitor not to be taken for granted; one sociologist wrote that African American men were twelve times more likely to become lawyers and fifteen times more likely to become doctors than they were to become professional athletes.[8] However, the coupling of sports as entertainment with social change has created a triangular liaison between sports, social change, and economics. The reason being that sponsors and advertisers of sporting events; a nearly five billion dollar spending group;[9] if not already, are fast becoming more and more self-aware of the impact that social change has on their sales and marketing plans. This as both television sponsors of and advertisers of sporting events seek to entice nearly seventeen million television viewers per regular season game to purchase their products and services.[10] And while sports and politics may seem like strange bedfellows,[11] it is often the confluence of sports and social change which can converge on society creating an overflow into something with the potential to be mutually benefitting. Like for example, the cooperation between sports and government or politics which culminates into the Olympic Games. Conversely, the relationship between sports and social change or sports and politics can become so constricting that it erupts like a volcano into the boycotting of or protesting of sporting events such as the Olympics or the NFL. Take, for example, the eruptions mentioned in the chapter on Economics which took place when the forty-fifth president of the United States and the former Speaker of the House Newt Gingrich each made disparaging remarks about professional African American athletes who dare to take a stand for social issues by speaking out publicly, philanthropy or actual protesting.

It is quite obvious that the relationship between sports and social change or sports and politics are the more high-profile relationships, but what about religion? Do sports as entertainment also intersect with religion? It can be argued that sports as entertainment does intersect with religion, especially when misguided patriotism and misconstrued nationalism masquerading as national pride have turned the United States flag, patriotism, and national pride into religious symbols and even idols. And for many Americans, the flag, patriotism, and national pride have become the predominant symbols of their faith. It is as if devotion to who evangelicals typically credit as being the omniscient creator of the universe has taken a back seat as it were to devotion to a flag and a song. It is also what many historians and scholars believe has come to represent misguided nationalism versus authentic patriotism; misguided because during and after the election of the forty-fifth president of the United States, patriotism and nationalism or national pride were erroneously being used synonymously. This, in spite of the fact that there is a vast chasm between Americans being patriotic and Americans being nationalistic or identifying with a misguided sense of nationalism or national pride. Patriotism is a sense of pride in the good–the best of the nation– especially when the nation accomplishes something historic like landing men safely on the moon and returning them safely to earth. However, nationalism is patriotism that has metaphorically speaking gone blind. As mentioned in this book's introduction, this type of nationalism or patriotism is an irrational sense of pride in America. It is being unreasonably and aberrantly prideful, regardless of what America does,[12] whether good–constructive such as helping allied forces defeat the Nazi's or bad–destructive such as racial segregation.

Historians and scholars cite the irony in how Africans and African Americans were forced to entertain their White enslavers just to stay alive before eventually being placed on auction blocks. Yet, the progeny of the enslaved are in modern times admiringly put on pedestals by the progeny of White enslavers. Placed on pedestals because of their value as entertainers, whether in the genres of film, music, art, or playing professional sports, yet their African and African American ancestors were once placed on auction blocks as chattel slaves predominantly as either agrarian laborers, craftsmen, or household servants. Furthermore, entertainment a way for contemporary African Americans and people of color is not merely a way to survive as some of their ancestors were compelled to do, but unlike their ancestors, they can often make a very lucrative living entertaining. And perhaps most importantly, entertainment can be used as a platform to support various sociopolitical and economic causes. Causes that can positively affect African Americans; who are the descendants of enslaved Africans; along with people of color in general and all of those who have been oppressed and marginalized for decades if not centuries.

Take, for example, America's National Football League controversy, more commonly known as the NFL anthem controversy mentioned briefly in the chapters on Social Change and Politics. The controversy officially began at the start of the regular playing season, September 6, 2016.[13] This was when NFL star quarterback Colin Kaepernick began kneeling instead of standing during the playing of America's national anthem, the Star-Spangled Banner. His kneeling was supposed to raise public awareness of police brutality against people of color and the need for criminal justice system reform. It was his peaceful demonstrations that many Americans believe were the reason why Kaepernick was essentially ousted from the league. And whether fans supported Kaepernick's demonstrations or opposed them, a large number felt personally inclined to distance themselves from watching the games on television, which led to a decline in viewership for the following years, 2017 and 2018. Viewership declined by over one and a half million and seven hundred thousand respectively during those years. However, there was a rebound in 2019 that essentially restored viewership to where it was when the 2016 season began.[14]

It has been argued that the fans were by and large African Americans and people of color who were not just showing solidarity with Kaepernick but also supporting the First Amendment rights of all Americans, including professional athletes. But it has also been argued that there were some followers and loyalists of the forty-fifth president of the United States; those who agreed with the president's sentiment mentioned in the chapter on Economics that NFL players who choose to kneel during the playing of the anthem instead of standing "should be fired or find something else to do;"[15] who also chose to decrease their viewership of televised NFL games. But the timing of the backlash displayed by the followers and loyalists of the forty-fifth president of the United States was such that it could not have been in direct opposition to Kaepernick because, by this time, he was already out of the league. No, they were now protesting subsequent NFL teams as well as individual players, who, after Kaepernick's departure from the league, either began kneeling or continued to kneel. Over time, the real motive for the initial kneeling protest by professional athletes like Kaepernick, amateur athletes, and fans who chose to remain seated during the anthem was metaphorically speaking lost in translation. Lost because what began as one man kneeling in order to draw attention to police brutality against people of color and the need for criminal justice system reform was misconstrued by some Whites and by a number of the American media as a narrative that essentially pitted African American athletes and entertainers against the United States flag and the United States military.

Just as there are many facets to the cooperation between sports and government or politics, there are also many facets to the historical clashes between sports and government or politics, whether it was Adolf Hitler's showcase of Aryan supremacist ideology being upstaged by the successes of African American athlete Jesse Owens at the 1936 Summer Olympics in Berlin, Germany. Or American heavyweight boxing champion Muhammad Ali, a conscientious objector to America's involvement in Vietnam's Civil War. Whose immovable stance against the war earned him both a 1967 criminal conviction for violating the United States military draft laws by his refusal to be inducted into the draft during the Vietnam War[16] and an indelible place in history as both an athlete and a global humanitarian. So, regardless of the nation, the particular sport, or the venue, sports and sociopolitical issues have certainly at times been strange bedfellows.[17] However, it is the grandest of grand sporting events, the Olympic Games, which has the longest and also the most tumultuous history of being upstaged by sociopolitical and even economic anxiety, activism, or crises.

Year	Host City/Country	Action Taken	Incitement(s)/Provocation(s)
1956	Melbourne, Australia	Boycott	Soviet invasion of Hungary
1964	Tokyo, Japan	Boycott	South Africa's apartheid regime

Year	Host City/Country	Action Taken	Incitement(s)/Provocation(s)
1968	Mexico City	Boycott, Protests	(1) Mexican Army kills protesting students (2) African American athletes Smith and Carlos raise fists in defiance of segregation in U.S.
1972	Munich, West Germany	Attack	Terror attack against Israeli athletic team's compound
1976	Montreal, Quebec	Boycott	(1) Quebec's debt as host (2) South Africa's apartheid regime
1980	Moscow, Russia	Boycott	Soviet invasion of Afghanistan
1984	Los Angeles, California	Boycott	Soviet retaliation for 1980 boycott
1988	Seoul, South Korea	Boycott	North Korea upset over not being allowed to co-host with South Korea
2008	Beijing, China	Protests	Treatment of Tibetan people by China
2014	Sochi, Russia	Criticism	(1) Russia's anti-gay law (2) Accusations of human rights abuses

—A History of Boycotts of the Olympic Games[18]

So, it is obvious that whether it is amateur competition or professional, sports are ingrained in American history and world history as a whole. Yet with the building of a nation being such a monumental task, it is difficult to envision America's Founding Fathers having time to participate in sports or any activity that was not directly related to nation-building or colonizing. However, just as the ancient Romans and the Greeks had their gladiator sports, wrestling, and chariot races,[19] and the North African Moors had their bullfighting and various other African countries their donkey racing,[20,21,22] there were archery and polo in China,[23] so too did America's George Washington adore his fox hunting,[24,25] as did Thomas Jefferson his chess playing.[26,27] Why even John Adams, in a letter to his friend Benjamin Rush exclaimed his fondness for a game he simply referred to as "Bat and Ball."[28,29]

So, it seems only fitting that taking the pulse of America as it relates to sports as entertainment should be done at the dorsal artery located in the foot, which of course conjures up images of the movement of an athlete. A very fitting representation of athleticism. And perhaps it is because sports are often considered by some Americans to be simply a pastime, a diversion from serious work or recreation,[30] that sports can indeed be metaphorically described as a relatively minor artery, such as the dorsalis pedis artery located in the foot. Yet sports are nonetheless a major part of not just American but Western society as a whole. Although, in addition to being considered the weakest pulse point, the foot is made up of relatively small bones, none of which by themselves might be considered vital. However, breaking even one of those twenty-six small bones in the human foot, although not totally debilitating, can lead to weeks' worth of crutches, days' worth of limping, and often months' worth of discomfort from the fracture of even the smallest bone in the foot.

Most of the "thrill of victory and the agony of defeat"[31] that the average sports fan experiences in relationship to their favorite team or individual player or performer is experienced most commonly via either television or radio. However, because professional sports are focused as much on entertainment as they are on athletic competition, the world's passion for sports is hardly diminished simply because of a fan's physical proximity to the field, pitch, court, ring, or track. Whether a fan is actually in the stadium, arena, stands, or watching via television thousands of miles away, the psychology of sports suggests that the connection of fans to sports is so strong that they become an invaluable part of their psyche. So much so that sports are believed to be beneficial to the psychological health of some fans by acting as a "buffer against depression and alienation while increasing self-esteem and self-worth."[32]

In addition, the psychology of sports and the relevance of sports as entertainment in American society also has the ability to quickly shift from mere pastime to the ignitor of social, economic, or political change. These sources of ignition do not necessarily have to be a country's government or a sport's governing body. They are quite often merely what takes place during a casual conversation between fans or while fans watch or listen to a monologue by a sports media television or radio personality. For example, a certain radio broadcast monologue by an unnamed Fox Sports radio talk show host which aired on SiriusXM Satellite Radio in America. Based upon the feedback provided to the show's host by listeners who chose to call in and voice their opinions, it was made quite clear that the host had no understanding of the implications entailed in chiming in on controversies chocked full of racial overtones, undertones, and proverbial dog whistles.

Furthermore, this listener feedback made it painfully clear that while the First Amendment Rights of all Americans should be respected, there was no shortage of African Americans and people of color who were exhausted and even exasperated at hearing someone who self-identifies as White discussing racialized topics as if they were an authority on the subject especially as it relates to African Americans. Perhaps this is not unlike the idea that America's institutions, the free press, or media being one of them, are simply metaphorical "mirrors" designed to reflect the pulse or condition of the hearts and minds of the general public. This idea was also mentioned in the chapter on Social Change. It would infer that the radio talk show callers were a reflection of an at large African American sentiment. So, perhaps what can be deduced from their responses to the previously mentioned unnamed Fox Sports radio talk show host is that: If a talk show host who self-identifies as White chooses to speak publicly on advertiser and paid subscription supported radio or television about racialized topics, especially as it relates to African American people; the host should either have a minimum of two African American guests on the show with the goal of creating real dialogue or else the host should play the role of an impartial umpire, an impartial third party.[33] Someone who merely guides the topic of conversation between the show's host and guests on the show and any callers. Another recommendation might be the use of the Socratic questioning method to engage the audience.

The repercussions felt by the unnamed Fox Sports radio talk show host were the fallout from the hosts pointed attempt to try and discount or marginalize an article which was written by an African American writer. The article and its writer, who the host was criticizing, was attempting to demonstrate that sports media culture, in general, is disproportionately White[34] when viewed through the lens of American styled college football, which is predominantly African American. However, in a critique of the article, the Fox Sports talk show host made at least one easily challengeable false equivalency while attempting to compare purported Black-on-Black crime; crimes where both the perpetrator and the victim are African American; and police or law enforcement-on-Black crime. The latter being instances where the perpetrator is a White law enforcement official, and the victim is a person of African American descent. This talk show host also incorrectly quoted FBI crime statistics to support his false equivalencies in a veiled attempt to paint the general population of African Americans in a stereotypically negative light. In addition, the callers to this show who sounded empathetic to the plight of African Americans and people of color were themselves marginalized. This is because it sounded as if their opinions were being challenged more harshly based upon whether the show's host thought that the caller might be African American or Latino based upon their perceived audible linguistic profile as opposed to White. The very sort of thing that one linguist has described as "the auditory equivalent of [racialized] profiling."[35] In such a case as this, the host could have even been rightfully accused of insulting some callers and belittling others based on their perceived ethnicity in what African Americans and people of color interpreted as a display of White privilege.

Like adding proverbial fuel to the proverbial fire, those who would subsequently complain to the network about this particular Fox Sports radio talk show host, and this particular episode would say that it appeared to have very little to do with sports or the actual article that was being critiqued. Because most of the ideas being espoused by the host sounded more like a sociopolitical discourse about how African Americans and people of color should do what successful people who self-identify as White do than a discussion about the sport of college football. It could be argued that it was merely a thinly veiled if veiled at all, diatribe against African American student athletes. Athletes who just happen to dominate American style football both in terms of the number of participants compared to those athletes[36] who self-identify as White as well as their exemplary on the field exploits. And if this discourse was indeed a diatribe against African Americans, it was also in turn apologetics for the mythical bootstrap mythos mentioned in the previous chapter on Religion. And if this was not enough to raise the ire of African Americans, listeners of color, and their sympathizers, then perhaps the fact that this same talk show host alluded to the notion that he believed that African American people should do a better job of policing their own communities would do the trick. This host, who self-identifies as White, was suggesting that because African Americans cannot control so-called Black-on-Black crime in their communities, they then default to the so-called race or racism card as a sort of knee jerk reaction to police brutality. The brutality, which the host implies, would be less frequent if African Americans did a better job of self-policing.

While this book has neither the room to do so nor is this chapter on Sports the appropriate place to deviate too far from its premise; however, it is always appropriate, and room should always be made to debunk racialized American myths. So, as for the myth of so-called Black-on-Black crime, it should be duly noted that Black-on-Black crime does not exist because, statistically speaking, most crimes are committed by a person of the same so-called race as the victim.[37] This is simply because Americans tend to live near people who look like the so-called racial or ethnic group that they themselves most closely identify with. This also means that most of their interpersonal interactions are likewise within that same so-called racial or ethnic group. So, it should come as no surprise that both perpetrators and victims are very likely to be of the same so-called racial or ethnic group. This is why critics believe that while talk shows like the previously mentioned show may see their foray into such racialized subject matter as merely attempting to portray their radio and television programming as edgy, highly charged, and opinionated. They should always pause and reflect on America's history as it relates to intergenerational racialized socioeconomic oppression before discussing racialized topics as if they were well versed in the social construct of race.

It is not that the critics are interested in censorship. They simply argue that, as mentioned in the previous chapter on Religion, because the free press; the media; helped perpetuate not only the bootstrap mythos but the invisible advantages of White privilege, they thereby possess a certain amount of perceived power. Power which allows those who self-identify as White to control not only the broadcast space that the news media occupies but also any narratives about the notion of race that is to be discussed inside that controlled space.[38] And this is why communications historians and scholars note that while it was not until 2011 that the United States Federal Communications Commission (FCC) voted to end the "fairness doctrine;"[39,40] a 1949 policy which attempted to hold both television and radio station licensees to a standard of neutrality in news reporting. It encouraged the presentation of news and public policy issues in the most balanced way possible. However, the proverbial writing was already on the wall with regard to the demise of the fairness doctrine as early as the presidency of Ronald Reagan[41] and the 1987 Meredith Corp. v. FCC case in the United States Court of Appeals. Because in Meredith Corp. v. FCC, the court ruled that the FCC was not constitutionally obligated to enforce the fairness doctrine.[42] Which meant that making sure that there was at least an appearance of equity between the protagonists and antagonists of any particular topic or issue in order to avoid the appearance of partisanship was unnecessary.[43,44]

Therefore, it should come as no surprise that the bootstrap mythos, the social psychology of an economic philosophy rooted in the ideology of the religious Protestant work ethic, permeates throughout all of America's pulse points, including sports. This is arguably not unlike microaggression that is imbibed in racially charged or racialized language epitomizing the bootstrap mythos. Language that conjures up Black-on-Black crime as something more heinous than it is, which is simply people who are part of the same ethnic group, yes at times abusing one another, but not due to inherent psychological biases against their own group. But simply because of their proximity to one another and the same logic applies to Whites victimized by other Whites. However, the illegitimacy of the microaggression displayed by those who self-identify as White during discussions about so-called race is that they, through conscious or subconscious displays of forgetfulness, assume that both African Americans and those who self-identify as White are all operating on a level playing field. And the truth is that they are not operating on a level playing field, and studies after studies presented throughout this book have up to this point made a rather reasonable attempt to prove this to be the case. These studies also suggest that the imprint of the bootstrap mythos: A tale of a quintessential self-made person. Vividly and with broad strokes being painted as a boot wearing White protagonist. Tugging with every ounce of strength they possess on those stubborn bootstraps. To transport themselves upward "from poverty to wealth and from obscurity to prominence,"[45] appears to be permanently etched in both the psyche of those who laud the mythos and as well in those who despise it.

However, African Americans and people of color contend that stories such as these too often, through conscious or subconscious displays of forgetfulness, leave out important details. Details such as how that particular self-made person is often purported to have gained an unfair advantage by bending the rules,[46,47] either through plain old-fashioned fraud or through some form of unethical favoritism.[48] How they, for lack of a better phrase, metaphorically speaking stabbed people in the back before climbing over them on their way to the top and successfully cheating under either unethical or outright illegal mechanisms or simply as a result of some form of unearned privilege or concession. And the emphasis here is not on something as frivolous as the bending of unwritten rules, such as is the case of a person who can successfully count cards at the casino playing blackjack or twenty-one. All the while knowing that although not illegal, it can still, depending upon the casino's location, get a suspected card counter banned or placed on a casino's undesirables list. No, this type of self-made swindler rises to the level of the angst and disgust hurled at some of the most renowned and revered titans of industry and "robber barons"[49] of America's Gilded Age. It was a post-Civil War period remembered by its apologists for its golden economic prosperity. Likewise, it was remembered by unapologetic historians and scholars for the social disfunction which underlay its gilded or thinly layered gold covering.[50] Or the more contemporary technology giants, all of whom were once painted as the "men who built America"[51] and the inventors of American philanthropy. Men who are instead being described by contemporary writers as inside traders, brutal, and Machiavellian[52] while others are accused of being anti-Semitic.[53] But what about the man who in order to become the forty-fifth president of the United States, "played to the most sordid instincts and prejudices of the electorate?"[54] A man who is seen not as unethical, illegal, or illegitimate. But thanks to bootstrap hyperbole, he and those like him throughout American post and modern history are instead viewed as "gentleman thieves" or modern-day Robin Hood's.

However, historians and scholars warn that although America's long, storied relationship with self-made wolves in sheep's clothing, whether gilded, titanic or tycoon should be lamented, the modern titans of industry and robber barons are much more sinister. This is because instead of preying on marks; the innocent victims of a traditional con game; they have recruited willing participants known as shills in a confidence scheme, which means that their would-be innocent victims are now theoretical accessories and accomplices. Would-be victims that Alienists might even describe as now in a sense being complicit.[55] And while to accuse the modern titans of industry and robber barons of being like pied pipers; masters of crowd psychology and behavior based on social identity;[56] might be too unsophisticated as a simile, the resemblance is striking. As a matter of fact, this phenomenon could even be compared to the Stanford Prison Experiment, a 1970s social psychology study conducted at Stanford University in which randomly selected young men were asked to take on the experimental roles of prison guards. The roles would either reveal the true inherent nature of humanity in general or the pervasiveness of "white tribalism,"[57] because without coaching, inducement, or coercion from the researchers conducting the experiment, the young men acting in the roles of prison guards, discriminated against, humiliated, beat, and starved their prisoners. Prisoners who like themselves were randomly selected, young men who instead of the role of guards were chosen to play the experimental role of prisoners. And it was this experiment which uncovered the idea that although individuals may possess inherent ideological biases which may lay, relatively speaking, dormant, these same discriminatory ideologies can become exacerbated when individuals are introduced into roles where systemic discrimination is present.[58]

There are some historians, scholars, and writers who believe that based on hard evidence, the forty-fifth president of the United

States gained some or arguably the majority of his personal wealth through unfair business advantage in the form of rule bending, deception, trickery, fraud, and other unethical behaviors described earlier in this chapter. And this same pathology of doing whatever it takes to be successful in business even if whatever means doing that which is unethical, immoral, illegal, or perhaps even criminal is contagious behavior. Although in the world of amateur or professional sports, the most commonly recognized symptom of this pathology is the use of performance enhancing drugs,[59] which is either against the rules of a particular sport, illegal, or both. And while the majority of cheating; seeking an unfair advantage; in sports is at the individual level, there are occasions where sports organizations have been found guilty of cheating; seeking an unfair advantage. Yet, it can be argued that it is ironically much easier to cheat in the world of business and politics than it is in the world of sports.

However, to be fair, it must be said that the point is not to single out Fox Sports, SiriusXM, or even the Fox Sports radio talk show host described earlier in this chapter. As if they are the only ones guilty of using the perceived power afforded them via White privilege to control the narratives about the racialization of African Americans and people of color. Narratives that are discussed on media platforms controlled by those who self-identify as White. In fact, there are plenty of both viewers and listeners of ESPN television and radio broadcasts who actually applaud both Fox Sports and ESPN for offering on-air employment opportunities to so many African Americans and people of color on television and radio. However, many of these same viewers and listeners have grown weary of what they perceive to be a large number of on-air personalities on television and radio who self-identify as White, who are not formally trained in nor have the background in how to report on issues that have to deal with the "psychocultural pathology of racism."[60] In addition, viewers, and listeners suffer from the fatigue of hearing the oft regurgitated false equivalencies used by these on-air personalities, personal biases, and racialized stereotypes. A lot of which is simply the manifestation of the on-air personalities desire to provide their often predominantly White male[61] audiences with the kind of shock and awe designed to purposely stoke controversy and invite the largest possible viewing or listening audience.[62]

However, this business model frequently leaves the show's host appearing too critical of African American athletes and people of color in general, thereby alienating those viewers and listeners who do not self-identify as White. Which when it comes to those who self-identify as White publicly critiquing African Americans and communities of color begs the question, Why not challenge those who self-identify as White to first look in the mirror and then sweep around their own proverbial front door before they attempt to sweep around someone else's?[63] And critics believe that this goes beyond television and radio personalities who self-identify as White, who use polarizing stories about African Americans and athletes of color to increase viewership or listenership, to increase network or individual show ratings. No, their primary critique is not that sports shows will at times focus more on the sociocultural aspects of sports stories versus the X's and O's; the fundamentals and strategies of the games; or perhaps recent scores and notable challenges related to either coaching or the acquisition of the services of talent (players). On the contrary, as this chapter has so far attempted to prove is that sports, not unlike social change, economics, politics, and religion, not only has a pulse; the ability to measure a being's aerobic capacity or "the ability of the [human] heart and lungs to supply the muscles with oxygen."[64] Or in America's case, it is its capacity as a nation to gasp, to inhale when its people are being oppressed. But then to exhale, to release, a metaphorical breath of life to supply those parts of its being which make it move, its people, with real freedom. This metaphorical pulse taking is the best way to gauge the wellness of a nation and supports the theory that there is an intimate relationship between sports, social change, economics, and even religion.

The previously mentioned question suggested that radio and television personalities should be challenged, held accountable whenever their words are deemed one-sided or uninformed. However, it could be argued that these are mere words, soundwaves, which like a small pebble dropped in a pond, create a ripple that quickly dissipates. It could also be argued that words do possess a type of power but that it is like the sound of thunder. By itself, thunder can be frightening but is relatively harmless. On the other hand, lightening is an action that is not only frightening but also possesses the power to be lethal. Take, for example, the accountability argument states that the majority of America's law enforcement or police officers are good people or good cops. While the counterargument usually posed as a question, asks, If the majority of America's police officers are indeed good cops, then why don't the ostensibly good ones ever challenge the unethical, criminal, and at times lethal actions of the bad ones? And in this argument, the bad ones are those on the front lines of America's criminal justice system. A system which has been described by activists as not being broken but is by design built to work the way it does.[65] Often protecting the White Privilege of officers who are guilty of the excessive use of force when confronting and subsequently apprehending men of color and African American men in particular.

Yet, in all fairness, the bad ones are no more likely than the good cops to make arrests or come face to face with armed suspects.

However, they are more likely to shoot an unarmed individual or an individual who is fleeing the scene of a suspected nonviolent crime.[66] And quite often these are instances where the alleged offense which warranted a "police–citizen encounter"[67] or confrontation in the first place might have only risen to the level of a misdemeanor crime. However, at times the encounters and confrontations lead to the shooting deaths of unarmed African American men and men of color. Critics of America's criminal justice system and social justice activists argue that such brutality is not a snapshot of the racialization of criminal justice but is instead representative of a long-term trend of "historically persistent"[68] behaviors, not merely isolated incidents.

So, who is there to challenge or critique publicly or behind closed doors, not only the unethical and sometimes criminal behavior and actions of White police officers? The ones who violate the civil rights of African American men, women, and people of color in general. And while police brutality may be the metaphorical lightning mentioned previously, Can the argument be made that the thunder of television and radio personalities does not precede the lightning but is simply the loud, often upsetting roar heard in response to lightning strikes? Because it is not only those in sports media or sports culture who have racialized axes to grind. Those individuals in the media who self-identify as White just happen to be part of something much-much bigger than themselves. They are a part of systems replete with the vestiges of chattel slavery, Jim Crow, and White privilege. So, it stands to reason that it is a lack of accountability which allows police unions– the police fraternity–to remain silent while maintaining their traditional defensive posture when it comes to White officers involved in unnecessary or excessive violence during arrests and in unjustifiable homicides. This, in spite of the fact that almost fifty percent of African American police officers surveyed agreed with a statement that suggested police officers, in general, are more likely to use physical force against African Americans and other minorities than against Whites in similar situations. This was in stark contrast to less than five percent of White police officers who agreed with the same statement.[69] Which by itself suggests that racialized biases are not merely isolated incidents involving a few bad apples. In fact, it supports the argument made by criminal justice writers and scholars that all of America's institutions and systems, not just its criminal justice system, have historically favored those who self-identify as White. So, it should come as no surprise that for example, the codification of the sport of baseball through the Black Codes of states like Georgia mentioned at the beginning of this chapter would usher the world of sports into America's family of racialized institutions and systems.

The idea of the often-nuanced socioeconomic institutions and systems is reminiscent of the difference between the word bias as a noun and the word biased. The verb is not mere conjecture but fact. Since it is individual biases that, over time, become systemic and institutional biases, lest any American ever forget that slavery was a social and racialized institution. So, whether law, custom, or practice, the interpersonal processes of White Americans extend beyond the random or isolated. They delve deeply into the economic, political, and educational systems and organizations of America.[70] This also speaks of consistent patterns and even policies that essentially penalize those who lack White privilege.[71] And so there is a reason why the integration of sports in America appears to have taken place over a shorter period of time and appears to be marked by only a few well known and highly publicized examples of African American and other athletes of color crossing the color line. It is because the color line was more than just the invisible line between African Americans and other athletes of color and those who self-identify as White. Instead of a sharply drawn line between the social constructs of the so-called Black and White as races, the integration of sports was more like a "series of ramparts, of which outer portions may be given up while inner bastions are still steadfastly defended."[72] So, the integration of sports was unlike the integration of society at large. Because although Africans, African Americans, and Whites had for centuries interacted socially, it was within the social construct of a racialized caste system, a subordinate relationship, and thus possessed a longer, seemingly more tumultuous history.

Africans, African Americans, and Whites were essentially forced to interact with one another. One group, those who identified as White, was compelled to interact with Africans and African Americans for the sake of economic investments and livelihoods. While the other group, Africans and African Americans, were often forced to acquiesce to the often outrageous, unsympathetic, and merciless whims of Whites. This was the social labor output required of Africans and African Americans in order to not be fined, corporally punished, or otherwise humiliated for social interactions between the two people groups that went awry. Whereas when it came to sports, African Americans were expressly forbidden from participating in sports alongside Whites during that same duration of time. From the "Gentleman's Agreement" of the 1890s in which professional baseball's National League agreed to or conspired to bar African American players from playing on its teams[73] to the unofficial 1916 "Caucasians-only policy" of the Professional Golf Association's (PGA) constitution[74] which was later officially inserted into the organization's constitution and bylaws as the clause requiring that PGA members be "professional golfers of the Caucasian race."[75] This represents the inner bastions of the color line mentioned previously.

Suggesting that the integration of sports in America, which at first glance appears to have taken place much more quickly than society at large, was just as stated, an appearance, an optical illusion, or perhaps was not unlike the mirage mentioned in the previous chapters on Politics and Religion.

Yes, "the color question"[76] as related to sports may have been partially answered, and "the drawing of the color line"[77] may have been blurred a bit by "liberal promoters and business backers [who] were willing to cash in on [the] growing notoriety" and box-office appeal of the likes of a few African American athletes.[78] But most of those athletes were so transcendent that their legacies left indelible marks not just on the psyche of American sports fans but on that of popular culture around the world. Such as professional heavyweight boxer Jack Johnson and professional baseball player Jackie Robinson, both of whom were previously mentioned in the chapter on Social Change. Or the story of professional golfer Charlie Sifford.[79] Or the unsung histories of a myriad of African American athletes who broke world records or broke barriers such as 1899 cycling sprint champion and world record holder Marshall "Major" Taylor.[80] Valmore "Val" James, who in 1981 became the first African American to play in the National Hockey League (NHL) when he was signed to New York's Buffalo Sabres through the 1982-1983 season, a feat that took place sixty five years after the NHL's founding.[81] However, even though the outer portions of the color line may have been given up or at least relaxed in order to exploit truly transcendent African American and athletes of color, it was the stories of America's forgotten African American sports legends who suffered the most damage because the color line's inner bastions are still being steadfastly defended.

So, just like for centuries, any clarion call loud enough to challenge the socioeconomic and political institutions of the enslavement of Africans and African Americans and later the institution of Jim Crow fell on the dull hearing of both Northern and Southern ears. Ears that were most likely stuffed with America's so-called "plantation economy" cash crops such as cotton, sugar cane, or tobacco. Likewise, there was no rallying cry by White Americans regarding the color line of sports. Because of America's racialized sports history, it should come as no surprise that one hundred and fifty plus years after emancipation in 1865 and a little over fifty years since the Civil Rights Act of 1964, only about one third of African Americans believe that police in their communities use the appropriate amount of force when encountering suspects. As opposed to three-quarters of those who self-identify as White, who believe that police in their communities use the appropriate amount of force when encountering suspects.[82] It is this socially divisive pathology on the part of those who self-identify as White which historians and scholars argue amounts to a "[refusal] to see [the] police as an inherently [racialized] institution."[83] This is not at all unlike the Antebellum generations who refused to challenge chattel slavery and the subsequent generations who refused to challenge Jim Crow.

Critics argue that not unlike their forefathers, contemporary generations of those who self-identify as White are likewise collectively refusing to challenge America's apparently overly brutish White police officers. In addition to this, it is the previously mentioned police unions who too frequently condemn the victims of police brutality yet defend guilty officers. This "Whitewashing bad people and throwing mud on good people" (Proverbs 17:15 MSG) serves only to reinforce the societal norms which allow the institutions and systems which keep the social construct of race in America alive. It is these collective complicities, not the phenomenon of the shared psychosis of the followers and loyalists of the forty-fifth president who were mentioned in the previous chapter on Religion, which continue to empower America's racialized caste system. This empowers the continuation of the illusory color line, not only in sports but throughout American society in general. Consider, for example, the way America's criminal justice system works at the local level. Local police, predominantly White prosecutors,[84,85] judges, defense attorneys, and even police unions to a certain extent all have to work together. With prosecutors who "depend on police officers to obtain convictions in their cases."[86] Likewise, police officers depend on prosecutors to administer the appropriate charges after arrests have been made by those officers. In addition to this, "chief prosecutors at the state level are typically chosen in popular elections and supported by police unions."[87]

So, over time a relationship develops that has been referred to as the "courthouse club" or the criminal justice system "brotherhood,"[88] which, for lack of a better phrase, is a "game" of consideration and reciprocation. It is a game that is played almost exclusively by those who self-identify as White, those who do the majority of the arresting, prosecuting, and sentencing. It is a game that can be likened to the fostering of a spirit of familiarity which can breed a type of partisanship that both writers, as well as criminal justice scholars, suggest is a threat to the impartiality that the system is supposed to uphold.[89,90] It is this lack of impartiality that disproportionately incarcerates African Americans and people of color[91] in comparison to those who self-identify as White. So, whether the subject is sports, social change, economics, politics, or religion, only a faint whisper can be heard challenging the racialized biases and the continuation of America's color line, which still exists even within the free press.

The moral to the story is that understanding other cultures is paramount, especially if writing or speaking publicly about a culture other than one's own. This is not meant to insinuate that Franz Boas' famous anthropological theory of relativism should be part of primary and secondary American school curriculum. But that some abecedarian semblance of his warning should be shared; that if ethnocentrism is not "scrupulously"[92] avoided; the wages that it produces is to be deceived into having an ethnocentric view of others. This often leads to individual biases and interpersonal processes, which are often the root of racialization. This idea of America's roots goes back to the issue posited in this book regarding the flaws in America's foundation. Flaws, which have, by default produced generations of not necessarily flawed people but flawed ideologies. Because of this, the vast majority of those who self-identify as White have a grandfather, father, uncle, brother, cousin, or even just a neighbor they know has racialized biases that have gone unchallenged. And probing even further might even uncover the fact that they also know someone who is a White supremacist group member or who simply has a radical ideology regarding the notion of race, ethnicity, gender, or religion that have also gone unchallenged. So, it makes perfect sense that if those who self-identify as White have historically been unwilling to even challenge their own family, friends, and associates, then the horrors of chattel slavery, Jim Crow, and in modern times brutish White police officers going unchallenged is an easily recognizable pattern. As such, there is no need to beg the question, If the views of racist family, friends, and associates are really and truly in the minority in America, then why not confront them? No, the question to be begged is, Why does it seem that instead of challenging racist family, friends, and associates of those who self-identify as White, it is African American people who are more likely to be challenged or confronted? Challenged, confronted, and even ostracized for uncovering and then challenging racism.

It is kind of like the idea of disciplining a neighbor's child for making unacceptable grades in school or for breaking a window with a baseball in the same fashion one would discipline one's own child. There is a very stark difference between disciplining one's own child and disciplining the neighbor's child. So, whenever someone who self-identifies as White feels empowered to critique African American people regarding some of the really divisive historically racialized issues in America, it is in its simplest abecedarian form comparable to disciplining a neighbor's child. Since no reasonable person would ever feel emboldened enough to consider disciplining the neighbor's child because that child did not take out the trash, individuals like the Fox Sports radio talk show host described earlier in this chapter should also focus more on influencing their own culture to do better and be better.

An additional moral to the story is that, while people who self-identify as White do have a First Amendment right to speak, it does not mean that they should exercise that right haphazardly. Take, for instance, the NFL owner who, during the height of the NFL protest era, exercised his right to critique NFL players who were exercising their First Amendment to protest by kneeling during the playing of America's national anthem. He felt as though it was acceptable to compare the NFL to a prison, implying that the players, most of whom are African Americans, were the prisoners, and the owners, who are predominantly White, are the wardens. Again, people who self-identify as White do have a First Amendment right to speak; however, it does not mean that they should exercise that right haphazardly. Even the Bible warns that "You will say the wrong thing if you talk too much—so be sensible and watch what you say"

(Proverbs 10:19 CEV). But in light of that owner's comments, a very small minority of those in sports media who self-identify as White could be heard challenging his racialized rhetoric. They did this by inserting the idea that they believed that what the anthem protests required was not that fewer African American men should kneel, but that more African American men should begin kneeling. However, none of these empathetic voices ever stopped to ask the questions, Why is it that NFL players who self-identify as White do not kneel? Why is it that those athletes who self-identify as White did not appear to be offended at the prison comments that the above mentioned NFL owner made? The final question, the proverbial million-dollar question, which has since the first public cries for the emancipation of enslaved Africans and African Americans perplexed African Americans and those who sympathize with their plight which is: Why more people who self-identify as White are not appalled at the daily displays of racialized White misbehavior, bigotry, and racism in America? It is rhetorical questions such as these that seem to infer that perhaps the reason why there seems to be a lack of NFL players who self-identify as White sympathizing with their African American teammates on the issue of racism is because White sympathizers are quite rare. Those Whites who side with African Americans and people of color are more often than not presupposed by their White peers to be liberals, leftists, weak, and naïve. There was even a time during America's segregationist history that they might have been called communists or, to borrow a phrase from Harper Lee's book *To Kill a Mockingbird*, "[Negro] lovers."[93]

So, does this mean that those who self-identify as White, those who passively sit by and watch others in their group oppress African Americans and people of color, should be given a free pass? Should they be allowed to hide behind the misguided American notion that

America is a country of individuals or the widely used dictum from English poet Geoffrey Chaucer which says that it is "[every] man for himself?"[94] Or the notion that it is not *their* fight, so why should they bother getting involved. Perhaps this is why when a racially biased American police officer assaults or even kills an African American person or a person of color during a routine traffic stop, White men in general, not all, but in general, see it as having nothing to do with them or their own individuality. In response to this logic, not only human rights activists but at least a handful of theologians; the ones who do not adhere to a politicized theology; argue that the phrase "It is not my concern" is a phrase that should be considered profanity. It should be viewed by those who self-identify as White; those who claim to be believers in, and followers of Christ; the same as any other swear or curse word. And it is this same hypocrisy present in America's churches that is present in American sports. Take, for instance, Jerry Jones, the majority owner of the NFL's beloved Dallas Cowboys. He very well may have been willing to bench, suspend, or fire players on his team who knelt during the playing of the national anthem during the height of the NFL protest era. An action he insinuated publicly that he was prepared to carry out. However, in years prior to the protest era, Jones had proven that he was more than willing to hire certain players who had been accused of often horrendous crimes. So, does it not sound hypocritical when any employer or organization publicly portrays itself as extremely honorable and respectful, yet would hire or continue to employ people who are violent toward women? Hypocritical when the same employer or organization would then consider it an act of outrageous proportion if a relatively small number of players on a team would dare to kneel during the playing of the national anthem.

The vitriol of America's former Speaker of the House Newt Gingrich, who believes that rich athletes of color who complain about racism in America need a therapist[95] and that of conservative right-wing American talk show host Laura Ingraham, who believes that professional athletes of color should just "[S]hut up and dribble"[96] instead of publicly expressing their outrage at acts of racism, go virtually unconfronted by those who self-identify as White. However, that is, of course, not the case with African Americans and people of color, who challenge the racialized rhetoric of the Gingrich's and Ingraham's of America and challenge the silence of White American's in response to such rhetoric. However, this challenge is not in the form of the traditional boisterous thunder but a counter-narrative that believes that athletes of color should actually be applauded, not ostracized. Applauded not only for using their platform as a tool for social change but also for attempting to earn as much income during their playing careers as they can. And while this book is not the place to expound on this narrative, its logic suggests that because of the racially divisive direction in which America has been headed arguably since the Civil Rights Act of 1964, the Voting Rights Act of 1965, and the Hate Crimes Prevention Act of 2009 that perhaps the right thing for African Americans who have the opportunity to do is to earn as much income as they can. To create as much wealth as they can. This in order to put their children and grandchildren in the optimum positions to limit their interactions with law enforcement, with unfriendly employers or situations where they do not have as many options to be treated fairly. Situations where they are forced to, as it were, bow down to White privilege, racialized bias, and microaggression in their daily lives. Again, this book is not the place for that conversation. Still, the narrative implies that while the wealth of African Americans and people of color will never be permitted by the powers that be in America to be used to radically change America's racialized institutions and systems, it can, however, be used as a bit of a buffer according to that narrative.

Once again, it also bears repeating that the eradication of tribalism or changing the condition of the human spirit of Americans will not be done using statistics and comprehensive research reports. However, some studies like the one published in the Journal of Sports Media explore the "implicit suggestion"[97] of "Whiteness as the norm"[98] in American sports, in spite of the fact that athletes of color often make up the statistical majority of some sports teams. An idea which undoubtedly has its roots in the history of the enslavement of Africans and African Americans and in the power of Whites over Africans and African Americans, which was later cleverly disguised within the Black Codes or Jim Crow laws. An idea which obviously became staunchly ingrained in the subconscious of the American psyche. Not only within its social, economic, and criminal justice institutions and systems but also within its organized sports. And it has been argued that any remaining negative residual effects of the integration of both collegiate and professional sports in the 1940s through the 1960s are the result of the racial biases remaining within. And not only within amateur sports bodies and professional sports organizations but also biases that still exist within the media that covers amateur and professional sports. Yes, in many respects, the past and the events that took place in the past are, as British novelist L. P. Hartley philosophized, like "[a] foreign country; they do things differently there."[99] However, racialized biases and racism, no matter how subtle within the media, are as deeply rooted in Whiteness as all of America's other institutions and systems where racism and discriminatory biases exist. So, the same overhaul of institutions, systems, and racially tinged ideologies that would need to take place in amateur and professional sports organizations would also need to transform sports media outlets.[100]

CHAPTER 6

EMIGRATION OR IMMIGRATION

Giving up doesn't always mean you are weak; sometimes it means that you are strong enough to let go.

–Author Unknown

W hat was America thinking when it emancipated 3,953,761 enslaved Africans and African Americans and left them to live in the same general population with their former enslavers, overseers, drivers, and various other proponents of slavery? How has that worked out? The answer to the second question, based upon the evidence and the ideas expressed in the previous chapters of this book, is that it was a failed experiment, but an adventure, nonetheless. Chocked full of all the thematic style and imagery of a Mark Twain novel, with an epic quest for freedom, the seduction of treasure, and teaming with perilous adventure. But whose end results turn out to reveal that the freedom was only imagined, the treasure was always just beyond the grasp of the protagonist's fingertips, and the adventure, while clearly unforgettable, "was all a dream."[1] And while the world is used to hearing about America's immigration (starting with the letter 'I') crisis; an influx of people on the outside attempting to get in; it is, however, not familiar with America's emigrant (starting with the letter 'E') crisis, which is people on the inside trying to get out. Nor is the world familiar with the idea of Africans and African Americans abandoning America in order to

avoid remaining part of the melting pot² experiment, which is not a
novel idea. Take, for example, the Compensated Emancipation
Proclamation Act of 1862 that was enacted eight months prior to
Lincoln's   Emancipation   Proclamation.   This   compensated
proclamation offered emancipated Africans and African Americans
in the District of Colombia $100 if they wanted to leave America and
relocate to Haiti or Liberia.³ So, the idea of Africans and African
Americans leaving the experiment as an act of self-liberation or
enticement from the United States government is not a completely
new one but has simply been revived.

As a matter of fact, more than three decades prior to Lincoln's
Emancipation Proclamation, Thomas Jefferson warned that he feared
emancipating Africans and African Americans and allowing them to
remain in the United States would only uncover "Deep rooted
prejudices... by the Whites"⁴,⁵ and "[T]en thousand recollections, by
the Blacks, of the injuries they have sustained..."⁶,⁷ Jefferson believed
that enslaved Africans and African Americans should be emancipated,
but that they should be colonized–returned–to Africa. Although,
when given a chance to emancipate the enslaved Africans and African
Americans he kept enslaved, an act of liberation which was the dying
wish of an old friend, Jefferson declined to free his own enslaved
Africans and African Americans. This, in spite of the fact that his
dying friend's money would have as part of his will recompensated
Jefferson, the will's executor, for his losses. Not only did Jefferson
refuse his friend and Revolutionary War hero Tadeusz Kościuszko's
dying wish, but Jefferson was vehemently opposed to emancipating
his enslaved Africans and African Americans en masse. Perhaps the
image that Jefferson's refusal conjures up is not unlike that of the
Apostle Peter, who not only denied Christ three times as prophesied
but did so with swearing. And it was Jefferson's refusal to be the

executor to Kościuszko's will which eventually led to Kosciuszko's estate being deemed in-testate.[8,9]

Perhaps this story, along with many others, is one reason why a generation later abolitionist and minister Moncure Conway lamented regarding Jefferson's apparent hypocrisy regarding enslavement, "Never did a man achieve more fame for what he did not do."[10,11] Which was perhaps merely a posthumous swipe at Jefferson taken in an attempt to expose the fact that Jefferson was never, at least not in the contemporary use of the word, a "counter-racist."[12-17] Jefferson merely spoke the "anti-slavery"[18,19] and "abolitionist"[20,21] language but was never truly active in the struggle. He was, in some regard, not unlike many of both his forbearers and his contemporaries. Not just the man-stealing (slaveholding) ministers, the women whipping missionaries, and the cradle-plundering church members that William Lloyd Garrison so despised.[22] But also those who occasionally spoke of their disgust for the enslavement of Africans and African Americans through the language of anti-slavery and abolitionism, yet had no sincere interest in racial equity or integration.[23,24] And although this book is using contemporary vernacular to describe them, Jefferson and those like him were far too intelligent not to understand that it takes more than not being a racist; a passive, inactive endeavor. Instead, one must be antiracist as previously mentioned in the chapter on Religion. There requires proactive searching for and finding the voices of Africans and African Americans.[25]

What was America thinking when it emancipated 3,953,761 enslaved Africans and African Americans and left them to live in the same general population with their former enslavers, overseers, drivers, and various other proponents of slavery? Yes, what was it thinking? And it is this rhetorical question which even after presenting chapters full of allusion, paragraphs chocked full of thoughts and ideas from antiquity, with heavy use of Antebellum vocabulary and narrative, and plenty of flash forwards to modern times that this book's introduction promised would be made available has failed to bring the philosophical reader one step closer to a possible answer. It can even be argued that the book's introductory assertion that America and its grand experiment is not an enigma has been proven false. Because to really understand what America was thinking when it emancipated 3,953,761 enslaved Africans and African Americans and left them to live in the same general population with their former enslavers, overseers, drivers, and various other proponents of slavery is arguably the quintessential unsolvable puzzle of puzzles. It could even be argued that this puzzle is right up there with science's Big Bang theory and philosophy's Problem of Evil.[26]

A good summary reiterates the main points of what was written prior and can also offer a single prevailing thought for the reader to ponder. Still, if a book has dual competing trains of thought, it does not automatically render the book ambiguous, wishy-washy, or too passive. So, perhaps this is not merely a story about the "fight-or-flight response"[27] referred to by psychologist and trauma specialist Peter A. Levine, in which "the objective is to get away from the source of threat."[28] No, this is not as simple as fighting versus running. Or in other words, fighting because there is no way to escape the threat once it is realized that the opportunity to run is either not available or has long passed. Instead, it appears to be an intriguing duality of the ideas of both fighting for America, which is fighting to stay, not just fighting the threat until a means of escape can be had, but actually hoping that the experiment is salvageable. Likewise, giving up on America, fleeing because the flight response worked exactly as it was designed to do which is to put as much distance between an individual and a threat as possible. Or perhaps it is a case where a fight has already been fought, and there is now a clear means of escape. In other words, this is simply believing that the experiment has run its course.

While this book has presented lots of evidence and reasons why Americans, African Americans, and people of color, in particular, may want to emigrate, to leave, it never pointedly asks the question, Why do Americans want to emigrate? The answer is probably best discovered by first attempting to understand why people on the outside of the experiment looking in, choose to come–to immigrate–to America. This is, of course, a generalization, but after taking into account those who immigrate to take advantage of educational opportunities that may not be available or readily available in their home country and those "workers in specialty occupations," who both America's government and many of its corporations welcome simply because it is thought that America "cannot otherwise obtain needed business skills and abilities from the U.S."[29] workforce in particular industries. What is left over after the two previously mentioned groups of immigrants is a rather rhetorical question: Why do people flee war torn or economically disadvantaged countries in order to live in America? And this book is filled with examples of why the argument can be made that people typically do not immigrate because America is some moral bastion of hope and goodwill. So, the answer must be something else. Perhaps the answer can be found in the fact that this book is filled with examples of how the argument can be made that a significant portion of any hope or goodwill emanating from America's shores and beckoning immigration stems from its abundance of resources. And any generosity, whether real or perceived, flows from America's abundance, its surplus, its excess, and not out of the abundance of its heart like the poor widow discussed in Luke 21:1-4 (author's paraphrase of NLT), whose two pennies was all that she had in comparison to the rich who only gave what they did not need.

So, it should come as no surprise that people often immigrate to America because they believe they have no choice but to commit to relocating and starting their lives over on foreign soil. And that they immigrate primarily for economic opportunities, but also in search of educational opportunities. It is, however, ironic that people flee war or civil war torn or economically disadvantaged countries to live in America only to realize that while America's Civil War ended over one hundred and fifty years ago, many of America's citizens still struggle with post-traumatic stress disorder handed down to them from generation to generation as a result of that war. Also, those who flee other countries realize that even though by definition African Americans are native-born United States citizens it is as if they possess a dual citizenship. They are American citizens, but even one hundred and fifty years after emancipation, they are as a people group still viewed by the majority not as Americans, but often as simply Africans in America. This even though they do not possess African citizenship. It was W. E. B. Du Bois; a champion of African and African American rights during the first half of the twentieth-century, who referred to this concept of dual citizenship as a "double consciousness."[30] And the idea of a "double consciousness"[31] was further elaborated on by those like provocative American poet Amiri Baraka who referred to the "double consciousness"[32] as "White ghosts."[33] Referring to the often invisible pressures of not just social prejudice against African Americans in America, but the unwritten rules and barriers that Frederick Douglass called color lines,[34] which divide the so-called races in America, in addition to classism.

So, it is the idea of what immigrants to America witness in the culture over time, which makes all the more ironic the familiar refrain of Americans who self-identify as White. Those Whites who emigrate and move to Mexico, Canada, South America, the Caribbean, Europe, Asia, Africa, or Australia. Who often do so in order to escape the tension and stresses that come along with America's previously mentioned abundance of resources, its surplus, and its excess, which unfortunately also includes its legacy of the transgenerational trauma[35] mentioned in the Chapter on Religion. And even though America is one of, if not the, wealthiest nations on the planet in various economic categories, whether it is the proverbial Promised Land or simply a means to an escape is totally in the eye of the beholder.[36]

As it has been stated ad nauseam within this book, the eradication of tribalism or changing the condition of the human spirit of Americans will not be done using statistics and comprehensive research reports. However, it is worth stating that in spite of its wealth America has child poverty rates that are appreciably higher than the nominal rich-world average.[37] One in five children in America suffers from food insecurity. Compared to its allies such as Germany, Japan, the United Kingdom, France, Australia, and Italy in the categories of poverty, hunger, health, peace, justice, and strong institutions, America consistently ranks toward the bottom. With an average ranking of about twenty-ninth when compared to forty-one other industrialized nations.[38] So, it goes without saying that just because America has a high national income does not make it the self-named Promised Land. However, in all fairness, the irony of the Promised Land moniker is that during the earlier history of America, both those who self-identified as White, as well as Africans and African Americans, liked to use the same motif. That of acquiring or being delivered to the Promised Land. Take, for example, George Washington's reference to the Western United States as the Promised Land containing "Milk and honey"[39] previously mentioned in the

chapter on Religion. Reminiscent of Israel's Promised Land, the
Western United States was America's Utopia–heaven on earth–
Shangri-la. Then there was the prayer of Robert Smalls, an enslaved
African American who was famously able to, through cunning and
guile, under the cover of darkness, deliver a Confederate supply ship
into the hands of the military of the United States, more commonly
referred to as the Union. Small's prayer was, "Oh Lord, we entrust
ourselves into thy hands. Like thou didst for the Israelites in Egypt,
guide us to our promised land of freedom."[40] And it is often
overlooked how two different groups of people on the same land,
professing the same God, through a similar prayer language and
phraseology of sorts; a kind of lingua franca; yet with starkly different
sets of motives and outcomes. Two nations within a nation living on
the same latitude and longitude, yet existing worlds apart from each
other.

   If the question has never been publicly begged before, it is
without a doubt being begged now thanks to a little help from the
provocative title of this book, and that is, Should not Africans and
African Americans once emancipated been provided with their own
state or perhaps a couple of states in which to live? This would have
afforded them physical space apart from their former enslavers,
overseers, drivers, and various other proponents of slavery. A closely
related follow-up question is, Did no one stop to think that the newly
emancipated would require space to rest their weary bodies, minds,
and spirits to in a sense "pull [themselves] together?"[41] No, not in the
traditional use of the expression, because the fact was, they had done
absolutely nothing within themselves to warrant the lives they were
essentially forced to live. Living and dying in the labor camps,
commonly referred to as plantations, and enduring the horrors
inflicted upon them by the wardens who ran them, commonly

referred to as owners. Nonetheless, it is difficult to argue against the idea, although critics of this book will undoubtedly try to, that the newly emancipated needed time and space to learn how to once again live as free men and women. To live as their ancestors did–most of whom we were free men, women, and children. This arrangement would, of course, have had an expiration date. Still, perhaps it might have been reasonable to allow a few generations to pass before any type of en masse re-integrating with Whites after the Civil War.

Of course, revising history based upon hindsight can be hollow unless, of course, its goal is to correct false narratives. Likewise, it is in some regard daft to think that one hundred and fifty years after the Emancipation Proclamation and all of the ugliness of the subsequent racialized divisiveness, America might once and for all put to bed the notions of racially motivated biases, bigotry, overt racism and the systems that help perpetuate them. However, if America is that metaphorical living, breathing, being referenced throughout the entirety of this book, then attempting to uncover "how it all went wrong," even though the relationship is irreparable is simply part of the psychology of the "need for closure (NFC)."[42] Much of America's history, chocked full of hyperbole and folk etymology, reads more like the Great American Novel mentioned in this book's introduction, where all's well that ends well,[43] than a historiography. The irony is that the NFC, politically speaking, is more of an American conservative need than a liberal one.[44] Yet a simple educated guess could argue that the majority of conservative historians as well as a few so-called religious scholars, do not want to hear a corrected version of the Founding Fathers narrative. Instead, they prefer the, even if well-intentioned, untruth. The "suggestio falsi" in which it is "easier to find a new audience than it is to write a new [narrative]."[45] The Founding Fathers narrative is the kind of stuff that folklore is stuffed full of, not the "unsettling truths"[46] about America's dehumanization of the American Indian, enslaved Africans, and African Americans previously mentioned in the chapter on Religion. And whether the folklore is referred to as revisionist history, the sanitization of harsh realities, or the romanization of antiquity, it can all be accused of falling into the illusion-of-truth effect.[47,48,49] This takes facts out of proper context, uses half-truths, and even bonafide lies. Through decades and even centuries of litany, iteration, and dramatic narrative recapitulation, it miraculously turns them into concrete facts.

This book was purposed to have something for every American regardless of what side of the social construct of race they find themselves on via the genetic lottery, as it were. Whether they are running toward the fire, meaning that in their eyes the glass is half full, and they see the experiment as still being a work in progress. Or whether they are running away from the fire, meaning that in their eyes the glass is half empty, and they see the experiment as something that was destined to fail because of the poorly laid foundation upon which it was constructed. The book was also purposed, as the book's title suggests as an attempt, even if a weak one, to substantiate the saga of Africans and African Americans in America. Those who, through this book's repetitious refrain, leave no doubt that they are the descendants of enslaved Africans. Those who even though they are tenth or perhaps even the fifteenth generation natural-born Americans, inclusion continues to elude them, and they have yet to be fully embraced by the only nation they have ever really known. Those who in spite of it all, still get a sense of pride when yet another African American becomes the first to break through some racialized socioeconomic, educational, or political barrier one hundred and fifty years after emancipation.

One thing that the book was not purposed to do, even though the provocative title might infer it, was to be a scathing rebuke of those Americans who self-identify as White. Those of whom not one individual is alive today who was an enslaver, overseer, driver, or various other proponent of the enslavement of Africans and African Americans as previously mentioned in the chapters on Politics and Religion. But if the book was purposed to substantiate the very long and storied saga of Africans and African Americans in America, it had to also be willing to present "unsettling truths"[50] not to individuals but to a patriarchal power structure. However, whether or not that power structure and those who embrace it are willing to accept the evidence presented here as fact is immaterial. The case has been made rather convincingly throughout the previous chapters of this book, with this final chapter serving only as a closing argument. So, there is no disputing the fact that they did inherit inclusion into the social construct of Whiteness even if they did not inherit wealth from their American ancestors. Likewise, they are also the recipients of the perpetration induced traumatic stress (PITS)[51,52] mentioned in the Chapter on Religion, which, again, through no fault of their own was handed down to them from their American ancestors. Either as part of America's slavery history or its racialized segregationist history. However, the reason why this book's attempt to substantiate the saga of Africans and African Americans in America is admittedly a weak one is twofold: (1) for people of color, being proud of African American achievements in spite of institutional and systemic racialized bias has worn thin; (2) not a new narrative, but a renewed narrative has been reborn, a countermovement per se, which sees the centuries of African American struggle for inclusion as mere vanity. Or in the words of the great abolitionist Frederick Douglass, "What, to the American slave, is your 4th of July?[53] So, this book's purpose is not weak in terms of its sincerity and the factual evidence it presents. But weak in terms of its ability to change the minds of those whose minds are already made up to leave America's grand experiment. Yes, there is a large segment of America's African American population and populations of people of color who believe that as a collective, they should not only be investing less time of their time being concerned with inclusion. And that they should also discontinue trying to educate those who self-identify as White about racism because the pathology of racism will always keep them from believing the experiences of African Americans and people of color.[54]

Perhaps this is because there has been a rather pervasive notion floating around America for quite some time. The notion that what African American communities and communities of color need most is a politician, statesman, or other leader. Someone who is unanimously recognized as the voice of the melanated segment of the nation within a nation. An individual who could more accurately, succinctly, and intelligently explain the nominal African diaspora worldview. Those who self-identify as White would finally be able to understand the African diaspora worldview and how it conflicts with the White worldview. But is not this idea of a perfect and enticing African American leader coming along at just the right moment to once and for all present the perfect case for the total inclusion of people of color into the fabric of America merely a pipe dream? Someone who would arrive on the scene with a message so profound, so revolutionary, that the majority of those who self-identify as White would be lured away from their White privilege by this melanated Pied Piper. This sort of thinking has worn thin because the truth of the matter is there has been no shortage of the most brilliant and even genius African Americans who have in the eyes of many, squandered their genius by investing too much time attempting to accurately, succinctly, and intelligently explain to White people the "truth [about] their society."[55]

So, it can thus be argued that if intellectual and charismatic African American giants like Frederick Douglass, Booker T. Washington, W. E. B. Du Bois, Martin Luther King, Jr., and Barack Obama could not make the African diaspora worldview plain and clear to those who self-identify as White then who can? Furthermore, it has been suggested that if all of the African American genius flung at the issue of institutional and systemic racialized bias was not for naught, then the historical emancipation of Africans and African Americans would not be seen as merely a celebration of freedom for African Americans and people of color. It would also be reverenced by those who self-identify as White because it not only represents African American freedom but it also represents American progress. Also, it can be argued that if the plethora of published writings, public speeches, and political wherewithal of Africa's and America's "Brightest and Best,"[56] has indeed not fallen on deaf ears, then why the modern refrain of "Make America Great Again?" A refrain that was once not only the pledge of the forty-fifth president of the United States to his followers and loyalists, but it was their rallying cry as well. It was a racially tinged dog whistle reminiscent of the tactics employed as part of the Southern Strategy mentioned in the chapters on Social Change and Politics. An ideology comprised primarily of and for the electorate and the elected who self-identified as White with no desire or inclination to suggest that America "go back to the United States Constitution and talk about making this a more perfect union..."[57] which is exactly what the emancipation acts and the subsequent constitutional amendments were attempting to do. No, the idea of a more perfect union would suggest equity between all Americans, while the racialized dog whistle of "Make America Great Again" would only serve in making America "White" again.

It was English poet Robert Southey who said, "Curses are like young chicken: they always come home to roost,"[58] in his epic poem "The Curse of Kehama." Inspired by his fear that Napoleon Bonaparte could be the Antichrist who ushers in the Apocalypse. How ironic that over two hundred years later, many historians and scholars believed that a leader with similar egotistical, authoritarian, and autocratic traits was elected as America's commander in chief in 2016. However, historians and scholars did stop short of using the terms dictator and tyrant to describe America's commander in chief, which were frequently used to describe Napoleon. So, perhaps the very boogie man that many African American parents had for decades taught their children about was not just a figment of their imagination but real-life flesh and blood antagonists. The same boogie man whom they either esoterically or perhaps often overtly blamed for many of the struggles of African Americans in America, the proverbial powers that be which are mentioned throughout this book. The same boogie man expressed through subtle language, subliminal messages, and references inferring that Whites have a hidden advantage over people of color. Not only that, but to take it a step further in saying that many successful Whites lied, cheated, used, abused, and often stole their way to the top of the socioeconomic or political food chain. So, the revelation of the feeling that many African Americans and people of color felt that "the man" was out to get them or out to suppress them was more than just an emotional feeling. Instead, it was an actual social, economic, and political strategy quite often hidden in plain sight, which is both a very powerful and very telling image. It is also a powerful testimony against the perpetrators of racialized bias who were adept at obfuscating their guilt, deflecting, and detracting it.

Adept at shifting blame and even crying foul when caught in the act of one of their often-elaborate discrimination schemes. Even going so far as to cry lunacy on the part of those who dared accuse them of racialized bias. Or as a clinical diagnosis might suggest, they were using psychological projection to transfer their own sense of guilt to those they were oppressing.[59]

There is another pervasive notion floating around America that has been perpetuated in America for generations. Which is that the Emancipation Proclamation, the ratification of the Fourteenth Amendment, and later the Civil Rights Act magically nullified any and all racially motivated biases, bigotry, and overt acts of racism. Furthermore, it was the Jim Crow laws in general and local politics in particular that always watered down any socioeconomic or political gains garnered by Africans and African Americans. So, there was never any broad sweeping legislation at the federal, state, county, parish, or local municipality level after the Emancipation Proclamation, the ratification of the Fourteenth Amendment, and later the Civil Rights Act. Nothing that said America is henceforth, now, and forevermore renouncing racially motivated biases, bigotry, overt acts of racism, and systemic racism. No one ever stood up to proclaim that America at every level of its personhood was willing to systematically scrutinize all of its laws and ordinances, both civil and criminal, searching for and eradicating any hint of White privilege and Black underprivilege that might remain.

So, instead of completely tearing down any remaining vestiges of slavery during Reconstruction and truly rebuilding the nation anew, the powers that be, in this case, federal, state, and local governments, simply picked and chose little by little, bits and pieces of the nation's faulty foundation to be repaired–revamped–reorganized. Never was there a broad sweeping policy in place to level the playing field between the newly freed 3,953,761 formerly enslaved Africans and African Americans and their former enslavers, overseers, drivers, and various other proponents of slavery. Maybe that was because the powers that be during Reconstruction were themselves either former enslavers, the sons or grandsons of enslavers, or former supporters of or beneficiaries of the enslavement of Africans and African Americans. And later, those powers that be were those who were opposed to integration in the 1950s and 1960s. Most of whom were the progeny of former enslavers, overseers, drivers, and various other proponents of slavery, or descendants of parents or grandparents who were Ellis Island immigrants from Europe. They knew that the full socioeconomic, educational, and political inclusion of African Americans into American society would erode their own White privilege. So, they too made sure that only the bare minimum was going to be done to eradicate bias and bigotry in laws and in ordinances. And very often, the rule of thumb was no harm, no foul, meaning that unless someone complained or better yet unless someone complained loudly enough, nothing would change.

As alluded to in the previous chapters of this book, being identified as either White or Black in America has never really been about skin pigmentation or the lack thereof, but about power. And likewise, it can be argued that the study of America's melting pot did not get its start with the notion of people of color being introduced to predominantly White societies. Instead, at the heart of the melting pot experiment is the different levels of the social construct of Whiteness[60] or the real beginning of White identity. For example, the Civil War is very often described in terms of brother against brother, North versus South, with the imagery of identical twins being somehow separated at birth. However, it is misleading to think that this was the case or that all Whiteness was created equally. Some

Northerners, those who supported the United States in the Civil War, more commonly referred to as the Union, may have shared common DNA with Southerners who supported the Confederacy and secession. They may have even intermarried into their families and had sustainable personal or business relationships, but this was at its core about interculturalism, not brotherhood. So, the Civil War was not the romanticized historical portrayal of a conflict between White brothers but was, most importantly, an intercultural conflict between what it meant to be a White Northerner and what it meant to be a White Southerner. And what it meant to be American in the northern or northeastern part of America versus the southern and southeastern part of America. It was perhaps a good example of the concept of motivational conflict psychology,[61] in which the Confederacy had to choose between two undesirable outcomes: (A) surrender; or (B) suffer near catastrophic casualties. On the other hand, the United States or the Union's choice was a good news-bad news choice: (A) restoring the Union with slavery, but with gradual emancipation; (B) restoring the union without slavery, but requiring an all-out dominant military victory with near catastrophic casualties.

Whether Tolstoy's historical fiction, *War and Peace*,[62] or Tzu's historical non-fiction, *The Art of War*,[63] it is not as difficult as some might think to make the leap from the conflict psychology of war to the conflict psychology of whether Americans should fight or flee the grand experiment. The core idea of choosing between two undesirable outcomes or a good news-bad news choice is applicable in times of war and in so-called times of peace. Take, for example, the fictitious story of an American who lived in a particular neighborhood, and their next-door neighbor's home was burglarized. Then a week later, another home belonging to another one of this American's neighbors was burglarized. Then sometime later, another resident who resided just one street over from this American had their automobile stolen and another resident's automobile was vandalized. And while this painstaking story of pirates in the working class could proceed ad nauseum, it does beg one abecedarian question, which is, Why on earth would this American willingly choose to remain in that neighborhood or city if she or he had the means and the wherewithal to leave that environment? Why install burglar bars on a home in the above described neighborhood, increase the electronic and hardware security of the home, purchase a firearm, and add a steering wheel locking mechanism to automobiles in addition to an already highly advanced automobile alarm system? Why hire a private security firm to patrol the neighborhood? While this might seem like a rather crude or even farfetched example, it is meant to underscore "the fight-or-flight response"[64] discussed earlier in this chapter. It is the idea that typically if one has both the means and the wherewithal to do so, it is very reasonable to assume that one would move to another neighborhood so that one might potentially have less fear of having one's home burglarized or automobile stolen. Yet one can also choose to essentially stay and resist, to fight. And perhaps it is the fact that both the flight choice and the fight choice each come with their own level of trauma, which in a sense makes the decision-making process even more daunting. It is not only daunting but also leaves the decision maker ripe for criticism, rebuke, and questions of why by onlookers and passersby regardless of the choice.

This is not unlike the idea that African Americans, who historically have not always been treated like or appreciated as full-fledged citizens by many of those who self-identify as White, often appear to roll up their proverbial sleeves and prepare to fight tooth-and-nail to vociferously defend themselves against the notion that they are somehow not American. The idea that they are others or somehow illegitimate in their own nation when it comes to the right to life, liberty, and the pursuit of happiness in America. This behavior begs the question, Why should African Americans and people of color continue with their fight response? Especially since history has consistently shown that whenever people of color encounter overt acts of racism, those who self-identify as White tend to see those instances as simply anomalies or one-offs rather than an indication of the continuation of systemic, multi-generational racism. And this question of why do people continue in a direction that is obviously fraught with known resistance; the fight response; is not unlike the question whether spoken out loud or suggested as a soft whisper after a natural disaster. Whether it is a hurricane along America's Gulf or Atlantic coast, mudslides, earthquakes, or wildfires out west, the question is almost always, Why would Americans continue to rebuild knowing that these types of disasters will eventually strike again? The answer is usually a resounding, often adamant, and even a fierce defense of the American way of life. This in spite of how perilous a situation may be. Yet the accompanying narrative is that this is simply the American Spirit of persevering, of never giving up, of living to fight another day, of refusing to be conquered.

It has been suggested that it is not as difficult as some might think to make the leap from the conflict psychology of war to the choice of whether to remain in America or emigrate. Well, it is likewise not as difficult as some might think to make the leap from the combat stress reaction of war; the combat stress or combat fatigue of war "known since Biblical times and . . . noted in professional literature since the American Civil War;"[65] to the stress reaction of living in America for people of color. And it can also be argued that the combat stress reaction experienced by people of color due to the centuries of oppression and racism in America is much more tragic than traditional war. With a few exceptions, there is typically a clearly defined end in a traditional war, which is simply the point at which the shooting and bombing stops. However, the metaphorical war that people of color participate in is multigenerational with no apparent end, without even the slightest glimmer of hope of a truce or peace treaty in sight. So, then Sun Tzu's warnings that: (1) fatigue can set in because "the general lays on unnecessary projects;"[66] (2) troops which are "easily changeable and lack plans"[67] are more easily worn down, and that (3) an exhausted and fatigued army is often viewed as ripe for attack by its enemies;[68] in the context of Africans living in America makes perfect sense. As does Tzu's idea that combatants should beware of attacking any enemy which is "well-regulated and [is an] imposing formation." It is this idea of the "well-regulated and imposing" foe that many would argue perfectly describes the power possessed by America's majority.

So, again, What was America thinking when it emancipated 3,953,761 enslaved Africans and African Americans and left them to live in the same general population with their former enslavers, overseers, drivers, and various other proponents of slavery in the hopes that everyone could all just let bygones be bygones? Although both enslaved and free Africans and African Americans fought valiantly in the Civil War, it is as if the literal end of the Civil War was merely the end of a conflict that pitted those who self-identify as White against others who self-identify as White. And in spite of the horrific amount of blood that was shed, it is as if this was only a sort of iron sharpening iron exercise. Part of a sinister plan in which the two sides would eventually form an alliance in the still ongoing metaphorical war between those who like themselves possess Whiteness[69] or White identity and those who do not. Metaphors aside, as the combatant with smaller numbers and fewer resources, it is no wonder that African Americans and people of color are weary of this fight.

This is not unlike the infamous story about a man who woke up one morning and found out that his spouse was having an affair with the gardener. He then discovers that the mailman was actually the biological father of this man's three children. To make matters worse, this man received word that he had not only been fired from his job of twenty years but that he would not receive any severance pay; neither would he qualify for unemployment compensation. If things were not already bad enough, it appeared as though the dollar for dollar match that his now former employer had been making to his retirement investment plan had been rescinded through some obscure fiduciary loophole. Then, on top of all of this, he found out that his mortgage company had gone bankrupt and declared insolvency. And as a result, through some strange rule of law, a law that of course, he did not quite understand, he discovered that the mortgage payments he had been making for fifteen years would be tied up in litigation. So, he either had to repay the amount in a lump sum or move out of his home with no hope of being able to access the home's equity in a sale. But just wait, things can and will get worse in this story; just call it the icing on the cake. Because even though he was at least a fifth generation American who could trace his American ancestry back at least 100 years, however, through some obscure loophole in U.S. citizenship law for people born in a particular U.S. island territory, he had to take a citizenship test.[70] This fictitious, gloomy, disheartening, and agonizing story might make for a popular blues song had it been penned by an American singer-songwriter like B.B. King, Muddy Waters, John Lee Hooker, or Robert Johnson. However, the problem America seems to have is not just that a segment of its population, African Americans and people of color, feel as though the fictitious worst-case scenario presented above could very easily represent an actual hour, a day, a week, a month, a year, a decade, or perhaps even the lifetime of the problems they face. In a most horrible sense of irony, the problem is that African Americans longanimously endured because they could never possess the power that having White identity bestows upon the recipient.

It was Paulo Freire who suggested that it is not only the oppressor who possesses power, but the oppressed also possess a certain kind of power. He wrote that, "[T]he great humanistic and historical task of the oppressed [is] to liberate themselves and their oppressors as well." That, "[o]nly power that springs from the weakness of the oppressed will be sufficiently strong to free both."[71] Yet no matter how deeply moving and intellectually stimulating those thoughts, it can be argued that in terms of the African American struggle against oppression, this liberation already took place during the non-violent Civil Rights Movement. Nevertheless, it still appears as though more of the vicious cycle of oppression ensued in spite of the strength of the liberating power that Freire was referring to. This is because the Civil Rights Acts and any new laws that aim to soften[72] the power of the oppressors is arguably only a "[F]alse generosity"[73] if it is not tied to totally dismantling the systems that perpetuate systemic racially motivated biases. That "moral disorder"[74] called prejudice of which Frederick Douglass spoke. So, perhaps the moral to the story is that those on the outside of America looking in have no choice but to be both in awe of and in bewilderment of those African Americans and people of color of both the past and modern times. In awe of those who are the possessors of the intestinal fortitude to stay and fight.

This fight instinct or fight reaction is what Levine was painting a picture of when he described how a human being's

"[M]uscles prepare to escape by increasing their tension level," the "[H]eart rate and respiration increase," as the entire "[M]etabolic system is flooded with adrenaline."[75] Those on the outside of America looking in are in awe of those enslaved Africans who fought to remain alive after being seized as human chattel and later trafficked as human cargo and then exported via the Atlantic Ocean. A journey from the west coast of Africa to Brazil could take as few as eighteen days or as many as one-hundred and fifty days[76] or more depending upon the weather and other mishaps. But those outsiders looking in at America are likewise bewildered at how so many human beings were able to individually and collectively fight the wretched living conditions in the holds of ships specifically designed to hold humans, not humans as-in voluntary passengers, but humans as-in captured human cargo. No, those on the outside of America looking in are not just lauding enslaved Africans for winning metaphorical battles. Enslaved Africans took every available opportunity to revolt. It was a mutinous and defiant attitude that, even if unsuccessful, told their enslavers that they would not go quietly into the night.[77] Lastly, these outsiders are also bewildered that the number of those who decided that death at sea, either by suicidal drowning or at the hands of the murderous crew was not more extensive. And perhaps those numbers would have been even larger had those enslaved Africans known what centuries of torment lie ahead of them and their progeny.

However, those very same bewildered outsiders are in awe of those enslaved Africans who once they had arrived on South American, Caribbean or North American soil fought to remain alive. So that even if they themselves would never again taste freedom, their offspring might one day feast on its splendor. This awe extends to those Africans and African Americans who fought in a civil war, which at the time offered them the mere rumor of emancipation. Only later to realize that while the literal war was over for Whites, the metaphorical and philosophical war was, in effect, just beginning for emancipated Africans. Those of whom still remembered their homelands and for those born on American soil. But bewilderment is not far behind the awe as outsiders cannot help but wonder if those valiant and often heroic Africans and African Americans may have shortly after emancipation began to realize that while there would always be that glimmer of hope of winning a handful of battles, they might never actually win the real war. The war against White privilege, White supremacist ideology, and the terroristic, guerrilla, and ambush style warfare of the likes of the Ku Klux Klan. This is in addition to the transgenerational stresses handed down from both the enslaved to their progeny and the transgenerational perpetration induced traumatic stress (PITS)[78,79] that former enslavers, overseers, drivers, and various other proponents of slavery handed down to their progeny.

So, after so much awe and bewilderment, it should not be too difficult for an outsider to understand the reasoning and rationale of those Americans who feel led not to continue the fight but instead to escape, to move on to greener pastures. Pastures with a smaller population of wolves; pastures that are just a little bit kinder and gentler. An environment with perhaps a little less racially motivated bias and hopefully, a lot fewer overt acts of racism. And frankly, who could blame them for moving on to countries, cities, neighborhoods, and neighbors who might warmly welcome and even appreciate them as opposed to simply tolerate them? Able to live not just in cultures that embrace diversity, but cultures that embrace inclusion. And it is because of America's tumultuous racialized history that even one hundred and fifty years after emancipation, it is still with bold confidence that far too many of those who self-identify as White, who can trace their ancestry back to America's slavery history, see themselves as the owners of America. Yet they see African Americans, who can also trace their ancestry back to America's slavery history, as mere visitors, guests in a country that African Americans and their ancestors helped build. Yet, instead of this continued exclusion creating a strong desire in African Americans and people of color to carry on the good-fight; the struggle of countless ancestors who had gone on before them. No, to the contrary, they believe that there is perhaps something to be said about wanting to just be left alone. That being ignored and made to feel invisible in a foreign country might actually feel like a big relief. That is, after the years, decades, and centuries of both the perceived and the real pressures of being under the microscope as it were. They believe that they are not necessarily running from or fleeing something inherently bad, but instead, they are running toward something better. But sadly enough, while individuals are often counseled to leave abusive relationships, many times when they do leave, instead of applauding them and even embracing their resolve to live their lives free from threats, they are considered quitters. They are even blamed for not trying harder to do their part to repair not a broken relationship, but an abusive one.

While there is in almost every situation the most minute flicker, the tiniest glimmer of hope, unfortunately, for the tide of racism and racially motivated bias in America to turn, America would require a Great Awakening. An awakening in which a clear majority of Americans who self-identify as White are willing to admit or acknowledge that as much as they love their parents, their grandparents, their uncles, aunts, and great uncles and great aunts. And as much as they have a particular pride for their family lineage and accomplishments, growing up, things were said either explicitly or implicitly, which revealed to them that they have an advantage.

Regardless of how slight the advantage and whether visible or invisible, they were made to feel just a little bit better than people of color. It was most likely not as overt as the ideology of White Supremacy but rather nuanced through drawing attention to cultural differences and things which were said or done. Motivated by the notion of race, as well as things left unsaid or undone. Inspired by the social construct of race, to make one think one is better even if the amount is minuscule. So, perhaps President Lyndon Baines Johnson's words of 1960 still ring true in America nearly sixty years later: That the "[L]owest White man" can actually be made to think and feel less insecure and less anxious about his own station in life if he is made to feel as if he is, "[B]etter than the best"[80] African American or person of color. And even as seemingly crude and even shocking as Johnson's 1960 words may sound, this same psychological defense mechanism[81] is apparently alive and well in modern-day America.

This modern phenomenon that sees Americans who self-identify as White, feeling as though people of color are edging them out of the workforce, while it is an erroneous notion, is not new. Almost since America's inception, those who self-identify as White have believed that they, by nature, expect to be first in line, and when they cannot be first in line, it must be the fault of someone else. In particular, someone who racialized society has constructed to be so-called Black, Brown, Red, or Yellow. So, it is with both trepidation and skepticism that African Americans; who are the descendants of enslaved Africans; and people of color, in general, find it difficult to believe that even a simple majority of those who self-identify as White would ever willingly take part in the type of Great Awakening being described in this book.

America's next migration may not be a migration of Americans moving from one part of the nation to another. It may very well be an emigration of Americans out of the country. It may not be as high-sounding, epic, Homeric, pseudo-Miltonic, grandiloquent as the Israelites exodus from Egypt, the Islamic prophet Muhammad's journey from Mecca to Medina, the Kashmiri Hindus being forced to flee the Kashmir valley in India, or even the First and Second Great Migrations of as many as six million African Americans from America's southern states to its northern, midwestern, and western states between 1910 and 1970.[82] However, it just may end up being a saga in its own right nonetheless. Instead of intransitive verbs like fleeing, escaping, or decamping, no, this emigration could more closely resemble a retreat. Not a retreat as in a military withdrawal, but instead just that much quieter or even secluded environment where authentic rest and relaxation can be found.[83] A sanctuary, not an asylum. A place to simply exhale after holding one's breath for years or decades.

While the goal of this book is not to implicitly offer emigration as a remedy for America's ills, one can only pray that because of the breadth and width of the research that went into this book, it may serve as some minuscule inspiration to those Americans who are torn between ideas of continuing to fight to make American that more perfect union or escaping America in its present imperfect state. Of course, any inspiration to be found in this little book is by no means on the grand scale of that which *The Columbian Orator*[84] did inspire the great Frederick Douglass, opening his eyes to his "wretched condition"[85] and the "horrible pit"[86] he was in as an enslaved African American. The inspiration, which unfortunately offered Douglass "no ladder upon which to get out"[87] of his condition. So, it is not the prognostication of this little book, but America's future election cycles will be the most reliable tell-tale sign of both the necessity of emigration and just how massive any appreciable emigration will be.

This book has made it exhaustively clear that the eradication of tribalism or changing the condition of the human spirit of Americans will not be done using statistics and comprehensive research reports. However, with regard to American emigration, a Gallup Poll found that when asked whether they would prefer to move permanently to another country as opposed to remaining in America, the number of women, in particular, expressing a desire to leave permanently increased from ten percent under President Obama to twenty percent under the presidency of the forty-fifth president of the United States. The combined gender age group of fifteen to twenty-nine-year olds who would prefer to emigrate almost doubled from about eighteen percent under Obama to thirty percent under the presidency of the forty-fifth president of the United States. In addition, the combined gender age group of thirty to forty-nine-year olds wanting to relocate essentially doubled from ten percent under Obama to nineteen percent under the presidency of the forty-fifth president of the United States. And among the poorest Americans, the number of those who would prefer to move permanently to another country as opposed to remaining in America nearly triples from about thirteen percent under Obama to thirty percent under the presidency of the forty-fifth president of the United States.[88] And again, the eradication of tribalism or changing the condition of the human spirit of Americans will not be done using statistics and comprehensive research reports. Yet, this type of research acts as both an indictment and a testimony not unlike the "evidence" (James 5:1-3 CEV) mentioned in the Chapter on Religion. However, this testimony is in opposition to a Declaration of

Independence that flows ever so smoothly, written with its own unique literary devices, poetic even without verse and meter. Yet, it remains largely unfulfilled in the lives of its people.[89] Dum vivimus vivamus: While we live, let us live.[90]

NOTES

Front Cover

1. "Population of the United States in 1860."

Back Cover

1. "U.S. and World Population Clock."

Dedication

1. George Newnes, 1893, p. 233.

2. African Proverb, *Our Day to End Poverty,* p. 199.

Introduction

1. Introduction epigraph, *Missionary Herald, Volume 76.*

2. See Cover, Note 1.

3. "Gloom, Despair, and Agony On Me" song lyrics, *Hee Haw.*

4. Sir Arthur Conan Doyle, p. 196.

5. William Winwood Reade, pp. 143–144.

6. Etymology, Works of Israel Zangwill.

7. Difference between patriotism and nationalism, Sydney J. Harris.

8. Sydney J. Harris.

9. Merriam-Webster.com.

10. William Shakespeare, All's Well That Ends Well; a Comedy. By Mr. William Shakespeare.

11. Where America got its name, *Cosmographiae Introductio,* p. vii.

12. Film quote, The Jacksons; an American Dream.

13. Contrast between pain and pleasure, *The Elements of Ethics.*

14. Film quote, *Trading Places.*

15. Antebellum use of term, second inaugural address of the late President Lincoln.

16. The Indians of the Americas.

17. Supports a general idea, *American Experience.*

18. The Gettysburg address delivered by Abraham Lincoln Nov. 19 at the dedication services on the battlefield.

19. Voices of the True-Hearted.

Chapter 1

1. Social Change epigraph, Jerry Glenn.

2. Social Change epigraph, E. Elaine Murdaugh, pp. 275–289.

3. Supports a general idea, "The Origins of the Presumption of Black Stupidity."

4. Reference, Jovana Drinjakovic.

5. Reference, Robin McKie.

6. Reference, "Pumping Myocytes."

7. Merriam-Webster.com.

8. Reference, "Pulse: MedicinePlus Medical Encyclopedia."

9. Mary Shelley.

10. Robert Louis Stevenson.

11. See Introduction, Note 6.

12. See Introduction, Note 6.

13. Walter Lynwood Fleming, p. 279.

14. Supplemental reference, The Jim Crow Encyclopedia: Greenwood Milestones in African American History, p. 84.

15. Supplemental reference, Montesquieu: The Spirit of the Laws.

16. Supplemental reference, An American Dilemma: The Negro Problem and Modern Democracy. Volume I, p. 558.

17. Supplemental reference, Combatting Human Trafficking: A Multidisciplinary Approach, p. 3.

18. Etymology, Molly Bawn, 1878.

19. "Who We Elect: Sheriffs."

20. "Debugging the System: Exterminating Myths About Lice."

21. "CDC - Lice - Head Lice - General Information - Frequently Asked Questions (FAQs)."

22. CDC

23. "Common humanity," Du Bois, The Souls of Black Folk: Essays and Sketches.

24. "Paradise Lost, Found and Lost Again."

25. "It's Your Brain's Fault You Make the Same Mistakes Over and Over."

26. "Why We Often Repeat the Same Mistakes."

27. "Haunts or Helps from the Past: Understanding the Effect of Recall on Current Self-Control," pp. 245-256.

28. James Truslow Adams, pp. 415-416.

29. See Introduction, Note 4.

30. See Introduction, Note 5.

31. Television quote, *Burn Notice.*

32. Supports general idea, Jane Adolphe.

33. Madison Park: A Place of Hope.

34. Tulsa Race Riot.

35. House Bill 591.

36. Buried in the Bitter Waters: The Hidden History of Racial Cleansing in America.

37. See Introduction, Note 6.

38. Our Punitive Society: Race, Class, Gender and Punishment in America.

39. NY State Senate.

40. U.S. Reports: Terry v. Ohio, 392 U.S. 1. 1967.

41. "American Race Relations and the Caste System."

42. "Colin Kaepernick Explains Why He Sat during National Anthem."

43. Pat McKissack.

44. Joel Schumacher.

45. "Parenting: Set Your Children's 'Defaults' Early."

46. The Experiment, 2011.

47. Theodore W. Allen.

48. Neologism, Jon Michael Spencer.

49. "White Privilege: Unpacking the Invisible Knapsack."

50. Supports a general idea, Joe R. Feagin.

51. Film quote, *The Matrix Revolutions*, 2003.

52. "Word," The Matrix Revolutions.

53. "Connection," *The Matrix Revolutions.*

54. "Give," The Matrix Revolutions.

55. "Anything," The Matrix Revolutions.

56. "Consumer-Lending Discrimination in the FinTech Era."

57. Neologism, Liz Fosslien, p. 185.

58. "Keying In To History."

59. "How Southern Socialites Rewrote Civil War History."

60. CNN, 19 Dec. 2019.

61. See Introduction, Note 17.

62. "The Problem of Ego Identity," pp. 189-198.

63. Thought Reform and the Psychology of Totalism: A Study of Brainwashing in China.

64. Ronald Reagan.

65. Stone of Hope - Prophetic Religion and the Death of Jim Crow, p. 105.

66. "The Southern Manifesto of 1956."

67. Manifesto of 1956.

68. Dog Whistles, Walk-Backs, and Washington Handshakes: Decoding the Jargon, Slang, and Bluster of American Political Speech.

69. Pillar of Fire: America in the King Years, 1963-65.

70. James Boyd. "Nixon's Southern Strategy 'It's All In the Charts'."

71. Race-Baiter: How the Media Wields Dangerous Words to Divide a Nation.

72. Equity: in Theory and Practice, p. 64.

73. Social Indicators of Equality for Minorities and Women: A Report of the United States Commission on Civil Rights, p. 53.

74. Equity as a Policy Goal, p. 6.

75. "Inequality, Equality, and Equity."

76. Essentials of Cultural Anthropology, p. 229.

77. Cultural Anthropology: An Applied Perspective, p. 283.

78. U.S.C. Title 4 - FLAG AND SEAL, SEAT OF GOVERNMENT, AND THE STATES.

79. Katharine Lee Bates.

80. See Chapter 1, Note 3.

81. See Chapter 1, Note 3.

82. See Chapter 1, Note 3.

83. See Chapter 1, Note 3.

84. See Introduction, Note 6.

85. Statue of Liberty, Ellis Island Immigration Museum: Statue of Liberty National Monument.

86. Reginald Heber.

87. "Swindlers and rascals," Du Bois, The Souls of Black Folk: Essays and Sketches.

88. "Internal development," Du Bois, The Souls of Black Folk: Essays and Sketches.

89. "Racial Bias in the US Opioid Epidemic: A Review of the History of Systemic Bias and Implications for Care."

90. Kaiser Family Foundation.

91. "The War on Drugs That Wasn't: Wasted Whiteness, 'Dirty Doctors,' and Race in Media Coverage of Prescription Opioid Misuse," pp. 664–686

92. An Introduction to Forensic Genetics.

93. The Physiology of Sexist and Racist Oppression.

94. Molly Bawn.

95. See Introduction, Note 6.

96. "Fair and full," A Compilation of the Messages and Papers of the Presidents.

97. The Works of John Adams Second President of the United States.

98. "Witnessed the scene," A Compilation of the Messages and Papers of the Presidents.

99. The United States' Role in the World.

100. "The Impeachment Hearing."

Chapter 2

1. Economics epigraph, Thomas P. Govan.

2. "No Pensions for Ex-Slaves."

3. Specific term use, Press and Speech Under Assault: The Early Supreme Court Justices, the Sedition Act of 1798, and the Campaign Against Dissent, p. 473.

4. Specific term use, The Debate Over Slavery: Antislavery and Proslavery Liberalism in Antebellum America.

5. Specific term use, Deliver Us from Evil: The Slavery Question in the Old South, p. 202.

6. Specific term use, A Necessary Evil? Slavery and the Debate Over the Constitution.

7. Specific term use, *Two Lectures on the Subjects of Slavery and Abolition*, p. 27.

8. Specific term use, Southern Slavery Considered on General Principles, Or, a Grapple with Abstractionists, p. 16.

9. Specific term use, Evil Necessity: Slavery and Political Culture in Antebellum Kentucky, pp. 1-19.

10. See Notes 3-9.

11. See Notes 3-9.

12. "Sugar Empire, "John Henrik Clarke, p. XVII.

13. "Cotton Kingdom, "John Henrik Clarke, p. XVII.

14. Acts and Joint Resolutions of the General Assembly of the State of South Passed at The Annual Session of 1864, p. 10.

15. See Introduction, Note 6.

16. Film quote, *Jerry Maguire*.

17. Specific term use, A Self-Renewing Society: The Role of Television and Communications Technology, p. 85.

18. Specific term use, *George Bush's War*, p. 79.

19. Microaggressions in Everyday Life: Race, Gender, and Sexual Orientation.

20. Microaggression Theory: Influence and Implications, p. 24.

21. "Jobs, Jobs, Jobs!" Donald Trump (realDonaldTrump).

22. "Black Workers Are Being Left behind by Full Employment."

23. Metro Monitor: An Index of Inclusive Economic Growth in the 100 Largest U.S. Metropolitan Areas.

24. The Color of Wealth: The Story Behind the U.S. Racial Wealth Divide.

25. Black Wealth-White Wealth a New Perspective on Racial Inequality

26. Supplemental reference, African Americans in the U.S. Economy.

27. Supplemental reference, African American Economic Development and Small Business Ownership.

28. Supplemental reference, Human Behavior in the Social Environment from an African American Perspective.

29. Supplemental reference, Race, Faith, and Politics: 7 Political Questions That Every African American Christian Must Answer.

30. Specific term use, "Yes, Social Security Is An 'Entitlement'."

31. Specific term use, "Glossary Term: Entitlement."

32. Specific term use, "What Are the Major Federal Safety Net Programs in the U.S.?"

33. World Bank Group, 2002.

34. Economic and Social Impacts of the Media. 2015.

35. "The Tax Cuts are so large," Donald Trump (realDonaldTrump).

36. "Biggest Tax Bill and Tax Cuts," Donald Trump (realDonaldTrump).

37. See Note 21.

38. "White Americans Gain the Most From Trump's Tax Cuts, a Report Finds."

39. Race, Wealth and Taxes: How the Tax Cuts and Jobs Act Supercharges the Racial Wealth Divide. 2018.

40. Supplemental reference, Changes in Health Coverage by Race and Ethnicity since Implementation of the ACA, 2013- 2017. 2019.

41. "Sessions Rescinds Justice Dept. Letter Asking Courts to Be Wary of Stiff Fines and Fees for Poor Defendants."

42. Merriam-Webster.com.

43. Frederick Douglass, Narrative of the Life of Frederick Douglass, An American Slave.

44. Specific term use, The Power of Resistance: Culture, Ideology and Social Reproduction in Global Contexts.

45. Specific term use, Defying Dixie: The Radical Roots of Civil Rights, 1919-1950, p. 108.

46. Specific term use, Jacked Up and Unjust: Pacific Islander Teens Confront Violent Legacies, p. 154.

47. Estimating Slavery Reparations: Present Value Comparisons of Historical Multigenerational Reparations Policies. 2nd ed., vol. 96, 2015.

48. Divergent Paths: Structural Change, Economic Rank, and the Evolution of Black-White Earnings Differences, 1940-2014. 2017.

49. The Impact of Affirmative Action on the Employment of Minorities and Women Over Three Decades: 1973-2003. 2012.

50. ADGN: An Algorithm for Record Linkage Using Address, Date of Birth, Gender, and Name. 2017.

51. Algorithmic Bias? A Study of Data-Based Discrimination in the Serving of Ads in Social Media. 2016.

52. Discrimination in Online Ad Delivery. 2013.

53. Beyond the Marketplace: Rethinking Economy and Society, p. 3.

54. Understanding Inequality, Poverty and Wealth Policies and Prospects. Policy Press, 2011, p. 1.

55. Encyclopedia of the City, p. 418.

56. "If a player wants the privilege," Donald Trump (realDonaldTrump).

57. "Dissent and Deviance in Intergroup Contexts," pp. 1-5.

58. Supplemental reference, "The Rules of Implicit Evaluation by Race, Religion, and Age," pp. 1804-1815.

59. Supplemental reference, From Foreclosure to Fair Lending: Advocacy, Organizing, Occupy, and the Pursuit of Equitable Credit.

60. Supplemental reference, "The Idea of Racial Hierarchy Remains Entrenched."

61. Fox News (FoxNews).

62. Specific term use, Whiteness of a Different Color: European Immigrants and the Alchemy of Race.

63. Specific term use, Whiteness: The Communication of Social Identity.

64. Specific term use, Towards the Abolition of Whiteness: Essays on Race, Politics, and Working Class History.

65. "Inequality - Status and Power."

66. Justice and the Politics of Difference, p. 64.

67. Specific term use, "Two Concepts of Oppression."

68. Supports general idea, Time on the Cross: The Economics of American Negro Slavery.

69. Supports general idea, Roll, Jordan, Roll: The World the Slaves Made.

70. Supports general idea, "Review: Slavery, Paternalism, and White Hegemony," pp. 1190-1198.

71. Specific term use, She Said/He Said: An Annotated Bibliography of Sex Difference in Language, Speech, and Nonverbal Communication.

72. Supports general idea, "Doing Our Own Work: A Seminar for Anti-Racist White Women."

73. Supports general idea, "Understanding Privilege and Oppression Handout."

74. Supports general idea, "Visions, Inc. and the MSU Extension Multicultural Awareness Workshop."

75. Martin Luther King.

76. Shakespeare: The Biography.

77. George Washington's Religion: The Faith of the First President.

78. Harriet Elizabeth Beecher Stowe.

79. An Introductory Dictionary of Theology and Religious Studies.

80. Pia Desideria.

81. Specific term use, The American Plutocracy, p. 126-127.

82. Specific term use, "The People's Jubilee." *The Democrat,* July 1887, pp. 257–258.

83. Specific term use, Records and Briefs of the United States Supreme Court: William Burns, Plaintiff in Error vs. The United States of America, p. 20.

84. See Note 81.

85. See Note 82.

86. See Note 81.

87. Romeo and Juliet.

88. Film quote, *Car Wash*.

89. "Populations Serving Vulnerable and Underserved Populations."

90. Neologism, James A. Michener.

91. Neologism, Desmond Tutu: A Biography.

92. Neologism, Rolf Hochhuth.

93. Television quote, *The Simpsons*.

94. "Race and Economic Opportunity in the United States: An Intergenerational Perspective."

95. The Creation of the American Republic 1776-1787.

96. "The Constitution of the United States: A Transcription."

97. Specific term use, The Framers' Coup: The Making of the United States Constitution.

98. The Framers' Coup: The Making of the United States Constitution.

99. "The Founding Fathers' Power Grab."

100. See Note 97.

101. See Note 99.

102. Proceedings of the Massachusetts Historical Society.

103. "Demagogues," Proceedings of the Massachusetts Historical Society.

104. See Note 95.

105. Unequal Gains: American Growth and Inequality since 1700.

106. See Note 96.

107. See Note 96.

108. Merriam-Webster.com.

109. See Note 14.

110. "Superficial Temporal Artery."

111. Illustrated Anatomy of the Head and Neck - E-Book, p. 134.

112. Supplemental reference, Empires of Oil: Corporate Oil in Barbarian Worlds.

113. Supplemental reference, "Empires with Expiration Dates."

114. See Note 112.

115. See Note 113.

116. Moral Functionalism.

117. "The Bill of Rights: A Transcription."

118. Specific term use, The Political Register, and Impartial Review: For MDCCLXX. Vol. 7, p. 157.

119. Specific term use, AMERICAN BABYLON: Christianity and Democracy before and after Trump, pp. 62-63.

120. Specific term use, Persecution Complex: Why American Christians Need to Stop Playing the Victim.

121. Conscience and Compromise: Forgotten Evangelicals of Nineteenth-Century Scotland, p. 247.

122. John Fox.

123. The Fate of the Apostles: Examining the Martyrdom Accounts of the Closest Followers of Jesus.

Chapter 3

1. Politics epigraph, The Complete Works of Aristotle.

2. "The Gilder Lehrman Institute of American History."

3. "Chapter CXXVIII. An Act to Define and Declare the Rights of Persons Lately Known as Slaves, and Free Persons of Color." 1866.

4. Joseph P. Bradley.

5. "The Supreme Court. The First Hundred Years. Landmark Cases. Plessy v. Ferguson (1896): PBS."

6. See Introduction, Note 6.

7. Supports general idea, "To Understand America - Read the Bible."

8. Supports general idea, Proclaim Liberty Throughout the Land: The Hebrew Bible in the United States: A Sourcebook.

9. "Convict servants, "A Collection of Statutes Connected with the General Administration of the Law; Arranged According to the Order of Subjects: With Notes.

10. "Britain's Transportation Act of 1717,"A Collection of Statutes Connected with the General Administration of the Law; Arranged According to the Order of Subjects: With Notes.

11. To Begin the World Over Again: How the American Revolution Devastated the Globe.

12. "Entering and Exiting the British Empire."

13. "Origins of the American Revolution."

14. All the Countries We've Ever Invaded: And the Few We Never Got Round To.

15. Specific term use, The Gentleman's and London Magazine: Or Monthly Chronologer. 1787.

16. Specific term use, *The Analytical Review.*

17. Command at Sea: Naval Command and Control since the Sixteenth Century.

18. See Note 13.

19. See Note 13.

20. Specific term use, "'He Was a Man of His Times.'"

21. Samuel P. Huntington.

22. Tryals Per Pais in Capital Matters: Or, Some Brief and Useful Observations Relating to Such Tryals.

23. Sabbath in Puritan New England.

24. Supplemental reference, The English Bible and the Seventeenth-Century Revolution.

25. Supplemental reference, "The Tanner Lectures on Human Values."

26. The True George Washington.

27. "Taking Your Carotid Pulse: MedlinePlus Medical Encyclopedia Image."

28. Specific term use, The Presumed Alliance: The Unspoken Conflict Between Latinos and Blacks and What It Means for America.

29. Supports general idea, "Colonial Enslavement of Native Americans Included Those Who Surrendered, Too."

30. Supports general idea, Women in Early America: Struggle, Survival, and Freedom in a New World, p. 80.

31. Supports general idea, Brethren by Nature: New England Indians, Colonists, and the Origins of American Slavery, p. 14.

32. Paulo Freire, Pedagogy of the Oppressed.

33. The Politics of Indian Removal: Creek Government and Society in Crisis.

34. Florida's Seminole Wars, 1817-1858 (The Making of America).

35. "Negroes and the Seminole War, 1835-1842."

36. *Reconstruction: America After the Civil War*, Public Broadcasting Service (PBS), 9 Apr. 2019.

37. Economic agendas, Reconstruction: America After the Civil War.

38. People's Party, Reconstruction: America After the Civil War.

39. Cry from the Cotton: The Southern Tenant Farmers' Union and the New Deal.

40. Film, The Great Debaters.

41. Jimmy Carter.

42. U.S. Reports: Roe v. Wade, 410 U.S. 113. 1972.

43. Blinded by Might: Why the Religious Right Can't Save America.

44. Randall Herbert Balmer, *Thy Kingdom Come*.

45. Randall Herbert Balmer, "The Real Origins of the Religious Right."

46. The Political Blame Game in American Democracy, p. 61.

47. See Note 44.

48. See Note 45.

49. See Note 44

50. See Note 45.

51. To the Right: The Transformation of American Conservatism.

52. "Soul winders," To the Right: The Transformation of American Conservatism.

53. See Note 44

54. See Note 45.

55. Pat Robertson: A Personal, Religious, and Political Portrait, p. 203.

56. "Food Insecurity and Hunger in Rich Countries—It Is Time for Action against Inequality," p. 1804.

57. Where Keynes Went Wrong: and Why World Governments Keep Creating Inflation, Bubbles, and Busts, pp. 269-270.

58. "John McCain Townhall."

59. See Chapter 2, Note 56.

60. Washington redskins, Donald Trump (realDonaldTrump).

61. Merriam-Webster.com.

62. "A Man of Certitude and Joy."

63. Specific term use, The Language and Politics of Exclusion: Others in Discourse.

64. The Conscience: Rediscovering the Inner Compass.

65. "District of Columbia Emancipation Act of 1862."

66. "Dabbled," "Cicero and Political Expediency."

67. "Roman of Romans," "Cicero and Political Expediency."

68. "Political faith," "Cicero and Political Expediency."

69. Friedrich Dürrenmatt.

70. "Compare Today's Unemployment with the Past."

71. "List of incidents of civil unrest in the United States."

72. Specific term use, Summary & Analysis of White Fragility: Why It's So Hard for White People to Talk About Racism.

73. Television quote, *Spenser.*

74. "About the Electors."

75. Specific term use, Spectres of 1919: Class and Nation in the Making of the New Negro.

76. Voter Identification Requirements: Voter ID Laws.

77. "Voter Identification Laws and the Suppression of Minority Votes."

Chapter 4

1. Religion epigraph, John Sayre.

2. Merriam-Webster.com.

3. Supports a general idea, Routledge Companion to Christianity in Africa.

4. Supports a general idea, "Animated map shows how Christianity spread around the world."

5. Supports a general idea, "What Does History Say about the First Christians of Africa?"

6. Supports a general idea, *Clement of Alexandria.*

7. Supports a general idea, "The First Christian Communities (1st Century)."

8. Supports a general idea, "The Story of Africa | BBC World Service."

9. Specific term use, The Slave Coast of West Africa, 1550-1750: The Impact of the Atlantic Slave Trade on an African Society.

10. Specific term use, Africa and Africans in the Making of the Atlantic World, 1400-1800.

11. Race and Mixed Race.

12. "Moral Dilemmas."

13. I'm a Fruit Inspector Because Jesus Told Christians to Judge Righteous Judgment.

14. Freedoms Unfinished Revolution: An Inquiry into the Civil War and Reconstruction, p. 13.

15. Slave States 2020.

16. Law and Morality, p. 25.

17. See Chapter 3, Note 45.

18. Classics of Moral and Political Theory, p. 78.

19. Film quote, *Gone In 60 Seconds.*

20. The New World: Volume 8. J. Winchester, 1844.

21. "1776-1865: From Bondage to Holy War."

22. Proceedings of the Southern Baptist Convention, 1845: Southern Baptist Convention Annuals, 22 Baylor University Libraries Digital Collections.

23. "American Presbyterian Churches—A Genealogy, 1706–1982."

24. Neologism, "What Would Jesus Do? The Rise of a Slogan."

25. Supports a general idea, *Diversity and Society: Race, Ethnicity,* and Gender. P. 144.

26. Supports a general idea, Atlanta, Cradle of the New South: Race and Remembering in the Civil Wars Aftermath, p. 170.

27. Supports a general idea, Social Research in the Judicial Process: Cases, Readings, and Text, p. 48.

28. "Political right," See Chapter 3, Note 44.

29. "Hard right," See Chapter 3, Note 44.

30. See Chapter 1, Note 43.

31. "How Many Israelites Left Egypt in the Exodus?"

32. "Select Parts of the Holy Bible, for the Use of the Negro Slaves, in the . . . "

33. Christian Slavery: Conversion and Race in the Protestant Atlantic World.

34. See Chapter 1, Note 43.

35. "How and Why Did Some Christians Defend Slavery?"

36. Max Weber.

37. "The White Protestant Roots of American Racism."

38. See introduction, Note 6.

39. "What Does It Mean That Good Works Are the Result of Salvation?"

40. Specific term use, Unsettling Truths: The Ongoing, Dehumanizing Legacy of the Doctrine of Discovery, pp. 58-66.

41. The Self-Made Man: Success and Stress-American Style, p. 10.

42. Pope Alexander VI, Pagans in the Promised Land: Decoding the Doctrine of Christian Discovery, pp. 125-127.

43. Pope Alexander VI.

44. See Note 40.

45. Specific term use, "Debates, Columbus, Sexism, and Racism."

46. John Winthrop, pp. 33–48.

47. "The Anglo-Saxon Myth in the United States," p. 183.

48. See Note 46.

49. See Note 40.

50. See Note 45.

51. John L. O'Sullivan

52. Trail of Tears (Landmarks of the American Mosaic), p. 202.

53. Princeton Legacy Library: Champions of the Cherokees: Evan and John B. Jones, p. 98.

54. Genocide and International Justice, p. 132.

55. Supports a general idea, The Merchants' Magazine and Commercial Review, Volume 24. 1851, p. 546.

56. Supports a general idea, *Harper's New Monthly Magazine, Volume 5*, p. 839.

57. Supports a general idea, American *Economist, Volumes 11-12*.

58. Men and Idioms of Wall Street: Explaining the Daily Operations in Stocks, Bonds and Gold. 1875, p. 3.

59. Manual of the Corporation of the City of New York For the Year 1849.

60. Film quote, *The Long Shadow*.

61. Supports a general idea, Empire of Mud: The Secret History of Washington, DC, p. 69.

62. Supports a general idea, Workers on Arrival: Black Labor in the Making of America, p. 26.

63. Supports a general idea, U.S. News & World Report, Volume 123, Issues 1-7, p. 68.

64. Film quote, *Independence Day*.

65. "James 5 Commentary - People's New Testament."

66. Etymology of phrase, Anne Thackeray Ritchie, *Mrs. Dymond*, 1886.

67. The Gospel According to St. Luke, with Maps, Notes and Introduction, p. 287.

68. See Chapter 2, Note 88.

69. Unpresidented: A Biography of Donald Trump, p. 117.

70. "Fact Check: Has Trump Declared Bankruptcy Four or Six Times?"

71. "Donald Trump's Business Plan Left a Trail of Unpaid Bills."

72. See Chapter 3, Note 56.

73. How to Save the U.S. Refugee Admissions Program, p. 1.

74. The Black Population: 2010, p. 3.

75. "Split Over Global Warming Widens Among Evangelicals."

76. What are the Two Greatest Commandments? (n.d.).

77. "The 'Great Commission' in Matthew 28:19 Is NOT What You've Been Taught."

78. Christianity, Atheism, Islam and the Need for Real Evangelical Leadership, p. 197.

79. "Why Donald Trump Is Tearing Evangelicals Apart."

80. "The Religion of Trump."

81. The Mighty and the Almighty: How Political Leaders Do God.

82. Andy Crouch, "Speak Truth to Trump."

83. See Note 81.

84. See Note 82.

85. See Note 81.

86. The Wilderness Deep Inside the Republican Party's Combative, Contentious, Chaotic Quest to Take Back the White House, p. 360.

87. Supports a general idea, "Here's What We Know So Far About Russia's 2016 Meddling."

88. Supports a general idea, "Senate Panel Backs Intelligence Agencies on Russia-Trump Conclusions."

89. Supports a general idea, Cyberwar: How Russian Hackers and Trolls Helped Elect a President: What We Don't, Can't, and Do Know.

90. Supports a general idea, The Mueller Report Illustrated: The Obstruction Investigation.

91. Protestant Presbyterian, "Presidential Candidate Donald Trump At the Family Leadership Summit."

92. Forgiveness, "Presidential Candidate Donald Trump At the Family Leadership Summit."

93. "From Divorce to Blackface: A Short History of US Political Taboos."

94. Congressional Record: Proceedings and Debates of the 86th Congress First Session, Volume 105, Part 3, p. 3482.

95. Church-State Cooperation without Domination: A New Paradigm for Church-State Relations, p. 114.

96. Unlocking V.O. Key Jr.: "Southern Politics" for the Twenty-First Century, pp. 17-18.

97. The End of White Christian America, p. 247.

98. Martin Luther King.

99. Specific term use, Divided by Faith: Evangelical Religion and the Problem of Race in America, p. 2.

100. Specific term use, Worship across the Racial Divide: Religious Music and the Multiracial Congregation, p. 4.

101. Specific term use, Healing the Racial Divide: A Catholic Racial Justice Framework Inspired by Dr. Arthur Falls.

102. Stephen Kneale, "The Myth of Self-Made Men and Self-Made Churches."

103. "Kind deed," "The Myth of Self-Made Men and Self-Made Churches."

104. "Encouragement," "The Myth of Self-Made Men and Self-Made Churches."

105. "Character," "The Myth of Self-Made Men and Self-Made Churches."

106. See Chapter 1, Note 53.

107. Neologism, John G. Cawelti, *Apostles of the Self-Made Man.*

108. Neologism, Henry Clay.

109. See Chapter 3, Note 72.

110. Lieber's Code and the Law of War, p. 2.

111. Francis Lieber, p. 41

112. Indian Education, Issues 256-360. Vol. 18, Bureau of Indian Affairs,

Education Branch   Department of The Interior, Washington, D. C., 1955, p.

158.

113. Sharing Ideas 1957 A Special Contribution: Cultural Factors in Social

Adjustment, p. 10.

114. Jews and Gentiles in Early America: 1654-1800.

115. "Is the United States of America in Bible Prophecy?"

116. Specific term use, Benjamin Franklin, *Benjamin Franklin: His Autobiography,*

p. 193.

117. See Note 40.

118. See Note 42.

119. See Note 45.

120. Specific term use, The Pharisees and the Sadducees: An Examination of

Internal Jewish History.

121. Works: Containing Several Political and Historical Tracts Not Included in Any Former Edition, and Many Letters Official and Private Not Hitherto Published. With Notes and a Life of the Author.

122. The Outcry Against the New Poor Law; Or, Who Is the Poor Man's Friend?

123. "Second land of promise," George Washington, *The Writings of George Washington: 1782-1785*, pp. 473-476.

124. "Land of promise," George Washington.

125. "Milk and honey," George Washington.

126. Reinhold Niebuhr, "The Protestant Churches and Lynching, 1919-1939."

127. Robert Moats Miller, "The Protestant Churches and Lynching, 1919-1939."

128. The Strangers Book: The Human of African American Literature.

129. God Against Slavery: And the Freedom and Duty of the Pulpit to Rebuke It, as a Sin Against God.

130. "Fighting for Public Testimony."

131. "Good Friday, Palm Sunday, Lincoln's Death and Appomattox."

132. See Note 116.

133. See Chapter 2, Note 97.

134. See Chapter 2, Note 99.

135. See Chapter 2, Note 102.

136. Langston Hughes, p. 190.

137. Trauma Trails, Recreating Song Lines: The Transgenerational Effects of Trauma in Indigenous Australia.

138. Rachel MacNair, Perpetration-Induced Traumatic Stress: The Psychological Consequences of Killing.

139. Rachel MacNair, "The Effects of Violence on Perpetrators," pp. 67–72.

140. See Note 137.

141. See Note 138.

142. See Note 139.

143. See Note 138.

144. See Note 139.

145. See Chapter 3, Note 32.

146. Campaigning for President in America, 1788-2016, p. 317.

147. Modern American Extremism and Domestic Terrorism: An Encyclopedia of Extremists and Extremist Groups, p. 1.

148. Neologism, Soul Work: Anti-Racist Theologies in Dialogue, p. 15.

149. Thomas S. Kidd, Who Is an Evangelical? The History of a Movement in Crisis, pp. 2-6.

150. Red State Christians: Understanding the Voters Who Elected Donald Trump, p. 11.

151. John Dean, Conservatives Without Conscience.

152. Neologism, Paul V. Kollman, Understanding World Christianity: Eastern Africa, p. 119.

153. Thomas S. Kidd, "How Many of the Founding Fathers Went to 'Seminary'?"

154. Harper Lee, To Kill a Mockingbird.

155. Specific term use, Why Evil Rules - If God Is -: A Question of Believers and Non-Believers Alike, p. 247.

156. Specific term use, *Gandhi and Non-Violence*, p. 147.

157. Specific term use, *Practical Pacifism*, p. 105.

158. Specific term use, The Social Psychology of Good and Evil, p. 169.

159. The Problem of Evil (Oxford Readings in Philosophy) 1st Edition.

160. See Introduction, Note 17.

161. Censura Literaria. Containing Titles, Abstracts, and Opinions of Old English Books, with Original Disquisitions, Articles of Biography, and Other Literary Antiquities, p. 396.

162. Herman Melville, p. 351.

163. Slavery in the United States: A Social, Political, and Historical Encyclopedia, p. 198.

164. *Harriet Tubman*, p. 80.

165. Alexander Milton Ross, pp. 105-106.

166. See Introduction, Note 17.

167. See Introduction, Note 17.

168. See Chapter 2, Note 96.

169. See Chapter 2, Note 96.

170. "Transcript of Northwest Ordinance (1787)."

171. See Chapter 2, Note 96.

172. See Introduction, Note 17.

173. See Introduction, Note 18.

174. See Introduction, Note 17.

175. See Note 1.

176. See Note 1.

177. The Dangerous Case of Donald Trump: 37 Psychiatrists and Mental Health Experts Assess a President: Updated and Expanded with New Essays.

178. "Perspective | In the Age of Trump, Let Psychiatrists Judge the Mental Health of Public Figures."

179. The Committee on Slavery and the Treatment of Freedmen...

180. Montesquieu.

181. See Chapter 1, Note 1.

182. See Chapter 1, Note 2.

Chapter 5

1. Sports epigraph, Los Angeles Herald, 1910.

2. Jim Crow Laws.

3. See Introduction, Note 6.

4. Specific term use, Black Dance in the United States from 1619 to 1970, p. 6.

5. Jeremiah and Lamentations Volume 2.

6. Hughley, DL (realDLHughley).

7. "Here Are Your Odds of Becoming a Professional Athlete (They're Not Good)."

8. Sport in Contemporary Society: An Anthology, p. 283.

9. "NFL Regular Season Sees Increases in TV Ad Spend, Ad Airings and Impressions."

10. "NFL Ratings Are Mostly Higher Heading into Super Bowl LIV."

11. William Shakespeare, *The Tempest*, p. 63.

12. See Introduction, Note 7.

13. "How Russian Trolls Inflamed the NFL's Anthem Controversy."

14. See Note 10.

15. See Chapter 2, Note 56.

16. Muhammad Ali: The Peoples Champ, p. 137.

17. See Note 11.

18. "A History of Boycotts of the Olympic Games."

19. A Journal of Natural Philosophy, Chemistry, and the Arts.

20. Making Sense of Bullfighting.

21. "5 Ancient African Games That Migrated to Western Societies to Become Sporting Events."

22. Framing Majismo: Art and Royal Identity in Eighteenth-Century Spain.

23. History of Sports in China.

24. Works: Life of George Washington.

25. "Watch One of George Washington's Favorite Sports in Person: Fox Hunting."

26. "Most Blessed of the Patriarchs": Thomas Jefferson and the Empire of the Imagination.

27. "Sports of the Founding Fathers."

28. The Great American Sports Book: A Casual but Voluminous Look at American Spectator Sports from the Civil War to the Present Time.

29. When Johnny Came Sliding Home: The Post-Civil War Baseball Boom, 1865-1870.

30. Etymonline.

31. Specific term use, Public Papers of the Presidents of the United States: Gerald R. Ford; Containing the Public Messages, Speeches, and Statements of the President, p. 336.

32. Sport Fans: The Psychology and Social Impact of Fandom, p. 182.

33. Merriam-Webster.com.

34. "Heisman Winner Lamar Jackson Being Overlooked Because of Lack of Diversity among College Football Writers."

35. Articulate While Black: Barack Obama, Language, and Race in the U.S, p. 186.

36. "College Football's Big Problem with Race."

37. "White Supremacists' Favorite Myths about Black Crime Rates Take Another Hit from BJS Study."

38. "Confronting Racism Is Not about the Needs and Feelings of White People."

39. Specific term use, *Communicating Politics Online*, p. 31.

40. Specific term use, The Encyclopedia of Civil Liberties in America: Volumes One-Three, p. 349.

41. To Make Men Free: A History of the Republican Party, p. 301.

42. The Federal Communications Commission: Front Line in the Culture and Regulation Wars, p. 105.

43. See Note 39.

44. See Note 40.

45. Supports a general idea, "Business-Managed Democracy."

46. Supports a general idea, Entrepreneurial Intensity: Sustainable Advantages for Individuals, Organizations, and Societies, p. 123.

47. Intrapreneuring in Action: A Handbook for Business Innovation.

48. "When Leaders Cheat, Companies Lose."

49. Specific term use, Robber Barons: The Lives and Careers of John D. Rockefeller, J.P. Morgan, Andrew Carnegie, and Cornelius Vanderbilt.

50. Historical Dictionary of the Gilded Age, pp. 81-82.

51. The American Mercury, p. 23.

52. Meet You in Hell Andrew Carnegie, Henry Clay Frick, and the Bitter Partnership That Transformed America, p. 36.

53. The American Axis: Henry Ford, Charles Lindbergh, and the Rise of the Third Reich, pp. 17-21.

54. Dissent: The History of an American Idea, p. 11.

55. Specific term use, "Presidential and Olympian Scandals: Why Are We Complicit?"

56. "The St. Pauls Riot: An Explanation of the Limits of Crowd Action in Terms of a Social Identity Model," pp. 1–21.

57. Specific term use, Pan-African Journal, 1970, p. 151.

58. Advances in Experimental Social Psychology, p. 241.

59. "Study Says Cheating May Help You Get Ahead, But You'll Lose More in The End."

60. Specific term use, Racism: from Slavery to Advanced Capitalism, pp. xiii – xiv.

61. "Radio Program Demographic Rankers."

62. Electronic Media Law, p. 259.

63. Song quote, *Sweep Around.*

64. Merriam-Webster.com.

65. "Artists 'Break the Silence' Of White Privilege At #Justice4Jamar Fundraiser."

66. Above the Law: Police and the Excessive Use of Force, p. 140.

67. The System in Black and White: Exploring the Connections between Race, Crime and Justice, p. 75.

68. Specific term use, The Supreme Court, Race and Civil Rights: from Marshall to Rehnquist, p. 403.

69. Police Attitudes toward Abuse of Authority: Findings from a National Study, p. 9.

70. Institutional Racism and Community Competence, pp. 7-9.

71. Institutional Racism: A Primer on Theory and Strategies for Social Change, p. 11.

72. Human Nature and Collective Behavior Papers in Honor of Herbert Blumer, p. 189.

73. Ethnicity, Sport, Identity: Struggles for Status, pp. 13+.

74. "Caucasians Only: Solomon Hughes, the PGA, and the 1948 St. Paul Open Golf Tournament," pp. 383–393.

75. Forbidden Fairways: African Americans and the Game of Golf, pp. 125-132.

76. "Color question," See Note 72.

77. "Color line," See Note 72.

78. "Notoriety," See Note 72.

79. "Jackie Robinson and 10 Other African American Pioneers in Sports."

80. "Marshall "Major" Taylor," See Note 72.

81. Breaking the Ice: The Black Experience in Professional Hockey, p. 177.

82. The Racial Confidence Gap in Police Performance: Survey of U.S. Adults Conducted Aug. 16 - Sept. 12, 2016.

83. Police: A Field Guide.

84. Supports a general idea, "A Study Documents the Paucity of Black Elected Prosecutors: Zero in Most States."

85. Supports a general idea, "How to Stop Mass Incarceration."

86. Do Exclusionary Rules Ensure a Fair Trial? A Comparative Perspective on Evidentiary Rules, p. 96.

87. Do Exclusionary Rules Ensure a Fair Trial?

88. Specific term use, Police State: How Americas Cops Get Away with Murder, pp. 321-322.

89. See Note 83.

90. See Note 84.

91. The Gap Between the Number of Blacks and Whites in Prison Is Shrinking.

92. Specific term use, *Morality and Cultural Differences*, p. 51.

93. Harper Lee.

94. Geoffrey Chaucer.

95. See Chapter 2, Note 61.

96. Sports Illustrated (SInow).

97. "Implicit suggestion," "Race Ideology Perpetuated: Media Representations of Newly Hired Football Coaches."

98. "Whiteness as the norm," "Race Ideology Perpetuated: Media Representations of Newly Hired Football Coaches."

99. L. P. Hartley.

100. See Note 96.

Chapter 6

Samuel Langhorne Clemons.

See Introduction, Note 6.

See Chapter 3, Note 65.

4. Thomas Jefferson, Notes on the State of Virginia.

5. "Liberty in the Air."

6. See Note 4.

7. See Note 5.

8. Friends of Liberty: Thomas Jefferson, Tadeusz Kosciuszko, and Agrippa Hull; A Tale of Three Patriots, Two Revolutions, and a Tragic Betrayal of Freedom in the New Nation.

9. Debunking Glenn Beck: How to Save America From Media Pundits and Propagandists.

10. Henry Wiencek.

11. Carter G Woodson.

12. Neologism, *Philosophy for a New Generation*, pp. 481-490.

13. Neologism, Mental Health: A Challenge to the Black Community, pp. 65-70.

14. Neologism, A Companion to African American Literature, p. 195.

15. Neologism, *Modern Peoplehood*, p. 248.

16. Neologism, The Good Society and the Inner World: Psychoanalysis, Politics and Culture, p. 76.

17. Neologism, The Oxford Handbook of Culture and Psychology, pp. 572-577.

18. Provides historical context to specific term use, "Antislavery or Abolition?" pp. 95–99.

19. Provides historical context to specific term use, *Abolitionism: A New Perspective.*

20. See Note 18.

21. See Note 19.

22. The Life and Writings of Frederick Douglass: Philip S. Foner.

23. See Note 18.

24. See Note 19.

25. See Chapter 4, Note 148.

26. See Chapter 4, Note 159.

27. Neologism, Peter A. Levine.

28. Peter A. Levine.

29. Immigration, *U.S. Department of Labor.*

30. Neologism, W. E. B. Du Bois, William L. Van Deburg, *Modern Black Nationalism: From Marcus Garvey to Louis Farrakhan,* p. 154.

31. Neologism, W. E. B. Du Bois, William L. Van Deburg.

32. Neologism, W. E. B. Du Bois.

33. Neologism, Amiri Baraka, Frances Causey, *The Long Shadow (2017).*

34. Neologism, Frederick Douglass, *The Color Line.*

35. See Chapter 4, Note 137.

36. Molly Bawn.

37. "Building the Future: Children and the Sustainable Development Goals in Rich Countries."

38. "Building the Future:"

39. See Chapter 4, Note 125.

40. Film quote, "The Challenge of Freedom," *Slavery and the Making of America.*

41. Provides historical context to specific term use, *Belgravia: A London Magazine,* p. 325.

42. Moral Psychology with Nietzsche.

43. See Introduction, Note 10.

44. See Note 39.

45. Public Speaking Super Powers: Unleash Your Inner Speaking Superhero and Communicate Your Message with Confidence.

46. See Chapter 4, Note 40.

47. Supports a general idea, "Frequency and the Conference of Referential Validity," pp. 107–112.

48. Supports a general idea, "People with Easier to Pronounce Names Promote Truthiness of Claims."

49. Supports a general idea, "Making up History: False Memories of Fake News Stories."

50. See Chapter 4, Note 40.

51. See Chapter 4, Note 138.

52. See Chapter 4, Note 139.

53. See Note 22.

54. Toni Bell, "If Trump Wins."

55. "Author Argues for the Value of Being 'Antiracist'."

56. See Chapter 1, Note 86.

57. See Chapter 3, Note 65.

58. Robert Southey.

59. Racism Essential Readings, p. 184.

60. "The Social Construction of Whiteness: Racism by Intent, Racism by Consequence," pp. 649–673.

61. The Resolution of Conflict: Constructive and Destructive Processes.

62. Leo Tolstoy.

63. Sun Tzu, *The Art of War.*

64. See Note 26.

65. Combat Stress Reaction: The Enduring Toll of War, p. 51.

66. "Unnecessary projects," Sun Tzu, *The Art of War.*

67. "Easily changeable," Sun Tzu, *The Art of War.*

68. "Ripe for attach," Sun Tzu, *The Art of War.*

69. See Note 56.

70. "How a Weird Law Gives One Group American Nationality but Not Citizenship."

71. See Chapter 3, Note 32.

72. See Chapter 3, Note 32.

73. See Chapter 3, Note 32.

74. See Note 22.

75. See Note 26.

76. Encyclopedia of the Middle Passage.

77. Literary device, Dylan Thomas, Mary Rives Bowman, *The Adventures in Literature Program,* p. 695.

78. See Note 138.

79. See Note 139.

80. "What A Real President Was Like."

81. "The Psychology of Racism."

82. "The Great Migration, 1910 to 1970."

83. Lexico Dictionaries.

84. Caleb Bingham.

85. "Wretched condition," See Chapter 2, Note 43.

86. "Horrible pit," See Chapter 2, Note 43.

87. No ladder," See Chapter 2, Note 43.

88. "Record Numbers of Americans Want to Leave the U.S."

89. "James 1:22."

90. Merriam-Webster.com.

WORKS CITED

"1776-1865: From Bondage to Holy War." *Pbs.org*, Public Broadcasting Service.

A Review of Doct; Emmons's Theory of God's Agency on Mankind, Addressed to the Congregational Clergy of New England: Also, a Refutation of the Views ... of the Moral Evil Existing in the Universe. John Sayre, 1821.

"About the Electors." National Archives and Records Administration, National Archives and Records Administration, www.archives.gov/electoral-college/electors.

Abraham, Anslie H. *Why Evil Rules - If God Is -: A Question of Believers and Non-Believers Alike.* Xlibris, 2011, p. 247.

Abrams, Abigail. "Here's What We Know So Far About Russia's 2016 Meddling." *Time*, Time, 18 Apr. 2019, time.com/5565991/russia-influence-2016-election/.

Ackroyd, Peter. *Shakespeare: The Biography.* Chatto and Windus, 2005.

Acts and Joint Resolutions of the General Assembly of the State of South Passed at The Annual Session of 1864. Julian A. Selby, Printer to the State, 1866, p. 10.

Adams, James Truslow. *The Epic of America.* Little, Brown and Company, 1931, pp. 415-416.

Adams, John Francis, and Charles Francis Adams. *The Works of John Adams Second President of the United States.* Vol. 4, Bolles and Houghton, 1851.

Adams, Marilyn McCord., and Robert Merrihew Adams. *The Problem of Evil (Oxford*

    Readings in Philosophy) 1st Edition. Oxford University Press, 1991.

Adgate, Brad. "NFL Ratings Are Mostly Higher Heading Into Super Bowl

    LIV." *Forbes*, Forbes Magazine, 29 Jan. 2020,

    www.forbes.com/sites/bradadgate/2020/01/22/nfl-ratings-are-mostly-

    higher-heading-into-super-bowl-liv/#2ffe00df1216.

Adolphe, Jane, et al. *St. Paul, the Natural Law, and Contemporary Legal Theory.*

    Lexington Books, 2012.

"Aerobic." Merriam-Webster.com. Merriam-Webster, 2020.

Aiton, Katie Scott. "A History of Boycotts of the Olympic Games." *Matador*

    Network, https://matadornetwork.com/sports/a-history-of-boycotts-of-

    the-olympic-games/.

Alim, H. Samy., and Geneva Smitherman. *Articulate While Black: Barack Obama,*

    Language, and Race in the U.S. Oxford University Press, 2012, p. 186.

"All's well that ends well." Merriam-Webster.com. Merriam-Webster, 2020.

Allen, Theodore W. Class Struggle and the Origin of Racial Slavery: The Invention

    of the White Race. New England Free Press, 1976.

Amadeo, Kimberly. "Compare Today's Unemployment with the Past." The

    Balance, The Balance, 7 Feb. 2020,

    www.thebalance.com/unemployment-rate-by-year-3305506.

American Economist, Volumes 11-12. The American Protective Tariff League, 1893.

Ansolabehere, Stephen, and Eitan D. Hersh. *ADGN: An Algorithm for Record*

    Linkage Using Address, Date of Birth, Gender, and Name. 2017.

Arthur, Karen, director. *The Jacksons: an American Dream*. 1992.

Artiga, Samantha, et al. *Changes in Health Coverage by Race and Ethnicity since Implementation of the ACA, 2013- 2017*. 2019.

Atkinson, Judy. *Trauma Trails, Recreating Song Lines: The Transgenerational Effects of Trauma in Indigenous Australia*. Spinifex Press, 2002.

"Author Argues for the Value of Being 'Antiracist'." *Morning Joe*, SiriusXM 118, 14 Aug. 2019.

Axt, Jordan R., et al. "The Rules of Implicit Evaluation by Race, Religion, and Age." *Psychological Science*, vol. 25, no. 9, 2014, pp. 1804–1815.

"Backstory." Merriam-Webster.com. Merriam-Webster, 2020.

Bailey, Garrick, and James Peoples. *Essentials of Cultural Anthropology*. Wadsworth, Cengage Learning, 2014, p. 229.

Baker, C. Truett. *Church-State Cooperation without Domination: A New Paradigm for Church-State Relations*. Xlibris US, 2010, p. 114.

Balleck, Barry J. *Modern American Extremism and Domestic Terrorism: An Encyclopedia of Extremists and Extremist Groups*. ABC-CLIO, 2018, p. 1.

Balmer, Randall Herbert. *Thy Kingdom Come: How the Religious Right Distorts the Faith and Threatens America; an Evangelicals Lament*. Basic Books, 2007.

---. "The Real Origins of the Religious Right." *POLITICO Magazine*, 27 May 2014.

Barbarin, Oscar A. *Institutional Racism and Community Competence*. United States Department of Health and Human Services, Public Health Service, Alcohol, Drug Abuse, and Mental Health Administration, National

Institute of Mental Health, Center for Minority Group Mental Health

Programs, 1982, pp. 7-9.

Barmash, Isadore. *The Self-Made Man: Success and Stress-American Style*. Beard Books,

2003, p. 10.

Barnes, Jonathan. *The Complete Works of Aristotle*. Translated by Benjamin Jowett,

Princeton University Press, 1998.

Bartlett, Robert, et al. "Consumer-Lending Discrimination in the FinTech Era."

2019.

Bassett, C. Jeanne. "House Bill 591: Florida Compensates Rosewood Victims and

Their Families for a Seventy-One-Year-Old Injury." *Scholarship Repository*.

Bates, Katharine Lee. *America the Beautiful: And Other Poems*. Thomas Y. Crowell

Company, 1911.

Batra, N. D. *A Self-Renewing Society: The Role of Television and Communications

Technology*. University Press of America, 1990, p. 85.

Bauer, Elizabeth. "Yes, Social Security Is An 'Entitlement'." Forbes, Forbes

Magazine, 5 Nov. 2018,

www.forbes.com/sites/ebauer/2018/11/05/yes-social-security-is-an-

entitlement/#ab46c54500da.

Bayer, Patrick, and Kerwin Kofi Charles. *Divergent Paths: Structural Change, Economic

Rank, and the Evolution of Black-White Earnings Differences, 1940-2014*. 2017.

Beaton, Andrew. "How Russian Trolls Inflamed the NFL's Anthem

Controversy." The Wall Street Journal, Dow Jones and Company, 22

Oct. 2018, https://www.wsj.com/articles/how-russian-trolls-inflamed-nfls-anthem-controversy-1540233979.

Belgravia: A London Magazine. United Kingdom, Chatto and Windus, 1884, p. 325.

Bell, Toni. "If Trump Wins." *The Body Is Not An Apology*, 10 Nov. 2016.

Berman, Robby. "It's Your Brain's Fault You Make the Same Mistakes Over and Over." *Big Think*, Big Think, 3 May 2019, https://bigthink.com/robby-berman/its-your-brains-fault-you-make-the-same-mistakes-over-and-over.

Berzon, Alexandra. "Donald Trump's Business Plan Left a Trail of Unpaid Bills." The Wall Street Journal, Dow Jones and Company, 9 June 2016, www.wsj.com/articles/donald-trumps-business-plan-left-a-trail-of-unpaid-bills-1465504454.

Better, Shirley. *Institutional Racism: A Primer on Theory and Strategies for Social Change.* Rowman and Littlefield Publishers, 2008, p. 11.

Bierman, A. K., and James A. Gould. *Philosophy for a New Generation.* Macmillan, 1981, pp. 481-490.

Bingham, Caleb. *The Columbian Orator: Containing a Variety of Original and Selected Pieces; Together with Rules; Calculated to Improve Youth and Others in the Ornamental and Useful Art of Eloquence.* Printed by Manning and Loring, for the Author, Etc., 1804.

Bird, Wendell R. *Press and Speech Under Assault: The Early Supreme Court Justices, the Sedition Act of 1798, and the Campaign Against Dissent.* Oxford University Press, 2016, p. 473.

Blackmun, Harry A, and Supreme Court of The United States. *U.S. Reports: Roe v.*

    Wade, 410 U.S. 113. 1972. Periodical. Retrieved from the Library of

    Congress, <www.loc.gov/item/usrep410113/>.

Blumer, Herbert. *Human Nature and Collective Behavior Papers in Honor of Herbert*

    Blumer. Edited by Tamotsu Shibutani, Transaction Books, 1973, p. 189.

Bongmba, Elias Kifon, editor. *Routledge Companion to Christianity in Africa.* Taylor

    and Francis, 2015.

Boorstein, Michelle. "Why Donald Trump Is Tearing Evangelicals Apart." The

    Washington Post, WP Company, 15 Mar. 2016,

    www.washingtonpost.com/news/acts-of-

    faith/wp/2016/03/15/evangelical-christians-are-enormously-divided-

    over-donald-trumps-runaway-candidacy/.

Borman, William. *Gandhi and Non-Violence.* State University of New York Press,

    1986, p. 147.

Bowens-Wheatley, Marjorie, and Nancy Palmer. Jones. *Soul Work: Anti-Racist*

    Theologies in Dialogue. Skinner House Books, 2003, p. 15.

Bowman, Mary Rives. *The Adventures in Literature Program.* Harcourt Brace and

    World, 1963, p. 695.

Boyd, James. "Nixon's Southern Strategy 'It's All In the Charts'." *New York Times,*

    17 May 1970.

Bradley, Joseph P, and Supreme Court of the United States. *U.S. Reports: Civil*

    Rights Cases, 109 U.S. 3. 1883. Periodical. Retrieved from the Library of

    Congress, <www.loc.gov/item/usrep109003/>.

Branch, Taylor. *Pillar of Fire: America in the King Years, 1963-65*. Simon and

Schuster, 1999.

Brockenbrough, Martha. *Unpresidented: A Biography of Donald Trump*. Feiwel and

Friends, 2018, p. 117.

Brown, Nikki L. M., and Barry M. Stentiford. *The Jim Crow Encyclopedia: Greenwood

Milestones in African American History*. Greenwood Press, 2008, p. 84.

Brydges, Egerton. *Censura Literaria. Containing Titles, Abstracts, and Opinions of Old

English Books, with Original Disquisitions, Articles of Biography, and Other

Literary Antiquities*. II, T. Bensley, 1807, p. 396.

Business Insider. "Animated map shows how Christianity spread around the

world." YouTube, 14 Aug. 2015, https://youtu.be/BJ0dZhHccfU.

"Business-Managed Democracy." *Business-Managed Culture - Wealth as Reward - Myth

of the Self-Made Man*,

www.herinst.org/BusinessManagedDemocracy/culture/wealth/self-

made.html.

Cashmore, Ernest, and James Jennings, editors. *Racism Essential Readings*. Sage,

2001, p. 184.

Causey, Frances, director. *The Long Shadow (2017)*. 2017.

Caves, Roger W. *Encyclopedia of the City*. Routledge, 2013, p. 418.

Cawelti, John G. *Apostles of the Self-Made Man*. University of Chicago Press, 1965.

CDC - Lice - Head Lice - General Information - Frequently Asked Questions

(FAQs)." *Cdc.gov*, Centers for Disease Control and Prevention,

https://www.cdc.gov/parasites/lice/head/gen_info/faqs.html.

Chappell, David L. *Stone of Hope - Prophetic Religion and the Death of Jim Crow*. The

University Of North Carolina, 2004, p. 105.

"Chapter CXXVIII. An Act to Define and Declare the Rights of Persons Lately

Known as Slaves, and Free Persons of Color." 1866.

"Character." Merriam-Webster.com. Merriam-Webster, 2020.

Charles River Editors, editor. *Robber Barons: The Lives and Careers of John D.*

Rockefeller, J.P. Morgan, Andrew Carnegie, and Cornelius Vanderbilt.

CreateSpace Independent Publishing Platform, 2016.

Charles, Mark, and Soong-Chan Rah. *Unsettling Truths: The Ongoing, Dehumanizing*

Legacy of the Doctrine of Discovery. IVP, an Imprint of InterVarsity Press,

2019, pp. 58-66.

Chaucer, Geoffrey. *Canterbury Tales*. United Kingdom, Kegan Paul, Trench and

Company, 1886, p. 51.

Cheever, George B. *God Against Slavery: And the Freedom and Duty of the Pulpit to*

Rebuke It, as a Sin Against God. American Reform Tract and Book Society,

1857.

Chetty, Raj, et al. "Race and Economic Opportunity in the United States: An

Intergenerational Perspective." 2018.

Clarke, Duncan. *Empires of Oil: Corporate Oil in Barbarian Worlds*. Profile Books,

2007.

Clarke, John Henrik, et al. *Marcus Garvey and the Vision of Africa*. Black Classic

Press, 2011, p. XVII.

Clay, Henry. *The Speeches of Henry Clay, Volume 1*. A. S. Barnes and Company, 1857.

Clemens, Samuel Langhorne, and John Sutton. TUCKEY. *Mark Twains Which Was*

   the Dream? and Other Symbolic Writings of the Later Years. Edited with an

   Introduction by John S. Tuckey. Berkeley and Los Angeles, 1967.

Coates, Julia. *Trail of Tears (Landmarks of the American Mosaic).* Greenwood, 2014, p.

   202.

Coffman, Elesha. "What Does History Say about the First Christians of

   Africa?" Christian History | Learn the History of Christianity & the

   Church, Christian History, 30 July 2019,

   https://www.christianitytoday.com/history/2008/august/what-does-

   history-say-about-first-christians-of-africa.html.

Cohen, Elliot D. "Two Concepts of Oppression." *Psychology Today*, Sussex

   Publishers, 27 Nov. 2014.

Collier, John. *The Indians of the Americas.* W.W. Norton, 1947.

"Colonial Enslavement of Native Americans Included Those Who Surrendered,

   Too." *Brown University*, 15 Feb. 2017, www.brown.edu/news/2017-02-

   15/enslavement.

Congressional Record: Proceedings and Debates of the 86th Congress First Session, Volume

   105, Part 3. United States Government Printing Office, 1959, p. 3482.

Conrad, Cecilia A., et al. *African Americans in the U.S. Economy.* Rowman and

   Littlefield Pub., 2005.

Cook, John W. *Morality and Cultural Differences.* Oxford University Press, 1999, p.

   51.

Correia, David, and Tyler Wall. *Police: A Field Guide.* Verso Books, 2017.

Craemer, Thomas. *Estimating Slavery Reparations: Present Value Comparisons of*

   Historical Multigenerational Reparations Policies. 2nd ed., vol. 96, 2015.

Crouch, Andy. "Speak Truth to Trump." ChristianityToday.com, Christianity

   Today, 10 Oct. 2016, www.christianitytoday.com/ct/2016/October-

   web-only/speak-truth-to-trump.html.

Cunningham, George B., and Trevor Bopp. "Race Ideology Perpetuated: Media

   Representations of Newly Hired Football Coaches." Journal of Sports

   Media, vol. 5, no. 1, 2010.

Daley-Harris, Shannon, et al. *Our Day to End Poverty.* Berrett-Koehler Publishers,

   2007, p. 199.

Dao, Zhi. *History of Sports in China.* DeepLogic.

Davidson, Robert. *Jeremiah and Lamentations Volume 2.* The Saint Andrew Press and

   John Knox Press, 1985.

Davis, Abraham L., and Barbara Luck. Graham. *The Supreme Court, Race and Civil*

   Rights: from Marshall to Rehnquist. Sage Publications, 1995, p. 403.

Davis, David Brion, and Gerald Sorin. "Antislavery or Abolition?" *Reviews in*

   American History, vol. 1, no. 1, 1973, pp. 95–99.

Dean, John W. *Conservatives Without Conscience.* Penguin Books; Reprint Edition,

   2007

"Debates, Columbus, Sexism, and Racism." *Inside the Issues with Wilmer Leon,* Urban

   View, 19 Oct. 2019.

Deggans, Eric. *Race-Baiter: How the Media Wields Dangerous Words to Divide a Nation.*

   Palgrave Macmillan, 2012.

DellaVigna, Stefano, and Eliana La Ferrara. *Economic and Social Impacts of the Media.*

    2015.

Denker, Angela. *Red State Christians: Understanding the Voters Who Elected Donald*

    Trump. Fortress Press, 2019, p. 11.

"Desperate Measures." *Burn Notice,* season 6, episode 11, USA Network, 8 Nov.

    2012.

Detweiler, Frederick G. "The Anglo-Saxon Myth in the United States." *American*

    Sociological Review, vol. 3, no. 2, 1938, p. 183.

Deutsch, Morton. *The Resolution of Conflict: Constructive and Destructive Processes.* Yale

    University Press, 1973.

DiAngelo, Robin. *Summary & Analysis: White Fragility; Why It's So Hard for White*

    People to Talk about Racism. Beacon Press, 2018.

Dickey, J. D. *Empire of Mud: The Secret History of Washington, DC.* Lyons Press, an

    Imprint of Rowman and Littlefield, 2016, p. 69.

"District of Columbia Emancipation Act of 1862." *C-SPAN3 American History*

    TV, C-SPAN3, 16 Apr. 2019.

"District of Columbia Emancipation Act of 1862." *C-SPAN3 American History*

    TV, C-SPAN3, 16 Apr. 2019.

"Doing Our Own Work: A Seminar for Anti-Racist White Women." The Leaven

    Center, 2003.

Douglass, Frederick. *Narrative of the Life of Frederick Douglass, An American Slave.*

    Anti-Slavery Office, 1845.

---. *The Color Line (1881)*. CreateSpace Independent Publishing Platform, 27 March

2012.

Doyle, Sir Arthur Conan. "Chapter 10." *The Sign of the Four*, 1890, p. 196.

Drinjakovic, Jovana. "Our Hearts Start Beating Before They're Fully

Formed." *Vice*, 13 Oct. 2016,

https://www.vice.com/en_us/article/aekyzj/our-hearts-start-beating-

before-theyre-fully-formed.

Du Bois, William Edward Burghardt. *The Souls of Black Folk: Essays and Sketches*. A.

C. McClurg and Company, 1907.

"dum vivimus vivamus." Merriam-Webster.com. Merriam-Webster, 2020.

Duncombe, Giles. *Tryals Per Pais in Capital Matters: Or, Some Brief and Useful

Observations Relating to Such Tryals*. Printed by the Affigns of Richard and

Edward Atkins Efquires, 1702.

Earle, Alice Morse. *Sabbath in Puritan New England*. Charles Scribner's Sons, 1891.

Eastland, Terry. "The Religion of Trump." Washington Examiner, 15 Jan. 2016,

www.washingtonexaminer.com/weekly-standard/the-religion-of-trump.

Eitzen, D. Stanley. *Sport in Contemporary Society: An Anthology*. Oxford University

Press, 2014, p. 283.

Elmesky, Rowhea, et al. *The Power of Resistance: Culture, Ideology and Social Reproduction

in Global Contexts*. Emerald Publishing, 2017.

Emerson, Michael O., and Christian Smith. *Divided by Faith: Evangelical Religion and

the Problem of Race in America*. Oxford University Press, 2000, p. 2.

Emery, Lynne F. *Black Dance in the United States from 1619 to 1970*. Dance Books,

    1988, p. 6.

Emmerich, Roland, director. *Independence Day*. Twentieth Century Fox, 1996.

"Entering and Exiting the British Empire." The British Empire,

    https://www.britishempire.co.uk/timeline/colonies.htm.

Ericson, David F. *The Debate Over Slavery: Antislavery and Proslavery Liberalism in*

    Antebellum America. New York University Press, 2001.

Erikson, Erik H. "The Problem of Ego Identity." *The Life Cycle*, 1981, pp. 189–

    198.

Espín Orlando O. *An Introductory Dictionary of Theology and Religious Studies*. Columba

    Press, 2007.

Evans, William David, et al. *A Collection of Statutes Connected with the General*

    Administration of the Law; Arranged According to the Order of Subjects: With

    Notes. E. Lumley, 1836.

Exshaw, John. *The Gentleman's and London Magazine: Or Monthly Chronologer*. 1787.

"Fact Check: Has Trump Declared Bankruptcy Four or Six Times?" The

    Washington Post, WP Company,

    www.washingtonpost.com/politics/2016/live-updates/general-

    election/real-time-fact-checking-and-analysis-of-the-first-presidential-

    debate/fact-check-has-trump-declared-bankruptcy-four-or-six-times/.

Falola, Toyin, and Amanda Warnock. *Encyclopedia of the Middle Passage*. Greenwood

    Press, 2007.

Fandos, Nicholas. "A Study Documents the Paucity of Black Elected Prosecutors:

   Zero in Most States." The New York Times, The New York Times, 7

   July 2015, www.nytimes.com/2015/07/07/us/a-study-documents-the-

   paucity-of-black-elected-prosecutors-zero-in-most-states.html?_r=0.

Farrar, Frederic William. *The Gospel According to St. Luke, with Maps, Notes and*

   Introduction. Cambridge University Press, 1882, p. 287.

Feagin, Joe R. The White Racial Frame Centuries of Racial Framing and Counter-

   Framing. Routledge, 2013.

Fehrenbach, Margaret J., and Susan W. Herring. *Illustrated Anatomy of the Head and*

   Neck - E-Book. Saunders, 2013, p. 134.

Ferguson, John. *Clement of Alexandria.* Twayne Publishers, 1974.

Ferguson, Niall. "Empires with Expiration Dates." *Foreign Policy*, 14 Oct. 2009,

   foreignpolicy.com/2009/10/14/empires-with-expiration-dates/.

Ferraro, Gary. *Cultural Anthropology: An Applied Perspective.* Thomson Wadsworth,

   2008, p. 283.

Fiala, Andrew G. *Practical Pacifism.* Algora Publishing New York, 2004, p. 105.

"Fight News Is Followed by Race Riots In Many Parts of the Country." Los

   Angeles Herald, 5 July 1910.

"Fighting For Public Testimony." *All The Difference*, 24 Oct. 2010.

"Fissile." Merriam-Webster.com. Merriam-Webster, 2020.

Fleming, Walter Lynwood. Documentary History of Reconstruction, Political,

   Military, Social, Religious, Educational and Industrial 1865 to the Present

   Time. Arthur H. Clark Co.: Cleveland, Ohio, 1906, p. 279.

Fogel, Robert William., and Stanley L. Engerman. *Time on the Cross: The Economics of*

   American Negro Slavery. Little, Brown and Company, 1974.

Foley, Barbara. *Spectres of 1919: Class and Nation in the Making of the New Negro.*

   University of Illinois Press, 2008.

Foner, Eric. "The Gilder Lehrman Institute of American History." *Civil War and*

   Reconstruction, 1861-1877 | Gilder Lehrman Institute of American History,

   www.gilderlehrman.org/history-now/essays/civil-war-and-

   reconstruction-1861-1877.

Foner, Philip S. *The Life and Writings of Frederick Douglass: Philip S. Foner.*

   International Publishers, 1950.

Ford, Lacy K. *Deliver Us from Evil: The Slavery Question in the Old South.* Oxford

   University Press, 2011, p. 202.

Ford, Paul Leicester. *The True George Washington.* J.B. Lippincott Company, 1897.

Fordney, Chris. "Keying In To History." *National Parks,* 2000.

Fosslien, Liz, and Duffy, Mollie West. *No Hard Feelings: The Secret Power of*

   Embracing Emotions at Work. United States, Penguin Random House

   LLC, 2019, p. 185.

Fox News (FoxNews). "If you're a multi-millionaire who feels oppressed, you

   need a therapist, not a publicity stunt.

   https://twitter.com/FoxNews/status/912031326685089792." 24

   September 2017, 12:09 p.m. Tweet.

Fox, John. *Fox's Book of Martyrs.* E. C. Biddle, 1840.

Franklin, Benjamin, and H. Hastings Weld. *Benjamin Franklin: His Autobiography.*

    Harper and Bros., 1849, p. 193.

Franklin, Benjamin, and Jared Sparks. *Works: Containing Several Political and Historical*

    Tracts Not Included in Any Former Edition, and Many Letters Official and Private

    Not Hitherto Published. With Notes and a Life of the Author. Benjamin

    Franklin Stevens, 1882.

Freire, Paulo. *Pedagogy of the Oppressed.* English Language ed., 1970.

Frey, Rebecca Joyce., and Dori Laub. *Genocide and International Justice.* Facts On File,

    2009, p. 132.

Friedheim, William. *Freedoms Unfinished Revolution: An Inquiry into the Civil War and*

    Reconstruction. New Press, 1996, p. 13.

Friedland, Roger, and A. F. Robertson. *Beyond the Marketplace: Rethinking Economy*

    and Society. Aldine De Gruyter, 1990, p. 3.

"Friedrich Dürrenmatt Quotes." *BrainyQuote*, Xplore.

Gary, Lawrence E. *Mental Health: A Challenge to the Black Community.* Dorrance,

    1978, pp. 65-70.

Genovese, E. D. *Roll, Jordan, Roll: The World the Slaves Made.* Vintage Books, 1976.

Gerbner, Katharine. *Christian Slavery: Conversion and Race in the Protestant Atlantic*

    World. University of Pennsylvania Press, 2018.

Gilmore, Glenda Elizabeth. *Defying Dixie: The Radical Roots of Civil Rights, 1919-*

    1950. Norton, 2009, p. 108.

Gipe, George. *The Great American Sports Book: A Casual but Voluminous Look at American Spectator Sports from the Civil War to the Present Time.* Doubleday, 1978.

Gish, Steven D. *Desmond Tutu: A Biography.* Greenwood Press, 2004.

Glenn, Jerry. "Faith, Love, and the Tragic Conflict in Hochhuth's 'Der Stellvertreter.'" German Studies Review, vol. 7, no. 3, 1984, pp. 481–498. JSTOR, www.jstor.org/stable/1428886.

Gless, Sabine, and Thomas Richter, editors. *Do Exclusionary Rules Ensure a Fair Trial? A Comparative Perspective on Evidentiary Rules.* Springer International Publishing, 2019, p. 96.

"Glossary Term: Entitlement." U.S. Senate: Glossary Term: Entitlement, 19 Jan. 2018, www.senate.gov/reference/glossary_term/entitlement.htm.

Gone In 60 Seconds. 2000.

Goodwin, William, et al. *An Introduction to Forensic Genetics.* John Wiley and Sons, 2007.

Gordon-Reed, Annette, and Peter S. Onuf. *"Most Blessed of the Patriarchs": Thomas Jefferson and the Empire of the Imagination.* Liveright Publishing Corporation, 2017.

Gorn, Elliott J. *Muhammad Ali: The Peoples Champ.* University of Illinois Press, 1995, p. 137.

Gorski, Philip S. *AMERICAN BABYLON: Christianity and Democracy before and after Trump.* Routledge, 2020, pp. 62-63.

Govan, Thomas P. "Was Plantation Slavery Profitable?" The Journal of Southern

    History, vol. 8, no. 4, Nov. 1942.

Green, Michael D. *The Politics of Indian Removal: Creek Government and Society in Crisis.*

    University of Nebraska Press, 1985.

Greenberg, David. "From Divorce to Blackface: A Short History of US Political

    Taboos." Politico, 10 Feb. 2019, www.politico.eu/article/from-divorce-

    to-blackface-a-short-history-of-us-political-taboos/.

Griffith, Samuel B. *The Art of War.* United Kingdom, Oxford University

    Press, 1963, pp. 111-158.

Grubbs, Donald. *Cry from the Cotton: The Southern Tenant Farmers' Union and the New*

    Deal. The University of Arkansas Press Fayetteville, 2000.

Guess, Teresa J. "The Social Construction of Whiteness: Racism by Intent,

    Racism by Consequence." *Critical Sociology*, vol. 32, no. 4, 2006, pp. 649–

    673.

"H-1B Program." *U.S. Department of Labor,*

    www.dol.gov/agencies/whd/immigration/h1b.

Hajnal, Zoltan, et al. "Voter Identification Laws and the Suppression of Minority

    Votes." *The Journal of Politics*, vol. 79, no. 2, 2017.

Hall, Russell E. "American Presbyterian Churches—A Genealogy, 1706–1982."

    Journal of Presbyterian History, 1982.

Hammond, Scott John, et al. *Campaigning for President in America, 1788-2016.*

    Greenwood, 2016, p. 317.

Harper's New Monthly Magazine, Volume 5. Harper and Brothers Publishers, 1852, p.
    839.

Harrell, David Edwin. *Pat Robertson: A Personal, Religious, and Political Portrait*.
    Harper and Row, 1987, p. 203.

Harris, Cecil. *Breaking the Ice the Black Experience in Professional Hockey*. Insomniac
    Press, 2003, p. 177.

Harris, Sydney J. *Strictly Personal*. H. Regnery Company, 1953.

Hartigan, Richard Shelly. *Lieber's Code and the Law of War*. Precedent, 1983, p. 2.

Hartley, L.P. *The Go-Between*. Hamish Hamilton, 1953.

Hartman, Chester, and Gregory Squires. *From Foreclosure to Fair Lending: Advocacy,
    Organizing, Occupy, and the Pursuit of Equitable Credit*. New Village Press,
    2013.

Hasher, Lynn, et al. "Frequency and the Conference of Referential
    Validity." *Journal of Verbal Learning and Verbal Behavior*, vol. 16, no. 1,
    1977, pp. 107–112.

"'He Was a Man of His Times.'" *The Prime Directive*, 5 Feb. 2009,
    https://francoistremblay.wordpress.com/2009/02/21/he-was-a-man-
    of-his-times/.

Healey, Joseph F. *Diversity and Society: Race, Ethnicity, and Gender*. Pine Forge Press,
    2010, p. 144.

Heber, Reginald, 1783-1826. Heber's Hymns: Illustrated. London: Sampson Low,
    Son, and Marston, 1867.

Hee Haw. CBS. CBS, Nashville. 1969-1997. Television.

Helfand, Michael. "To Understand America - Read the Bible." *The Forward*, 2 July

2019, https://forward.com/life/faith/426832/to-understand-america-

read-the-bible/.

Henley, Nancy, and Barrie Thorne. *She Said/He Said: An Annotated Bibliography of*

Sex Difference in Language, Speech, and Nonverbal Communication. Know, 1975.

Hickson, Mark, and Larry Powell. *The Political Blame Game in American Democracy.*

Lexington Books, 2017, p. 61.

Higgins, Andrew. "Split Over Global Warming Widens Among

Evangelicals." The Wall Street Journal, Dow Jones and Company, 28

Sept. 2007, www.wsj.com/articles/SB119094053528242085.

Hill, Christopher. *The English Bible and the Seventeenth-Century Revolution.* Penguin,

1994.

Himma, Kenneth Einar, and Brian Bix. *Law and Morality.* Routledge, 2016, p. 25.

Himmelstein, Jerome L. *To the Right: The Transformation of American Conservatism.*

Univ. of California Press, 1992.

Hochhuth, Rolf. *The Deputy, a Christian Tragedy.* Translated by Clara Winston,

Grove Press, 1964.

Hornsey, Matthew J. "Dissent and Deviance in Intergroup Contexts." *Current*

Opinion in Psychology, vol. 11, 2016, pp. 1–5.

Hosenball, Mark. "Senate Panel Backs Intelligence Agencies on Russia-Trump

Conclusions." Reuters, Thomson Reuters, 3 July 2018,

www.reuters.com/article/us-usa-trump-russia-cyber/senate-panel-backs-

intelligence-agencies-on-russia-trump-conclusions-idUSKBN1JT2YB.

Hosseinpour, Reza. *Making Sense of Bullfighting*. Punto Rojo Libros S.L., 2014.

"How Many Israelites Left Egypt in the Exodus?" GotQuestions.org, 13 Sept.

   2016.

How to Save the U.S. Refugee Admissions Program. International Crisis Group, 2018, p.

   1.

Howard, M. W. *The American Plutocracy*. Holland Publishing Company, 1895, pp.

   126-127.

Hughes, Langston, et al. *The Collected Poems of Langston Hughes*. Vintage Classics,

   1994, p. 190.

Hughley, DL (realDLHughley). "The #NFL would rather a black man have

   #Concussion than a #Conscience! But they'll accept drug dealers,

   murderers, and wife beaters–I ain't gotta tell y'all some of you guys are

   #CowboyFans! #TeamDl.

   https://twitter.com/RealDLHughley/status/1092112894324400129." 3

   February 2019, 9:29 a.m. Tweet.

Humphrey, Norman Daymond. "American Race Relations and the Caste System."

   Psychiatry, vol. 8, no. 4, 1945.

Hungerford, Margaret Wolfe. *Molly Bawn*. 1878.

Huntington, Samuel P. *The Clash of Civilizations and the Remaking of World Order*.

   Penguin, 1997.

Huprich, Steven. "Presidential and Olympian Scandals: Why Are We

   Complicit?" Psychology Today, Sussex Publishers, 26 Jan. 2018,

   www.psychologytoday.com/us/blog/personality-matters/201801/presidential-and-olympian-scandals-why-are-we-

complicit.

Hyslop, James H. *The Elements of Ethics*. C. Scribner's Sons, 1905.

I'm a Fruit Inspector Because Jesus Told Christians to Judge Righteous Judgment. 23 Jan.

2017, reformedblogging.blogspot.com/2017/01/im-fruit-inspector-

because-jesus-told.html.

Indian Education, Issues 256-360. Vol. 18, Bureau of Indian Affairs, Education

Branch Department of The Interior, Washington, D. C., 1955, p. 158.

"Inequality - Status and Power." *Status and Power - Age, Aging, Job, Social, Differences,*

and Age - JRank Articles, medicine.jrank.org/pages/905/Inequality-Status-

power.html.

"Inequality, Equality, and Equity." *Psychology Today*, Sussex Publishers, 7 Mar. 2019,

www.psychologytoday.com/us/blog/unseen-and-

unheard/201903/inequality-equality-and-equity.

Innocenti Report Card 14. "Building the Future: Children and the Sustainable

Development Goals in Rich Countries." UNICEF Office of Research

(2017). Print.

Irving, Washington. *Works: Life of George Washington*. G. P. Putnam, 1860.

Irwin, Katherine, and Karen Umemoto. *Jacked Up and Unjust: Pacific Islander Teens*

Confront Violent Legacies. University of California Press, 2016, p. 154.

"Is the United States of America in Bible Prophecy?" *GotQuestions.org*, 9 Nov.

2004.

Izzo, Paul F. "Cicero and Political Expediency." *The Classical Weekly*, vol. 42, no.

11, 1949, pp. 168–172. *JSTOR*, www.jstor.org/stable/4342549.

Jackson, Frank. "Functionalism, Moral." *International Encyclopedia of Ethics*, 2013.

Jacobs, Tom. "The Idea of Racial Hierarchy Remains Entrenched." *Pacific*

Standard, 1 Aug. 2014, psmag.com/books-and-culture/study-suggests-

racial-hierarchy-remains-entrenched-americans-psyches-87225.

Jacobson, Matthew Frye. *Whiteness of a Different Color: European Immigrants and the*

Alchemy of Race. Harvard University Press, 1998.

"James 1:22." *The Passion Translation*, BroadStreet Publishing Group, LLC., 2017.

James 5 Commentary - People's New Testament." *Bible Study Tools*,

www.biblestudytools.com/commentaries/peoples-new-

testament/james/5.html.

James, Geoffrey. "When Leaders Cheat, Companies Lose." Inc.com, Inc., 10 Feb.

2014, www.inc.com/geoffrey-james/when-leaders-cheat-companies-

lose.html.

Jamieson, Kathleen Hall. *Cyberwar: How Russian Hackers and Trolls Helped Elect a*

President What We Don't, Can't, and Do Know. Oxford University Press,

2018.

Jarrett, Gene Andrew. *A Companion to African American Literature*. John Wiley and

Sons, 2013, p. 195.

Jaspin, Elliot. *Buried in the Bitter Waters: The Hidden History of Racial Cleansing in*

America. Basic Books, 2008.

Jazynka, Kitson. "Watch One of George Washington's Favorite Sports in Person:

Fox Hunting." *The Washington Post*, WP Company, 9 Nov. 2015.

Jefferson, Thomas. *Notes on the State of Virginia.* Wells and Lilly, 1829.

Jemail, Jimmy, et al. "SPORTS OF THE FOUNDING FATHERS." Vault, 4 July

1955, https://www.si.com/vault/1955/07/04/603005/sports-of-the-

founding-fathers.

Jerry Maguire. TriStar, 1997.

"John McCain Townhall." CNN, 10 Oct. 2008.

Johnson, Elizabeth Ofosuah. "5 Ancient African Games That Migrated to

Western Societies to Become Sporting Events." *Face2Face Africa*, 2 Aug.

2018, https://face2faceafrica.com/article/5-ancient-african-games-that-

migrated-to-western-societies-to-become-sporting-events.

Jones, Robert P. *The End of White Christian America.* Simon and Schuster

Paperbacks, 2017, p. 247.

Jones, Thomas B. "Caucasians Only: Solomon Hughes, the PGA, and the 1948 St.

Paul Open Golf Tournament." *Minnesota History*, 2003, pp. 383–393.

Kaiser Family Foundation. "Opioid Overdose Deaths by Race/Ethnicity." 2017.

Kaminski, John P. *A Necessary Evil? Slavery and the Debate Over the Constitution.*

Madison House, 1995.

Kerr-Dineen, Luke. "Here Are Your Odds of Becoming a Professional Athlete

(They're Not Good)." *USA Today*, Gannett Satellite Information

Network, 28 July 2016, ftw.usatoday.com/2016/07/here-are-your-odds-

of-becoming-a-professional-athlete-theyre-not-good.

Khazan, Olga. "Why We Often Repeat the Same Mistakes." *The Atlantic*, Atlantic

    Media Company, 28 Feb. 2016,

    https://www.theatlantic.com/science/archive/2016/02/why-mistakes-

    are-often-repeated/470778/.

Kidd, Thomas S. *Who Is an Evangelical? The History of a Movement in Crisis.* Yale

    University Press, 2019, pp. 2-6.

Kijakazi, Kilolo. *African American Economic Development and Small Business Ownership.*

    Taylor and Francis, 2014.

King, Martin Luther. "I Have A Dream." National Archives,

    www.archives.gov/files/press/exhibits/dream-speech.pdf.

---. "Martin Luther King Interview on 'Meet the Press.'" NBC, Washington, D.C.,

    17 Apr. 1960.

Kirtzman, Andrew. "A Man of Certitude and Joy." *The New York Times*, The New

    York Times, 2 Feb. 2013, www.nytimes.com/2013/02/02/opinion/ed-

    koch-a-man-of-certitude-and-joy.html.

Klarman, Michael J. *The Framers' Coup: The Making of the United States Constitution.*

    Oxford University Press, 2018.

Kneale, Stephen. "The Myth of Self-Made Men and Self-Made Churches."

    Building Jerusalem, 29 May 2017.

Knetsch, Joe. *Florida's Seminole Wars, 1817-1858 (The Making of America).* Arcadia

    Pub., 2003.

Kollman, Paul V., and Cynthia Toms Smedley. *Understanding World Christianity:*

    Eastern Africa. Fortress Press, 2018, p. 119.

---. "How Many of the Founding Fathers Went to 'Seminary'?" The Gospel

Coalition, 3 July 2019,

https://www.thegospelcoalition.org/blogs/evangelical-history/many-

founding-fathers-went-seminary/.

Kurtulus, Fidan Ana. *The Impact of Affirmative Action on the Employment of Minorities*

and Women Over Three Decades: 1973-2003. 2012.

Lambrecht, Anja, and Catherine Tucker. *Algorithmic Bias? A Study of Data-Based*

Discrimination in the Serving of Ads in Social Media. 2016.

Law, Robin. *The Slave Coast of West Africa, 1550-1750: The Impact of the Atlantic Slave*

Trade on an African Society. Clarendon Press, 1991.

Laycock, Stuart. *All the Countries We've Ever Invaded: And the Few We Never Got Round*

To. History Press, 2013.

Lee, Bandy X. *The Dangerous Case of Donald Trump: 37 Psychiatrists and Mental Health*

Experts Assess a President: Updated and Expanded with New Essays. Thomas

Dunne Books, an Imprint of St. Martin's Press, 2019.

Lee, Harper. *To Kill a Mockingbird.* J. B. Lippincott and Co., 1960.

Leiter, Brian. *Moral Psychology with Nietzsche.* Oxford University Press, 2019.

Lewis, Hunter. *Where Keynes Went Wrong: and Why World Governments Keep Creating*

Inflation, Bubbles, and Busts. Axios Press, 2011, pp. 269-270.

"Liberty in the Air." *Slavery and the Making of America*, season 1, episode 2, 9 Feb.

2005.

Lie, John. *Modern Peoplehood.* Harvard University Press, 2004, p. 248.

Lieber, Francis. *The Miscellaneous Writings of Francis Lieber.* J. B. Lippincott and

    Company, 1881, p. 41.

Lifton, Robert Jay. *Thought Reform and the Psychology of Totalism: A Study of*

    Brainwashing in China. The University of North Carolina Press, 2012.

Lincoln, Abraham. *Second inaugural address of the late President Lincoln.* James Miller,

    New York, 1865. Pdf. Retrieved from the Library of Congress,

    <www.loc.gov/item/scsm000283/>.

Lindert, Peter H., and Jeffrey G. Williamson. *Unequal Gains: American Growth and*

    Inequality since 1700. Princeton University Press, 2016.

Link, William A. *Atlanta, Cradle of the New South: Race and Remembering in the Civil*

    Wars Aftermath. University of North Carolina Press, 2013, p. 170.

"Lisa's Rival." *The Simpsons,* season 6, episode 2, 11 Sept. 1994.

Lockwood, Matthew. *To Begin the World Over Again: How the American Revolution*

    Devastated the Globe. Yale University Press, 2019.

Loh, Wallace D. *Social Research in the Judicial Process: Cases, Readings, and Text.* Russell

    Sage Foundation, 1984, p. 48.

Lowndes, Coleman. "How Southern Socialites Rewrote Civil War History."

    Vox.com, Vox Media, 25 Oct. 2017.

Lui, Meizhu, et al. *The Color of Wealth: The Story Behind the U.S. Racial Wealth Divide.*

    New Press, 2006.

MacNair, Rachel. *Perpetration-Induced Traumatic Stress: The Psychological Consequences of*

    Killing. Authors Choice Press, 2005.

---. "The Effects of Violence on Perpetrators." *Peace Review*, vol. 14, no. 1, 2002,

    pp. 67–72.

Mangan, James A., and Andrew Ritchie, editors. *Ethnicity, Sport, Identity: Struggles for*

    Status. Routledge, Taylor, and Francis Group, 2008, pp. 13+.

Marchesi, Julia, director. *Reconstruction: America After the Civil War*, Public

    Broadcasting Service (PBS), 9 Apr. 2019.

Markowitz, Michael W., and Delores D. Jones-Brown. *The System in Black and*

    White: Exploring the Connections between Race, Crime and Justice. Praeger, 2001,

    p. 75.

Marti, Gerardo. *Worship across the Racial Divide: Religious Music and the Multiracial*

    Congregation. Oxford University Press, 2018, p. 4.

Martin-Joy, John. "Perspective | In the Age of Trump, Let Psychiatrists Judge the

    Mental Health of Public Figures." *The Washington Post*, WP Company, 30

    Jan. 2020.

Massey, Alana. "The White Protestant Roots of American Racism." The New

    Republic, 26 May 2015.

The Matrix Revolutions. 2003.

Maxwell, Angie. *Unlocking V.O. Key Jr.: "Southern Politics" for the Twenty-First Century*.

    Edited by Todd G. Shields, The University of Arkansas Press, 2011, pp.

    17-18.

Mays, Dorothy A. *Women in Early America: Struggle, Survival, and Freedom in a New*

    World. ABC-CLIO, 2004, p. 80.

McBride, Alex. "The Supreme Court . The First Hundred Years . Landmark Cases

. Plessy v. Ferguson (1896): PBS." Thirteen.org,

www.thirteen.org/wnet/supremecourt/antebellum/landmark_plessy.ht

ml.

McConnell, Terrance. "Moral Dilemmas." *Stanford Encyclopedia of Philosophy*,

Stanford University, 16 June 2018, plato.stanford.edu/entries/moral-

dilemmas/.

McCutcheon, Chuck. *Dog Whistles, Walk-Backs, and Washington Handshakes: Decoding

the Jargon, Slang, and Bluster of American Political Speech*. ForeEdge, 2014.

McDowell, Sean. *The Fate of the Apostles: Examining the Martyrdom Accounts of the

Closest Followers of Jesus*. Routledge, 2016.

McIntee, Michael. "Artists 'Break the Silence' Of White Privilege At

#Justice4Jamar Fundraiser." *The UpTake*, 16 Feb. 2016,

theuptake.org/2016/02/16/artists-break-the-silence-of-white-privilege-

at-justice4jamar-fundraiser/.

McIntosh, Peggy. "White Privilege: Unpacking the Invisible Knapsack." Peace and

Freedom Magazine, 1989.

McKie, Robin. "Heart Cells Beating in a Petri Dish Offer New Hope to Heart

Patients." *The Guardian*, Guardian News and Media, 2 Feb. 2014,

https://www.theguardian.com/science/2014/feb/02/stem-cell-

research-heart-disease-long-qt.

McKissack, Pat, and Fredrick McKissack. *Rebels Against Slavery*. Scholastic, 1999.

McLoughlin, William G. *Princeton Legacy Library: Champions of the Cherokees: Evan and*

    John B. Jones. Princeton University Press, 1990, p. 98.

Meldrum, Patricia. *Conscience and Compromise: Forgotten Evangelicals of Nineteenth-*

    Century Scotland. Wipf and Stock, 2007, p. 247.

Melville, Herman, and Robert Penn Warren. *Selected Poems of Herman Melville.* David

    R. Godine, 1967, p. 351.

Men and Idioms of Wall Street: Explaining the Daily Operations in Stocks, Bonds and Gold.

    1875, p. 3.

Mendoza, Moises. "How a Weird Law Gives One Group American Nationality

    but Not Citizenship." *Public Radio International,* 11 Oct. 2014.

Menikoff, Aaron. "How and Why Did Some Christians Defend Slavery?" The

    Gospel Coalition, The Gospel Coalition, 31 Oct. 2017.

Micheau, Antoine, and Denis Hoa. "Superficial Temporal Artery." IMAIOS,

    IMAIOS, 15 Jan. 2020, www.imaios.com/en/e-Anatomy/Anatomical-

    Parts/Superficial-temporal-artery.

Michener, James A. *Hawaii: A Novel.* Dial Press Trade Paperbacks, 1959.

Miller, Arthur G. *The Social Psychology of Good and Evil.* The Guilford Press, 2004, p.

    169.

Miller, Derek L. *The United States' Role in the World.* Cavendish Square, 2019.

Miller, L. Scott. "The Origins of the Presumption of Black Stupidity." *The Journal*

    of Blacks in Higher Education, no. 9, 1995.

Miller, Robert Moats. "The Protestant Churches and Lynching, 1919-1939." Vol.

    42, no. 2, 1957, pp. 118–131., doi:10.2307/2715687. Accessed 21 Aug.

    2019.

Missionary Herald, Volume 76. Riverside Press, 1880.

Montesquieu, et al. *Montesquieu: The Spirit of the Laws.* Cambridge University Press,

    1989.

Montesquieu. *The Spirit of Laws.* Translated by Thomas Nugent, vol. 1, Robert

    Clarke and Company, 1873.

Morgan, Michael L. *Classics of Moral and Political Theory.* Hackett Publishing

    Company, 2011, p. 78.

Morin, Amy. "Study Says Cheating May Help You Get Ahead, But You'll Lose

    More In the End." Forbes, Forbes Magazine, 9 May

    2016, www.forbes.com/sites/amymorin/2016/05/07/study-says-

    cheating-may-help-you-get-ahead-but-youll-lose-more-in-the-

    end/#79d0134e65ef.

Morris, Michael H. *Entrepreneurial Intensity: Sustainable Advantages for Individuals,*

    Organizations, and Societies. Quorum, 1998, p. 123.

Motley, Eric L. *Madison Park: A Place of Hope.* Zondervan, 2017.

Moyers, Bill D. "What A Real President Was Like." *Washington Post,* 13 Nov. 1988.

Murdaugh, E. Elaine. "The Apostate Ethic: The Alternative to Faith in

    Hochhuth's Der Stellvertreter." *Seminar: A Journal of Germanic Studies,* vol.

    15, no. 4, 1979, pp. 275–289.

"My Enemy, My Friend." *Spenser: For Hire,* season 3, episode 2, 4 Oct. 1987.

Myrdal, Gunnar. *An American Dilemma. the Negro Problem and Modern Democracy.*

　　Volume I. Transaction Publishers, 1996, p. 558.

Nagel, Stuart S. *Equity as a Policy Goal.* Social Philosophy and Policy Center, 1983,

　　p. 6.

Nakayama, Thomas K., and Judith N. Martin. *Whiteness: The Communication of Social*

　　Identity. Sage Publications, 1999.

Nash, Gary B., and Graham Russell Gao Hodges. *Friends of Liberty: Thomas Jefferson,*

　　Tadeusz Kosciuszko, and Agrippa Hull; A Tale of Three Patriots, Two

　　Revolutions, and a Tragic Betrayal of Freedom in the New Nation. Basic Books,

　　2008.

Neiwert, David. "White Supremacists' Favorite Myths about Black Crime Rates

　　Take Another Hit from BJS Study." Southern Poverty Law Center, 23

　　Oct. 2017.

Netherland, Julie, and Helena B. Hansen. "The War on Drugs That Wasn't:

　　Wasted Whiteness, 'Dirty Doctors,' and Race in Media Coverage of

　　Prescription Opioid Misuse." *Culture, Medicine, and Psychiatry*, vol. 40, no.

　　4, 2016, pp. 664–686.

Newcomb, Steven T. *Pagans in the Promised Land: Decoding the Doctrine of Christian*

　　Discovery. Fulcrum Publishing, 2008, pp. 125-127.

Newell, Margaret Ellen. *Brethren by Nature: New England Indians, Colonists, and the*

　　Origins of American Slavery. Cornell University Press, 2016, p. 14.

Newman, Eryn J., et al. "People with Easier to Pronounce Names Promote

　　Truthiness of Claims." *Plos One*, vol. 9, no. 2, 2014.

Newnes, George, editor. *The Strand Magazine, Volume 5*. George Newnes, 1893, p.

233.

Nicholson, William. *A Journal of Natural Philosophy, Chemistry, and the Arts*. D. N.

Shury, 1806.

Nikolova, Hristina, et al. "Haunts or Helps from the Past: Understanding the

Effect of Recall on Current Self-Control." *Journal of Consumer Psychology*,

vol. 26, no. 2, 2016, pp. 245–256.

"No Pensions for Ex-Slaves." National Archives and Records Administration,

National Archives and Records Administration,

www.archives.gov/publications/prologue/2010/summer/slave-

pension.html.

Olcott, Charles. *Two Lectures on the Subjects of Slavery and Abolition*. 1838, p. 27.

Oliver, Melvin L., and Thomas M. Shapiro. *Black Wealth-White Wealth a New*

Perspective on Racial Inequality. Routledge, 2006.

Oluo, Ijeoma. "Confronting Racism Is Not about the Needs and Feelings of

White People." The Guardian, Guardian News and Media, 28 Mar. 2019,

www.theguardian.com/commentisfree/2019/mar/28/confronting-

racism-is-not-about-the-needs-and-feelings-of-white-people.

"Origins of the American Revolution." *C-SPAN3 American History TV*, C-SPAN3,

20 Oct. 2019.

Pak, Eudie. "Jackie Robinson and 10 Other African American Pioneers in

Sports." Biography.com, A&E Networks Television, 23 Jan. 2020,

www.biography.com/news/jackie-robinson-black-athletes-first-sports.

Palmer, Michael A. *Command at Sea: Naval Command and Control since the Sixteenth Century*. Harvard University Press, 2007.

Palmiotto, Michael. *Combating Human Trafficking: A Multidisciplinary Approach*. CRC Press, 2015, p. 3.

Pan-African Institute, and Pan-African Students Organization. *Pan-African Journal Volume 3*. Pan-African Journal, 1970, p. 151.

"Parole." Merriam-Webster.com. Merriam-Webster, 2020.

"Pastime (n.)." Etymonline, www.etymonline.com/word/pastime.

Paul, Joanne. "Paradise Lost, Found and Lost Again." *History Today*, Nov. 2017.

Pencak, William. *Jews and Gentiles in Early America: 1654-1800*. University of Michigan Press, 2005.

Perry, Andre M. "Black Workers Are Being Left behind by Full Employment." *Brookings*, Brookings, 26 June 2019, www.brookings.edu/blog/the-avenue/2019/06/26/black-workers-are-being-left-behind-by-full-employment/.

Phillips, Carron J. "Heisman Winner Lamar Jackson Being Overlooked Because of Lack of Diversity among College Football Writers." New York Daily News, 30 Aug. 2017.

Pinchot, Gifford, and Ron Pellman. *Intrapreneuring in Action: A Handbook for Business Innovation*. Berrett-Koehler, 1999.

Polage, Danielle C. "Making up History: False Memories of Fake News Stories." *PsycExtra Dataset*, 2012.

Pollard, Christina M., and Sue Booth. "Food Insecurity and Hunger in Rich

    Countries—It Is Time for Action against Inequality." *International Journal*

    of Environmental Research and Public Health, vol. 16, no. 10, 2019, p. 1804.

"Population of the United States in 1860;" Internet Archive, Washington, D.C.:

    Govt. Print. Off, 1 Jan. 1864,

    archive.org/details/populationofusin00kennrich/page/n9.

Populations Serving Vulnerable and Underserved Populations." *U.S. Centers for*

    Medicare and Medicaid Services, cms.gov.

Porter, Kenneth Wiggins. "Negroes and the Seminole War, 1835-1842." *The*

    Journal of Southern History, vol. 30, no. 4, 1964.

Post, Washington. *The Mueller Report Illustrated: The Obstruction Investigation.* Scribner,

    2019.

Pratt, Lloyd. *The Strangers Book: The Human of African American Literature.* University

    of Pennsylvania Press, 2016.

"Presidential Candidate Donald Trump At the Family Leadership Summit." *C-*

    SPAN Road to the White House, C-SPAN3, 18 July. 2015.

Proceedings of the Massachusetts Historical Society. Vol. 17, The Society, 1903.

Proceedings of the Southern Baptist Convention, 1845: Southern Baptist

    Convention Annuals, Baylor University Libraries Digital Collections.

Public Papers of the Presidents of the United States: Gerald R. Ford; Containing the Public

    Messages, Speeches, and Statements of the President. United States Government

    Printing Office, 1975, p. 336.

"Pulse: MedlinePlus Medical Encyclopedia." *MedlinePlus*, U.S. National Library of

   Medicine.

"Pumping Myocytes." *CELLS Alive!* https://www.cellsalive.com/myocyte.htm.

Rackaway, Chapman. *Communicating Politics Online*. Palgrave MacMillan, 2014, p. 31.

"Radio Program Demographic Rankers." Radio & Television Business Report, 21

   Mar. 2013, www.rbr.com/radio-program-demographic-rankers/.

Rapley, Rob, director. *"American Experience" The Abolitionists*. 2013.

Rastogi, Sonya D., et al. *The Black Population: 2010*. United States Census Bureau,

   2011, p. 3.

Ray, Julie, and Neli Esipova. "Record Numbers of Americans Want to Leave the

   U.S." *Gallup.com*, Gallup, 28 Feb. 2019,

   https://news.gallup.com/poll/245789/record-numbers-americans-

   leave.aspx.

Reade, William Winwood. *The Martyrdom of Man*. Trübner and Company, 1872, pp.

   143-144.

*Records and Briefs of the United States Supreme Court: William Burns, Plaintiff in Error vs.

   The United States of America*. Judd and Detweiler, 1925, p. 20.

Reicher, S. D. "The St. Paul's Riot: An Explanation of the Limits of Crowd

   Action in Terms of a Social Identity Model." *European Journal of Social

   Psychology*, vol. 14, no. 1, 1984, pp. 1–21.

Reifel, Ben. *Sharing Ideas 1957 A Special Contribution: Cultural Factors in Social

   Adjustment*. 1957, p. 10.

"Retreat." *Lexico Dictionaries*, Lexico Dictionaries.

Rice, Lincoln. *Healing the Racial Divide: A Catholic Racial Justice Framework Inspired by Dr. Arthur Falls.* Pickwick Publications, 2014.

Richardson, Heather Cox. *To Make Men Free: A History of the Republican Party.* Basic Books, 2014, p. 301.

Richardson, James Daniel. *A Compilation of the Messages and Papers of the Presidents.* Bureau of National Literature and Art, 1901.

Ridge, Tess, and Sharon Wright. *Understanding Inequality, Poverty and Wealth Policies and Prospects.* Policy Press, 2011, p. 1.

Riggins, Stephen Harold Ed. *The Language and Politics of Exclusion: Others in Discourse.* Sage Publications, Inc., 1997.

Ritchie, Anne Thackeray. *Mrs. Dymond.* Tauchnitz, 1886.

Roberts, Diane. "College Football's Big Problem With Race." *Time,* Time, 12 Nov. 2015, time.com/4110443/college-football-race-problem/.

Rodriguez, Junius P., editor. *Slavery in the United States: A Social, Political, and Historical Encyclopedia.* Vol. 1, ABC CLIO, 2007, p. 198.

Roediger, David R. *Towards the Abolition of Whiteness: Essays on Race, Politics, and Working Class History.* Verso, 1994.

Rogers, Karl. *Debunking Glenn Beck: How to Save America From Media Pundits and Propagandists.* Praeger, 2011.

"Ronald Reagan Radio Commentary on the Welfare Queen, October 1976." *SoundCloud,* Slate Voice.

Ross, Alexander Milton. *Recollections and Experiences of an Abolitionist, from 1855 to 1865.* Rowsell and Hutchison, 1875, pp. 105-106.

Rustin, Michael. *The Good Society and the Inner World: Psychoanalysis, Politics and Culture.* Verso, 1991, p. 76.

Ryczek, William J. *When Johnny Came Sliding Home: The Post-Civil War Baseball Boom, 1865-1870.* McFarland, 1998.

Sadler, Roger L. *Electronic Media Law.* Sage Publications, 2005, p. 259.

Santoro, Taylor N, and Jonathan D Santoro. "Racial Bias in the US Opioid Epidemic: A Review of the History of Systemic Bias and Implications for Care." Cureus, 14 Dec. 2018.

Schoenly, Lorry. "Debugging the System: Exterminating Myths About Lice." *CorrectionsOne,* 29 Jan. 2013.

Schultz, David, and Joh R. Vile, editors. *The Encyclopedia of Civil Liberties in America: Volumes One-Three.* Sharpe Reference, 2005, p. 349.

Schultz, Michael, director. *Car Wash.* Universal Pictures, 1976.

Schumacher, Joel, director. A Time to Kill. 1996.

See, Letha A. *Human Behavior in the Social Environment from an African American Perspective.* Taylor and Francis, 2013.

"Select Parts of the Holy Bible, for the Use of the Negro Slaves, in the . . ." Internet Archive, Printed by Law and Gilbert, 1 Jan. 1970.

Semeraro, Eleanor. "NFL Regular Season Sees Increases in TV Ad Spend, Ad Airings and Impressions." Broadcasting & Cable, 14 Jan. 2020, www.broadcastingcable.com/news/nfl-regular-season-increases-tv-ad-spend-impressions.

Shakespeare, William, and Kermode, Frank. The Tempest. United

    Kingdom, Harvard University Press, 1958, p. 63.

---. *All's Well That Ends Well: A Comedy. By Mr. William Shakespeare.* Printed for J.

    Tonson, and the Rest of the Proprietors, 1734.

---. *Romeo and Juliet: A Tragedy in Five Acts.* G. H. Davidson, 1800.

Shearer, Chad, et al. *Metro Monitor: An Index of Inclusive Economic Growth in the 100*

    Largest U.S. Metropolitan Areas. 2018.

Shelden, Randall G. Our Punitive Society: Race, Class, Gender and Punishment in

    America. Waveland Press, 2010.

Shelley, Mary. *Frankenstein; or, The Modern Prometheus.* Lackington, Hughes,

    Harding, Mavor and Jones, 1818.

Signil, Christopher. *Race, Faith, and Politics: 7 Political Questions That Every African*

    American Christian Must Answer. Creation House, 2012.

Simpson, Matthew C. "The Founding Fathers' Power Grab." The New Republic,

    29 Sept. 2016, https://newrepublic.com/article/137310/founding-

    fathers-power-grab.

Sinnette, Calvin H. *Forbidden Fairways: African Americans and the Game of Golf.*

    Sleeping Bear Press, 1998, pp. 125-132.

Skolnick, Jerome H., and James J. Fyfe. *Above the Law: Police and the Excessive Use of*

    Force. The Free Press, 1993, p. 140.

Slave States 2020, worldpopulationreview.com/states/slave-states/.

Smith, Jean Edward. *George Bush's War.* Henry Holt, 1992, p. 79.

Solomon, Robert M. *The Conscience: Rediscovering the Inner Compass*. Genesis Books,

    2010.

Solomon, Zahava. *Combat Stress Reaction: The Enduring Toll of War*. Springer, 2013,

    p. 51.

Soloveichik, Meir Y., et al. *Proclaim Liberty Throughout the Land: The Hebrew Bible in*

    the United States: A Sourcebook. Toby Press, 2019.

Sorin, Gerald. *Abolitionism: A New Perspective*. Praeger, 1972.

Southern Slavery Considered on General Principles, Or, a Grapple with Abstractionists. Rudd

    and Carleton Publishers, 1861, p. 16.

Southey, Robert. *The Curse of Kehama ... The Third Edition*. Longman, Hurst, Rees,

    Orme and Brown, 1812.

Spence, Carma. *Public Speaking Super Powers: Unleash Your Inner Speaking Superhero*

    and Communicate Your Message with Confidence. Author Academy Elite, 2018.

Spence, Gerry. *Police State: How Americas Cops Get Away with Murder*. St. Martin's

    Publishing Group, 2015, pp. 321-322.

Spencer, Jon Michael. *The New Colored People: The Mixed-Race Movement in America*.

    New York University Press, 1997.

Spencer, Nick. *The Mighty and the Almighty: How Political Leaders Do God*. Biteback

    Publishing Limited, 2017.

Spencer, Thomas. *The Outcry Against the New Poor Law; Or Who Is the Poor Man's*

    Friend? Price Twopence, 1841.

Spener, Philipp Jacob, and Kurt Jacob Aland. *Pia Desideria*. De Gruyter, 1964.

Sports Illustrated (SInow). "Shut up and dribble' — Fox News's Laura Ingraham

to LeBron and Kevin Durant after their criticism of

President Trump.

https://twitter.com/SInow/status/964512313175871488." 16 February

2018, 6:50 a.m. Tweet.

Standiford, Les. *Meet You in Hell Andrew Carnegie, Henry Clay Frick, and the Bitter

Partnership That Transformed America.* Three Rivers Press, 2006, p. 36.

Statue of Liberty, Ellis Island Immigration Museum: Statue of Liberty National

Monument, New Jersey/New York. [Washington, D.C.]: National Park

Service, U.S. Department of the Interior, 1999.

Stevenson, Robert Louis. *The Strange Case of Dr. Jekyll & Mr. Hyde.* Longmans,

Green and Co., 1886.

Stowe, Harriet Elizabeth Beecher. *Uncle Tom's Cabin; or, Life Among the Lowly.*

Ward, Lock, and Tyler, 1876.

"Subhuman." Merriam-Webster.com. Merriam-Webster, 2020.

Sue, Derald Wing. *"Microaggressions in Everyday Life: Race, Gender, and Sexual

Orientation".* John Wiley and Sons, 2010.

Sullivan, Shannon. *The Physiology of Sexist and Racist Oppression.* Oxford University

Press, 2015.

Swackhamer, Conrad, and Making of America Project. The United States

Democratic Review. Washington, D.C.: Langtree and O'Sullivan, 1837-

40, 184159.

Sweeney, Latanya. *Discrimination in Online Ad Delivery.* 2013.

"Taking Your Carotid Pulse: MedlinePlus Medical Encyclopedia Image."

    MedlinePlus, U.S. National Library of Medicine.

Tallant, Harold D. *Evil Necessity: Slavery and Political Culture in Antebellum Kentucky*.

    The University Press of Kentucky, 2015, pp. 1-19.

Tankersley, Jim. "White Americans Gain the Most From Trump's Tax Cuts, a

    Report Finds." The New York Times, The New York Times, 11 Oct.

    2018, www.nytimes.com/2018/10/11/business/trump-tax-cuts-white-

    americans.html.

Taylor, Jim. "Parenting: Set Your Children's 'Defaults' Early." *Psychology Today*,

    Sussex Publishers, 13 July 2011,

    https://www.psychologytoday.com/us/blog/the-power-

    prime/201107/parenting-set-your-childrens-defaults-early.

---. *Your Children Are Listening: Nine Messages They Need to Hear from You*. The

    Experiment, 2011.

Taylor, Marian, and Nathan I. Huggins. *Harriet Tubman*. Houghton Mifflin, 1997,

    p. 80.

Taylor, Steve. "The Psychology of Racism." *Psychology Today*, Sussex Publishers,

    https://www.psychologytoday.com/us/blog/out-the-

    darkness/201801/the-psychology-racism.

"Temporary Questioning of Persons in Public Places; Search for Weapons." *NY

    State Senate*, 17 Aug. 2019,

    https://www.nysenate.gov/legislation/laws/CPL/140.50.

"The 'Great Commission' in Matthew 28:19 Is NOT What You've Been

    Taught." Berean Patriot, 30 Oct. 2018, www.bereanpatriot.com/the-

    great-commission-in-matthew-2819-is-not-what-youve-been-taught/.

The American Mercury. United States, Mercury Publications, 1943, p. 23.

The Analytical Review; Or History of Literature, Domestic and Foreign, on an Enlarged Plan,

    Containing Scientific Abstracts of Information and Interesting Works, Published in

    English; A General Account of Such As Are of Less Consequence, With Short

    Characters; and or Reviews, of Valuable Foreign Books; Also the Literary

    Intelligence of Europe. Vol. 21, 1795.

"The Bill of Rights: A Transcription." *National Archives and Records Administration,*

    www.archives.gov/founding-docs/bill-of-rights-transcript.

"The Challenge of Freedom." *Slavery and the Making of America*, season 1, episode 4,

    16 Feb. 2005.

"The Constitution of the United States: A Transcription." National Archives and

    Records Administration, https://www.archives.gov/founding-

    docs/constitution-transcript.

"The First Christian Communities (1st Century)." Discover a Video on the

    History of the First Christian Settlements, https://www.the-map-as-

    history.com/History-of-christianity/the-first-christian-communities-1st-

    century.

The Gap Between the Number of Blacks and Whites in Prison Is Shrinking. Pew Research

    Center, 2017.

The Gettysburg address delivered by Abraham Lincoln Nov. 19at the dedication services on the

 battle field. Boston, Mass.: Published by M.T. Sheahan, Jan. 11.

 Photograph. Retrieved from the Library of Congress,

 <www.loc.gov/item/2004671506/>.

"The Impeachment Hearing." *PBS News Hour*, 4 Dec. 2019.

The Merchants' Magazine and Commercial Review, Volume 24. 1851, p. 546.

The New World: Volume 8. J. Winchester, 1844.

"The People's Jubilee." *The Democrat,* July 1887, pp. 257–258.

The Political Register, and Impartial Review: For MDCCLXX. Vol. 7, Printed for Henry

 Beevor, 1770, p. 157.

The Racial Confidence Gap in Police Performance: Survey of U.S. Adults Conducted Aug. 16 -

 Sept. 12, 2016. Pew Research Center, 2016.

"The Right to Tell: The Role of Mass Media in Economic Development." *World*

 Bank Group, 2002.

"The Southern Manifesto of 1956." *US House of Representatives: History, Art &*

 Archives, history.house.gov/Historical-Highlights/1951-2000/The-

 Southern-Manifesto-of-1956/.

"The Story of Africa| BBC World Service." BBC News, BBC,

 https://www.bbc.co.uk/worldservice/africa/features/storyofafrica/inde

 x_section8.shtml.

"The Tanner Lectures on Human Values." *Home - The Tanner Lectures on Human*

 Values - The University of Utah, https://tannerlectures.utah.edu/.

The Wilderness Deep Inside the Republican Party's Combative, Contentious, Chaotic Quest to

    Take Back the White House. Back Bay Books, 2016, p. 360.

The Williams Brothers. "Sweep Around." Malaco Records, 1986.

Thomas, Cal, and Ed Dobson. *Blinded by Might: Why the Religious Right Can't Save*

    America. Zondervan Pub. House, 2000.

Thornton, John. *Africa and Africans in the Making of the Atlantic World, 1400-1800.*

    Cambridge University Press, 1998.

Tipps, Havens, and Linda Zimbler. *Social Indicators of Equality for Minorities and*

    Women: A Report of the United States Commission on Civil Rights. United

    States Government Printing Office, 1978, p. 53.

Tischauser, Leslie Vincent. *Jim Crow Laws.* Greenwood, 2013.

Tolstoy, Leo. *War and Peace.* Walter Scott Publishing Company, 1920.

Toobin, Jeffrey, et al. "How to Stop Mass Incarceration." The New Yorker,

    www.newyorker.com/magazine/2015/05/11/the-milwaukee-

    experiment.

Torino, Gina C., et al. *Microaggression Theory: Influence and Implications.* John Wiley

    and Sons, 2019, p. 24.

Trading Places. 1983.

"Transcript of Northwest Ordinance (1787)." *Ourdocuments.gov,*

    www.ourdocuments.gov/doc.php?flash=false&doc=8&page=transcript.

Trotter, Joe William. *Workers on Arrival: Black Labor in the Making of America.*

    University of California Press, 2019, p. 26.

Trump Attacks Late Congressman; Nancy Pelosi Delays Sending Impeachment

Articles to Senate; Interview With Sen. Chris Van Hollen (D-MD). Aired

3-3:30p ET." *CNN Newsroom*, CNN, 19 Dec. 2019.

Trump, Donald (realDonaldTrump). "President should not be telling the

Washington Redskins to change their name-our country has far bigger

problems! FOCUS on them, not nonsense.

https://twitter.com/realDonaldTrump/status/387565483303923712." 8

October 2013, 6:09 a.m. Tweet.

---. (realDonaldTrump). "The Tax Cuts are so large and so meaningful, and yet the

Fake News is working overtime to follow the lead of their friends, the

defeated Dems, and only demean. This is truly a case where the results

will speak for themselves, starting very soon. Jobs,

Jobs, Jobs!

https://twitter.com/realDonaldTrump/status/943489378462130176."

20 December 2017, 6:32 a.m. Tweet.

---. "Biggest Tax Bill and Tax Cuts in history just passed in the Senate. Now these

great Republicans will be going for final passage. Thank you to House

and Senate Republicans for your hard work and commitment!

https://twitter.com/realDonaldTrump/status/936941673124425728."

20 December 2017, 4:54 a.m. Tweet.

---. "If a player wants the privilege of making millions of dollars in the NFL, or

other leagues, he or she should not be allowed to disrespect-our Great

American Flag (or Country) and should stand for the National Anthem.

If not, You're Fired. Find something else to do!

https://twitter.com/realDonaldTrump/status/911654184918880260."

23 September 2017, 11:11 a.m. Tweet.

Tulsa Race Riot: A Report by the Oklahoma Commission to Study the Tulsa Race

Riot of 1921. 2001.

"U.S. and World Population Clock." *Population Clock*, www.census.gov/popclock/.

U.S. News & World Report, Volume 123, Issues 1-7. U.S. News Publishing

Corporation, 1997, p. 68.

U.S.C. Title 4 - FLAG AND SEAL, SEAT OF GOVERNMENT, AND THE

STATES, https://www.govinfo.gov/content/pkg/USCODE-2011-

title4/html/USCODE-2011-title4-chap1.htm.

"Umpire." Merriam-Webster.com. Merriam-Webster, 2020.

Underhill, Wendy. Voter Identification Requirements: Voter ID Laws. 19 Jan.

2017.

"Understanding Privilege and Oppression Handout." Vanderbilt University.

United States, Congress, Senate, The Committee on Slavery and the Treatment of

Freedmen... *Report: To Accompany Bill S. No. 99.* Government Printing

Office, 1864. 38th Congress, 1st session, House Report 615.

Upchurch, Thomas Adams. *Historical Dictionary of the Gilded Age.* Scarecrow Press,

2009, pp. 81-82.

Vaca, Nick Corona. *The Presumed Alliance: The Unspoken Conflict Between Latinos and*

Blacks and What It Means for America. Harper Perennial, 2004.

Valentine, D. T. *Manual of the Corporation of the City of New York For the Year 1849*.

    McSpedon and Baker Printers, 1849.

Valsiner, Jaan. *The Oxford Handbook of Culture and Psychology*. Oxford University

    Press, 2014, pp. 572-577.

Van Deburg, William L. *Modern Black Nationalism: From Marcus Garvey to Louis

    Farrakhan*. New York University Press, 1997, p. 154.

Vicchio, Stephen J. *George Washington's Religion: The Faith of the First President*. Wipf

    and Stock Publishers, 2019.

"Visions, Inc. and the MSU Extension Multicultural Awareness Workshop."

Voices of The True-Hearted. Merrihew and Thompson, 1846.

Waldseemüller Martin, et al. *Cosmographiae Introductio*. 1507, p. vii.

Wallace, Max. *The American Axis: Henry Ford, Charles Lindbergh, and the Rise of the

    Third Reich*. St. Martin's Publishing Group, 2004, pp. 17-21.

Walsh, Edward. "Carter Attacks Reagan Tax Cut, Seeks Debates." Washington

    Post, 18 July 1980.

Wann, Daniel L., and Jeffrey James. *Sport Fans: The Psychology and Social Impact of

    Fandom*. Routledge, 2019, p. 182.

Washington, Denzel, director. *The Great Debaters*. Metro-Goldwyn-Mayer, 2007.

Washington, George, and Worthington Chauncey. Ford. *The Writings of George

    Washington: 1782-1785*. Putnam's, 1891, pp. 473-476.

Waxman, Olivia B. "Good Friday, Palm Sunday, Lincoln's Death and

    Appomattox." Time, Time, 14 Apr. 2017,

    https://time.com/4738248/enums/.

Weber, Max. Protestant Ethic and the Spirit of Capitalism. Wilder Publications,

    2018.

Website Services & Coordination Staff, and US Census Bureau. "The Great

    Migration, 1910 to 1970." *U.S. Census*, 1 Mar. 1994.

Weisburd, David, and Rosann Greenspan. *Police Attitudes toward Abuse of Authority:*

    Findings from a National Study. United States Department of Justice, Office

    of Justice Programs, National Institute of Justice, 2000, p. 9.

Wellhausen, Julius, and Mark Edward. Biddle. *The Pharisees and the Sadducees: An*

    Examination of Internal Jewish History. Mercer University Press, 2001.

"What Are the Major Federal Safety Net Programs in the U.S.?" *UC Davis Center*

    for Poverty Research, poverty.ucdavis.edu/article/war-poverty-and-todays-

    safety-net-0.

What are the Two Greatest Commandments? (n.d.). Retrieved from

    http://www.the-ten-

    commandments.org/whatarethetwogreatestcommandments.html

What Does It Mean That Good Works Are the Result of

    Salvation?" *GotQuestions.org*, 8 July 2013.

"What Would Jesus Do? The Rise of a Slogan." *BBC News*, BBC, 8 Dec. 2011.

White, Byron Raymond, and Supreme Court of The United States. *U.S. Reports:*

    Terry v. Ohio, 392 U.S. 1. 1967.

"Who We Elect: Sheriffs." *Sunday Civics with L. Joy Williams*, Urban View, 1 Sept.

    2019.

Wiedel, Jason. *Persecution Complex: Why American Christians Need to Stop Playing the Victim.* CrowdScribed, 2014.

Wiehe, Meg, et al. *Race, Wealth and Taxes: How the Tax Cuts and Jobs Act Supercharges the Racial Wealth Divide.* 2018.

Wiencek, Henry. *Master of the Mountain: Thomas Jefferson and His Slaves.* Farrar, Straus and Giroux, 2013.

Wikipedia contributors. "List of incidents of civil unrest in the United States." *Wikipedia, The Free Encyclopedia.* Wikipedia, The Free Encyclopedia, 23 Jan. 2020. Web. 11 Feb. 2020.

Wilson, Carter A. *Racism: from Slavery to Advanced Capitalism.* Sage Publications, 1996, pp. xiii – xiv.

Wilson, William J. "Review: Slavery, Paternalism, and White Hegemony." *American Journal of Sociology*, vol. 81, no. 5, Mar. 1976, pp. 1190–1198.

Winthrop, John. "A Modell of Christian Charity." *Collections of the Massachusetts Historical Society, Volume 27*, Charles C. Little and James Brown, 1838, pp. 33–48.

Wonneberg, D. A. *Christianity, Atheism, Islam and the Need for Real Evangelical Leadership.* FriesenPress, 2016, p. 197.

Wood, Gordon S. *The Creation of the American Republic 1776-1787.* W. W. Norton and Company, 1969.

Woodson, Carter G., and Rayford W. Logan. "Association for the Study of Negro Life and History., 1968." *The Journal of Negro History*, vol. 53, 1968.

Wyche, Steve. "Colin Kaepernick Explains Why He Sat during National Anthem."

   NFL.com, National Football League, 28 Aug. 2016.

Yalom, Victor, et al. "Peter Levine on Somatic Experiencing." Psychotherapy.net.

Young, H. Peyton. *Equity: in Theory and Practice*. Princeton University Press, 1994,

   p. 64.

Young, Iris Marion. *Justice and the Politics of Difference*. Princeton University Press,

   1990, p. 64.

Young, Ralph F. *Dissent: The History of an American Idea*. New York University

   Press, 2015, p. 11.

Zack, Naomi. *Race and Mixed Race*. Temple University Press, 1993.

Zanardi, Tara. *Framing Majismo: Art and Royal Identity in Eighteenth-Century Spain*.

   Pennsylvania State University Press, 2016.

Zangwill, Israel. *Works of Israel Zangwill*. American Jewish Book Company, 1921.

Zanna, Mark P., editor. *Advances in Experimental Social Psychology*. Vol. 31, Academic

   Press, 1999, p. 241.

Zapotosky, Matt. "Sessions Rescinds Justice Dept. Letter Asking Courts to Be

   Wary of Stiff Fines and Fees for Poor Defendants." *The Washington Post*,

   WP Company, 21 Dec. 2017.

Zarkin, Kimberly, and Michael J. Zarkin. *The Federal Communications Commission:*

   Front Line in the Culture and Regulation Wars. Greenwood Press, 2006, p.

   105.

INDEX

Lightning Source UK Ltd.
Milton Keynes UK
UKHW022046190121
377353UK00003B/411